The Life and Times of
RICHARD III

OVERLEAF LEFT Genealogy of the Kings of
England from Edward III to Henry VII,
showing the rival claims of the Houses
of York and Lancaster. Henry VI appears
in the medallion just above the fold, and
Edward IV, Richard III and Henry VII
in the central medallions below.
OVERLEAF RIGHT Richard III and his
Queen, Anne Neville, from a late
fifteenth-century manuscript.

Iohn a Gaunt had in wyffe Blanch
Bedstar a latu Surford thys fir
st he had vi chyldern Iohn Edward Iohn
& hur henry viii Whilix quene of por
tugale Elsabeth countes of brithingto
& by y ii p uris Constans he had later
quene of Spayne and by y uris ka
ter he had iii Ione countes of westmor
lond Iaerr p was a Cardinall Thomas duke
of Exetor Iohn erle of Sunset Thys Iohn
had vi chyldern Iary Erle of Souset Mar
garete countes of Deuenshyre Thomas
Ione quene of Scottis Edmude duke of Som
set y dyde at sent Albons Iohn duke of So
mset The whych Iohn had a doughter nm
lyd Margarite countes of Riche
mod & moth to kyng
Henry vi

Henry v y so
off steri y viii
was crownyd kyng aft
y deth off hys father
he was a dowghti man i alma
ner off warre & coquernd stormady
iv a gret parte off France & weddyd y
dowghter off y kyng off France whos
name was katery & dyde & lyeth at
westmnster

Hery the iiii the sone off Iohn
Iohans duke off laminster was
crownyd kyng at westmst i y day off
set Edward of essex thys was a deuow
te ma to god but he had gret trobyll
both off hys ennys &
also off hys owne pe
pill but trowth the
helxe off god he had y
bett off thez aftward
in gret sikenes he dyde &
was biuryd at caterbery

Hery the vi was
sone to harry y v
& he was crownyd
at westmnst in y yere
off ower lord mi cccc
xxxb & ys buurd at wyndsor

Edwarde y iiii after y cquest of
ynglond sone & eyre of y most
myghthfull prince Ric lute duke of
porke Whych was very eyre of y
realme of ynglond & franne as en
tule & leguos aft y dysere of hys
fad he was duke of porke &
very a per of y realmes a
foue sayd And y iiii
day of march by y
trewe pepull throlth y grace
of god he was chos to be kyng
& reseyud y kyngdom of yng
lond Whych was deu to hym by
Iust tytyll of Eritas & he was
crolbnyd kyng at westmnst
in y xxbiii day of y mo
nyth of Iune y zere of o
lorde mi cccc lxi & lyethe bur
ryd at wundesor & rapnyd xxii
zeres

Owyn todder mar
ryd iii quene
katern y was wyffe un
to kyng henry y v & had
by har Edmude perse of tychemed Iaspr &
Edward the sayd Edmude maryd w mar
garete y was dobter & eyer un to Iohn
dbke of Somersett

Richard y was sonne to Richard Debke
of yorke & brother un to kyng Ed
ward y iiii was kyng after hys brother &
rapnyd ii yeres & lyth buuryd at
leator

The Life and Times of
RICHARD III

Anthony Cheetham

Introduction by Antonia Fraser

WELCOME RAIN
NEW YORK

Additional titles in the **Life and Times** series,
published under the General Editorship of Antonia Fraser include:

Elizabeth I by Neville Williams (1-56649-198-3)
Henry VIII by Robert Lacey (1-56649-199-1)
Victoria by Dorothy Marshall (1-56649-036-7)

First WELCOME RAIN edition 1998
Published by WELCOME RAIN
New York, New York

First published in 1972 by
Weidenfeld & Nicolson
An imprint of the Orion Publishing Group
Orion House, 5 Upper St Martin's Lane
London WC2H 9EA

ISBN 1-56649-038-3
M 10 9 8 7 6 5 4 3 2 1

© George Weidenfeld
and Nicolson Limited
and Book Club
Associates 1972

Series designed by Paul Watkins
Layout by Margaret Downing

Filmset by Keyspools Limited, Golborne, Lancs
Printed in Great Britain by
Butler & Tanner Ltd, Frome and London

Contents

Introduction

THE MOST CONTROVERSIAL KING in English history – his passionate admirers would still not deny this title to Richard III, while continuing to see in him the most maligned of our sovereigns. As for those nourished beyond redemption on the black legend of Crookback Dick, even they must admit that his reign contains a spectacular historical problem in the deaths of the Princes in the Tower, the exact truth about which is still not known even after a lapse of five hundred years. Of course the trouble with this type of riddle, as Anthony Cheetham ably shows in a highly readable new biography, is that although it arouses the detective instinct in us all, at the same time there is the risk of its overshadowing the whole reign – to say nothing of the true personality of the man himself.

Thus it is especially valuable to have the fact of Richard's early life unrolled, including his own position in the complex family tree of York and Lancaster, for without this it is impossible to assess the man. It is a youth of promise, both military and administrative, including a decisive action at Tewkesbury and excellent handling of the North on his brother's behalf, as a result of which he was termed by those in a position to know 'our full tender especial good lord of York'. By the age of thirty he had been made Hereditary Warden of the Western Marches of Scotland by Edward as a reward for his good services to the Crown. Hard-working, brave, small in stature but still handsome (not in fact a hunchback, although one shoulder may have been slightly higher than the other), the ascetic figure of Richard presents a strong contrast to his brother the King, a golden-haired giant in youth but becoming 'overweight and oversexed' with age, and loaded with the problems that his indulgent marriage to Elizabeth Woodville had landed on the country in the shape of her grasping relations.

Indeed it is in this contrast that Anthony Cheetham looks for the source of Richard's trouble with the old régime on his brother's death; this plodding, even Puritanical, character, disliking the free and easy ways of his brother's Court. Even the usurpation is seen in the context of the terrible disaster that the minority of a child king could bring upon a country, Richard in his short reign concentrating on much constructive work towards better government. There still remains the problem of the young Princes' fate: here Anthony Cheetham is in no sense concerned to whitewash his subject. He contributes instead a lucid discussion of the evidence – showing incidentally how much of it derives from subsequent Tudor propaganda – at the end of which he demonstrates how, if Richard was guilty, at least it accords with the straightforward personality of the man, a man who was so far from being Shakespeare's calculating villain, that he probably possessed if anything 'too little guile rather than too much'.

Antonia Fraser

Acknowledgments

Photographs and illustrations were supplied by, or are reproduced by kind permission of the following. The pictures on pages 17, 74, 96, 131 are reproduced by gracious permission of H.M. the Queen; on pages 3, 33, 40, 41, 81 by gracious permission of the Duke of Buccleuch and Queensberry; and on page 79 (below) by courtesy of the Archbishop of Canterbury (copyright reserved by the Church Commissioners). Archives Nationales: 86–7; Bibliothèque Municipale, Arras: 39, 60; Christopher Barker: 111, 125/1, 125/2, 152; Bodleian Library, Oxford: 38/1, 38/2, 132/1, 132/2, 144/1; BPC: 157; British Museum: 2, 10–11, 13, 14–15, 22, 23/1, 23/2, 30–1, 34, 36/1, 36/2, 42–3, 50/1, 51, 57, 78/2, 83, 88, 103, 107, 108, 113, 116/1, 116/2, 119, 126, 134–5, 145/1, 145/2, 145/3, 152, 154, 155, 167, 174, 178, 179–80, 191, 200; Bibliothèque Royale, Brussels: 64, 65; R. A. J. Bunnett: 92; Camera Press: 210/2; Dean and Chapter, Canterbury: 78–9; Jack Casselden: 212; Castle Museum, York: 192/2; Musée Condé, Chantilly: 89; College of Arms: 84; Courtauld Institute of Art: 80, 170/2, 206; Department of the Environment (Crown Copyright): 192/1; C. M. Dixon: 164, 165; Entwhistle Photography: 78–9; Bibliothèque Centrale, Ghent: 45, 66, 67, 70; Giraudon: 39, 60, 89, 99, 169; Guildhall Library: 121, 210/1; Staatsarchiv Hamburg: 62; Bob Harding: 140; Michael Holford: 171; Henry E. Huntington Library & Art Gallery: 144/2; Lambeth Palace Library: 79/2; Edward Leigh: 53, 209; Mansell Collection: 48, 122, 203; National Gallery: 54; National Monuments Record: 12, 24, 25, 47, 92, 170; National Portrait Gallery, London: 128, 149, 183; National Portrait Gallery, Scotland: 96; Trustees of the Pierpont Morgan Library, New York: 50/2; Master and Fellows of Queens' College, Cambridge: 53; Reverend Ridgway: 199; Royal Commission for Historical Monuments (Crown Copyright): 161; Master and Fellows of St John's College, Cambridge: 137; Society of Antiquaries: 48, 122, 157; George Spearman: 100, 104–5, 104/2, 105/2, 105/3, 115; Penny Tweedie: 133; Musée de Versailles: 169; Victoria and Albert Museum: 61, 72, 158, 166, 172, 175, 176, 192/3, 193, 207, 213; Dean and Canons, Windsor: 100, 104–5, 104/2, 105/2, 115; Worshipful Company of Skinners: 16; Walker Art Gallery, Liverpool: 196–7; York City Libraries: 95.

Picture research by Jasmine Spencer.
Maps drawn by Design Practitioners Limited.

1 York and

Lancaster  1452-61

At THE NORTHAMPTONSHIRE CASTLE of Fotheringhay, on 2 October 1452, Cicely, Duchess of York, gave birth to a son, who was christened Richard after his father. The Duchess was renowned for her beauty and for her enduring devotion to her husband. Known as 'the Rose of Raby', she had married comparatively late, in her mid-twenties, and accompanied her husband on his tours of duty in the French territories conquered by Henry v and in the Irish pale. Undaunted by the hazards of war, travel or continual pregnancy, she had already borne ten children in three different countries before the young Richard first saw the light of day. Six of these children – three boys and three girls – had survived the rigours of infancy: in 1452 Richard's eldest brother Edward was ten years old, Edmund was nine, and George was four.

All three inherited something of their mother's looks and robust constitution. Richard, the last of Cicely's surviving children, seems to have inherited neither: a weak and sickly child, he struggled through his early years, causing an anonymous rhymster to comment, with a note of surprise, that 'Richard liveth yet'. In looks and height he would later resemble his father, a shortish man with plain, forthright features.

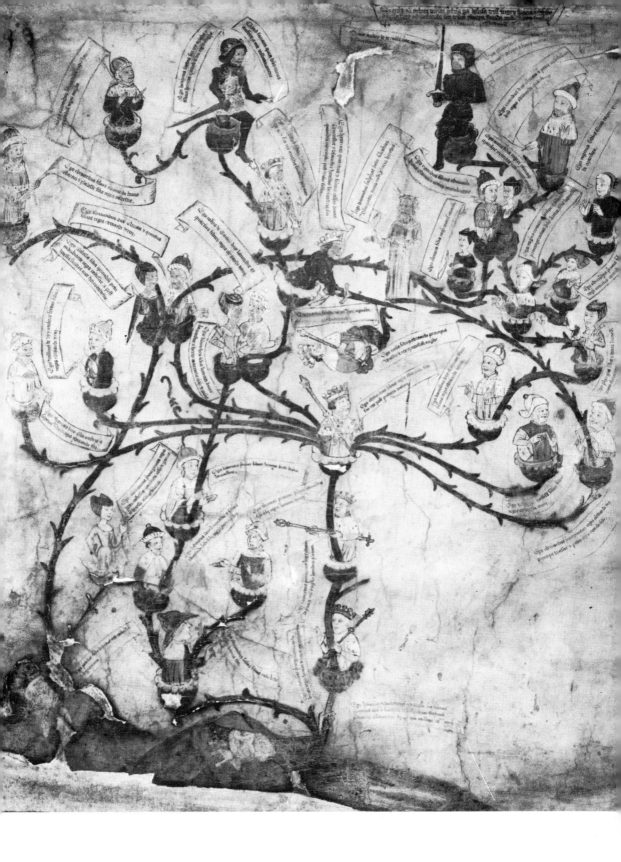

Henry VI and Margaret
of Anjou, with their
courtiers. The kneeling
figure presenting a book to
the Queen is John Talbot,
Earl of Shrewsbury.

14

Richard, Duke of York, was the greatest magnate and land-owner in the kingdom, excepting the king himself. From his mother, Anne Mortimer, he inherited the vast Welsh border estates of the earldom of March, the earldom of Ulster and the Irish lordships of Connaught, Trim and Clare; from his father, Richard, Earl of Cambridge, the dukedom of York and the earldoms of Rutland and Cambridge. Through both his parents York also inherited the royal blood of Edward III. On the one side he traced his descent from Lionel, Duke of Clarence, second son of Edward III; on the other he was the grandson of

16

Henry VI, a portrait by an unknown artist.

Edward III's fourth son, Edmund of Langley. These family relationships are of more than passing interest: their shadow lies across the short and violent span of Richard's life, and stains the whole chapter of English history known as the Wars of the Roses.

The fortunes of the House of York were founded on the fact that their royal descent was arguably better than that of the reigning House of Lancaster. For while York could claim descent from the second son of Edward III, Henry VI could trace his only from Edward's third son, John of Gaunt. King Henry

17

thus owed his crown more to the successful usurpation of his grandfather, Henry Bolingbroke, than to the legitimate laws of inheritance.

These dynastic subtleties might well have remained purely academic, if the kingdom had not been wracked, in the years preceding Richard's birth, by a series of crises that left the King bankrupt, the barons at each others' throats and the country shorn of its empire overseas. King Henry himself was most to blame. At a time when the King was expected to be his own prime minister and commander in chief combined, Henry was interested only in charity and prayer. This saintly incompetent allowed his ministers to pillage the royal coffers to the tune of about £24,000 a year. Nor was he able to devise an effective policy towards the besetting problem of his dwindling possessions in France. Henry v's great conquests had saddled his son with an embarrassing legacy – crushingly expensive to maintain, humiliating to abandon. In 1444 his advisers persuaded the King that he must cut his losses, come to terms with the French and marry a French princess. The bride chosen by Henry's advisers was Margaret of Anjou, daughter of René, Duke of Anjou, and niece of the French King, Charles VII. Although she was only fifteen years old, Margaret's dazzling looks, her lively intelligence and her impetuous energy soon wrought a transformation in the routine of her husband's Court. With more gratitude than foresight she also linked her fortunes – and the King's – with the second-rate ministers who had made her a Queen. But the French truce negotiated by her favourite protégé, William de la Pole, Earl (later Marquess and Duke) of Suffolk, lasted only two years. In 1448 the province of Maine was ceded to the French: in 1449 Normandy went the same way. By now the country was baying for the blood of the appeasers whom it held responsible for these disasters – Suffolk, Somerset and Queen Margaret.

In the following spring discontent boiled over into open rebellion. Suffolk was assassinated. Jack Cade and an army of Kentish rebels marched on London and forced the King to flee from his own capital. The Bishop of Salisbury was murdered by his flock who 'spoiled him unto the naked skin, and rent his bloody shirt into pieces and bare them away with them and made boast of their wickedness'.

Someone had to call a halt. Richard, Duke of York had already identified himself as an opponent of the Court party and as a long-standing enemy of John Beaufort, Duke of Somerset. In 1445 Somerset had blocked the renewal of York's appointment as the King's Lieutenant in France. Four years later he had engineered York's removal from the Court to an honourable exile as Lieutenant of Ireland. By 1451 it was also beginning to look as if York, or his eldest son Edward, would one day inherit the Crown. Henry's three uncles had all died childless, and the King still had no children by his French wife.

Cade's rebellion provided York with an excuse to return from Ireland and seek a confrontation with the King. Faced with the evidence of his misgovernment, Henry caved in and agreed to put matters right by consulting his Parliament in October. Parliament was solidly for York. Among the many reforms they demanded were Somerset's imprisonment and York's recognition as the King's chief councillor. But by December Queen Margaret was once again calling the tune. Somerset was reinstated and Parliament was prorogued. When it reassembled in May 1451 one Thomas Young of Bristol was committed to the Tower for proposing that York should be named as heir apparent. As far removed from power as ever he was in Ireland, York retired to his castle of Ludlow in the Welsh Marches.

The struggle between the reformers and the Court party had now assumed the character of a vicious personal duel between York and Somerset. With Henry refusing to name his heir, York was afraid that his rival might persuade the Queen to override his legitimate claims. For Somerset too had a claim to the throne through his descent from John of Gaunt and his mistress Catherine Swynford. Early in 1452 York was ready to try again – this time with an army at his back. In a proclamation issued at Ludlow on 3 February, he protested that he was 'the King's true liege man': his reforms had been negated 'through the envy, malice and untruth of the said Duke of Somerset' who 'laboureth continually about the King's Highness for my undoing and to corrupt my blood, and to disherit me and my heirs'. When York's army reached London he found the city's gates closed, and Henry at Blackheath with a force that outnumbered his own. Anxious to avoid bloodshed

'The said Duke of Somerset . . . laboureth continually about the King's Highness for my undoing'

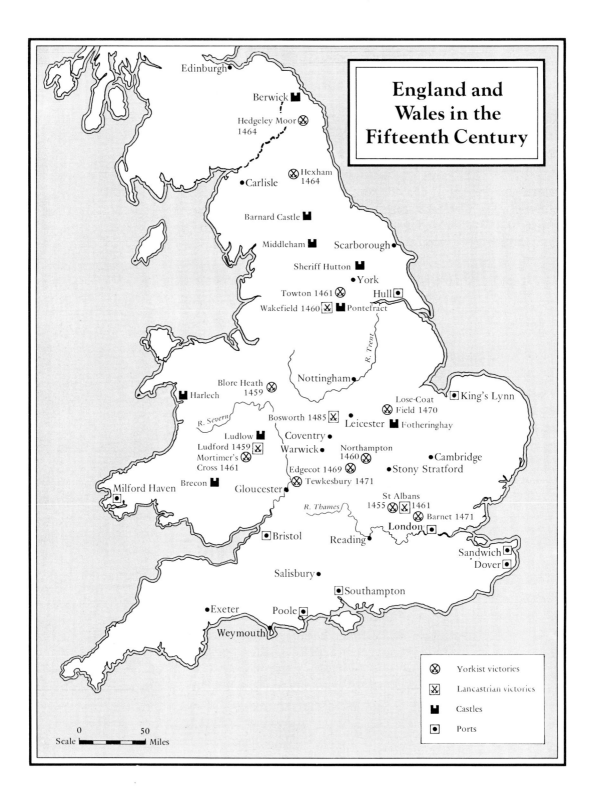

England and
Wales in the
Fifteenth Century

Edinburgh•

Berwick ▉

Hedgeley Moor ⊗
1464

Hexham ⊗
1464

•Carlisle

Barnard Castle ▉

Middleham ▉   Scarborough•

Sheriff Hutton ▉

•York

Towton 1461 ⊗   Hull ▣

Wakefield 1460 ☒ ▉ Pontefract

R. Trent

Nottingham•

Blore Heath ⊗
1459

▉ Harlech

Lose-Coat ⊗
Field 1470

▣ King's Lynn

R. Severn

Bosworth 1485 ☒   Leicester•   ▉ Fotheringhay

Ludlow ▉
Ludford 1459 ☒   Coventry•
Mortimer's ⊗   Warwick•   Northampton ⊗
Cross 1461   1460

•Cambridge

Edgecot 1469 ⊗   •Stony Stratford

Brecon ▉   Tewkesbury 1471

Milford Haven ▣   Gloucester•

R. Thames   St Albans
1455 ⊗ ☒ 1461

Barnet 1471 ⊗

London• ▣

▣ Bristol   Reading•

Sandwich ▣
Dover ▣

Salisbury•

▣ Southampton

•Exeter   Poole ▣

Weymouth

⊗ Yorkist victories

☒ Lancastrian victories

▉ Castles

▣ Ports

0   50
Scale ▮▮▮▮▮ Miles

at any price, the King induced York to surrender on the promise that Somerset would be arrested and tried. But the Queen would not give up the new favourite who had taken Suffolk's place in her affections. The King, always putty in her hands, was induced to break his word. York, who had obediently given himself up, was forced to undergo the humiliation of swearing a public oath never again to take up arms against the King.

Thus, in the year of Richard's birth, the kingdom already teetered on the brink of civil war. In the twelve months that followed, two events of cardinal importance sufficed to push it over the edge. On 17 July 1453 John Talbot, veteran of countless battles and sieges in the English reconquest of France, was killed at the battle of Castillon, and the last English army in France was annihilated by French cannon. By the year's end Bordeaux had fallen, Guyenne acknowledged Charles VII and the Hundred Years' War was at an end. At Henry's accession thirty years before, the Plantagenet dominions in France had embraced Normandy, Picardy, Ile de France and Gascony: now only Calais and the Channel Islands remained. An irreparable blow was dealt to English pride. Henry's government was branded with the stigma of defeat, and his French Queen became a symbol of England's shame. The defeated soldiers returning from the wars roamed the countryside in armed bands, a menace to the already disintegrating fabric of public order. Most important of all, the loss of empire dissolved the restraining bonds of patriotism which had held the domestic squabbles of the aristocracy in check.

Worse was to follow. Less than a month after Castillon, a bout of insanity deprived King Henry of speech and sense.

Her husband's madness brought out both the best and the worst in Queen Margaret. Still only twenty-three years old, she devoted her spectacular energy and courage to the defence of Henry's rights. But she was deaf to the real grievances of the Court's political opponents, construing their reforms as a direct assault on the royal prerogatives. While Somerset could do no wrong in her eyes, she had conceived a special loathing for the Duke of York. Without Henry's moderating influence, the Crown now became an instrument of faction. Queen Margaret did not hesitate to press her claims. In October her position was much strengthened when she gave birth to a son, Edward of

The Fifteenth-Century Wool Trade

Wool has been described as 'the flower and strength and revenue and blood of England', and during the late medieval period it was undoubtedly the principal source of wealth to the country. The revenue derived from the trade brought wealth both to secular merchants and to the great monasteries. Thus many of the fine houses and churches built in the fifteenth century were based upon wool.

BELOW In 1353, Edward III agreed that the export of wool should be entirely controlled by the body of merchants organised as the Company of the Staple at Calais. The Merchants of the Staple thus became a very powerful and wealthy body. In this illustration from Jean de Wavrin's *Chronique d'Angleterre*, the Master of the Staple is shown in audience with Duke Albert of Bavaria.

ABOVE Sheep-shearing from a late fifteenth-century manuscript. BELOW Much of the English wool was exported to the great trading cities of Flanders – Ghent, Bruges and Ypres – where it was made into cloth. Dyers at work, from 'Des Proprietez des Choses', a manuscript written in Bruges for Edward IV in 1482, by Jean du Ries.

Lancaster. This was a harsh blow to York's chances but popular feeling still ran high in his favour. The prospect of another long royal minority had little appeal for the Commons who assembled in Parliament early in 1454 to settle the question of the regency. Despite the protests of the Court, Richard of York was declared 'protector and defenser' on 27 March.

The protectorship did not survive the year's end. In December King Henry recovered his wits and formally recognised his son. Somerset, who had been committed to the Tower twelve months previously, was released, and York's ministers were dismissed. Both the Queen and Richard were now set on bringing matters to a head. York withdrew to Sendal Castle in Yorkshire and set about raising an army in conjunction with

William Grevel's house in Chipping Campden, Gloucestershire. Grevel was one of the wealthiest wool merchants of the fifteenth century and he built this fine town house from his wool revenues.

Ludlow Castle, the headquarters of Richard, Duke of York and his supporters in 1459.

his brother-in-law, the Earl of Salisbury. The Queen and Somerset summoned their supporters to a meeting of the Great Council at Leicester. The Yorkists mobilised first and marched south, and with an army of about three thousand men, they collided with the royal army at St Albans. In the first pitched battle of the Wars of the Roses, York was completely victorious. Somerset was slain and the King himself received a flesh wound from a Yorkist arrow.

York's dilemma was that he still claimed to act in the King's name. But, while the King was ruled by the Queen, his only sanction lay in superior force. The next three years were characterised by an armed truce during which the Queen's party slowly regained lost ground. The resurrected protectorship which York forced on the King was again abolished. A hollow reconciliation staged at St Paul's in March 1458 produced no real solutions, and the Duke of York confined himself warily to his estates.

The Yorkists entered the next round of hostilities with only two positive gains. The Merchants of the Staple, the most influential financial organisation in the country, backed them rather than the King as the best hope for a return to good government. The second was that the captaincy of Calais passed, on Somerset's death, to Cicely Neville's young nephew, Richard Neville, Earl of Warwick. Both as a refuge and as a springboard for invasion, Calais was an asset of incalculable value.

As usual the country at large suffered greater hardship than the principals who had brought about the breakdown of central government. The following summary by an anonymous chronicler, though biased in favour of the Yorkists, probably gives a fair picture:

In this same time, the realm of England was out of all good governance, as it had been many days before, for the king was simple

The Green Court of Knole Park in Kent. The great gatehouse was built by Cardinal Bourchier, Archbishop of Canterbury from 1454 to 1486.

and led by covetous counsel, and owed more than he was worth. His debts increased daily, but payment was there none: all the possessions and lordships that pertained to the crown the king had given away, some to lords and some to other simple persons, so that he had almost nought to live on. And such impositions as were put to the people, as taxes, tallages, and quinzimes, all that came from them was spent on vain, for he held no household he maintained no wars. For these misgovernances, and for many

others, the hearts of the people were turned away from them that had the land in governance, and their blessing was turned into cursing.

In Devonshire the Courtenay family terrorised the countryside in pursuit of private vendettas. In Northumberland the Nevilles took full advantage of their temporary ascendancy over the Percies. In 1457 the French launched a raid on Sandwich and burned it to the ground.

Early in 1459, York's youngest son, Richard, then in his seventh year, first felt the impact of war. With the Queen's party openly preparing for an armed challenge, Richard's father no longer considered Fotheringhay a safe refuge for his two younger sons, George and Richard. He therefore decided to move them to the greater isolation and superior defences of his great castle at Ludlow, where they joined his two older boys, the seventeen-year-old Edward, Earl of March, and his sixteen-year-old brother Edmund, Earl of Rutland. As it turned out, this was a most unfortunate decision. By early autumn the Queen's army was gathered at Coventry, poised to march on Ludlow. Despite the arrival of Richard Neville, Earl of Salisbury and his son Warwick, the Duke of York was heavily outnumbered. On the night of 13 October, with the royal army encamped only a mile from Ludlow, he heard that Warwick's most experienced troops – a contingent of the Calais garrison – had defected to seek the King's pardon. The news broke his nerve. The Yorkist leaders took to their heels and made for the Welsh coast. The Duke, who took with him only his elder sons, left his army, his wife and the rest of his family to fend for themselves. He and Edmund sailed for Ireland: Warwick and the others took refuge in Calais.

The Duchess Cicely and her two younger sons were not harshly treated. They were put into the custody of Richard's aunt, the Duchess of Buckingham, and lived on one of Buckingham's manors. In the following year the two boys were attached to the household of Thomas Bourchier, the Archbishop of Canterbury. Late in June 1460 they heard the welcome news that their brother Edward had landed at Sandwich with Salisbury and Warwick. On 2 July the three Earls were welcomed in London, where only the Tower held out for King

Henry. Then the Yorkists marched north: once again the Lancastrians were inadequately prepared. When the two armies clashed on 10 July, south of Northampton, the Yorkists carried the day in less than an hour. The Queen had wisely remained in Coventry during the battle and fled with Prince Edward, first to Harlech Castle in Wales, then to Scotland. King Henry was taken in his tent. For a second time he suffered the indignity of being rescued from his councillors in a pitched battle, and was taken back to London to sanction a Yorkist government.

But York, returning from Ireland in mid-September, had more ambitious plans. The clumsy fiction of the protectorship could be taken away as easily as it was granted. On 10 October he informed the astonished Lords in the Painted Chamber that he claimed the Crown by right of inheritance. Many of those present looked on York as a reformer rather than a candidate for the throne, and were not ready to depose the King in his favour. After much debate a compromise was reached: Henry would continue to rule for his natural life, but on his death the Crown would pass to York and his heirs. In the meantime York was to be Prince of Wales, Duke of Cornwall, Earl of Chester – and Protector of the Realm.

While the embarrassed Yorkist lords were arguing over their leader's claims, Queen Margaret was busy canvassing support to put another army in the field. In great secrecy a Lancastrian army was assembled at Hull. She was rewarded with total success. On 9 December York divided his strength, sending Edward west to pacify Wales, while he marched north to deal with the Queen. On the last day of December, the Lancastrians launched a surprise attack on Wakefield where the Protector was lodged. Although heavily outnumbered, York did not run away as he had at Ludlow. He and his son Edmund were killed on the battlefield. His brother-in-law Salisbury was taken and executed. The heads of the Yorkist leaders were impaled on the gates of York. The wars had entered a new and bloodier phase.

For the next three months confusion reigned as the country waited for the final battle that would decide the issue. The Prior of Croyland described the panic engendered by Queen Margaret's northerners as they marched on London:

> ... the northmen ... swept onwards like a whirlwind from the north, and in the impulse of their fury attempted to overrun the

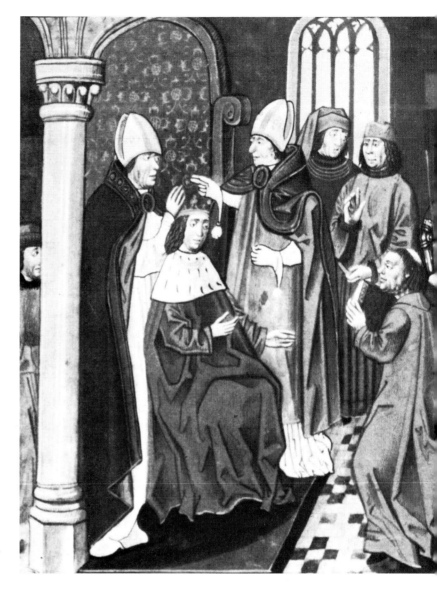

The coronation of
Edward IV, which took
place in Westminster
Abbey on 28 June 1461.
The King was crowned by
Cardinal Bourchier.

whole of England. At this period too, fancying that everything
tended to insure them freedom from molestation, paupers and
beggars flocked forth from those quarters in infinite numbers, just
like so many mice rushing forth from their holes, and universally
devoted themselves to spoil and rapine, without regard of place or
person. ... Thus did they proceed with impunity, spreading in vast
multitudes over a space of thirty miles in breadth, and, covering
the whole surface of the earth just like so many locusts, made their
way almost to the very walls of London.

Early in February came news that Edward had crushed the Earls of Pembroke and Wiltshire at the battle of Mortimer's Cross. Warwick, who had charge of London, advanced to block the northerners' march on the capital at St Albans. Early in the morning of 17 February the Queen's advance guard entered the town. By mid-afternoon Warwick's left wing had crumbled and he fled westward with the remnants of the army, hoping to join forces with Edward.

London now lay undefended. York's Duchess, who had already lost a husband, a son and a brother, boarded a ship bound for the Low Countries with George and Richard. Mysteriously, Margaret refused to seize the prize that was hers for the taking. Ten days later she had lost her chance. Edward and Warwick entered London in triumph on 26 February. Hugely relieved at their deliverance from the northerners, the citizens gave them a jubilant welcome. But the hero of the hour was Edward of York. Not yet nineteen years old, exceptionally tall and good-looking, he had already given proof of his ability as a commander of men at Mortimer's Cross. After York's death at Wakefield and Warwick's rout at St Albans, only his swift action had saved London from a Lancastrian sacking. He inherited all his father's charms without any of the rancour and suspicion generated by years of political in-fighting. There were no dissenting voices when he was proclaimed King at Paul's Cross on 4 March 1461.

The affair was, of course, carefully staged according to custom with an eye to its propaganda value. The real decision had already been taken by an inner circle of Yorkist leaders meeting at Baynard's Castle. The events leading to Edward's election were described by the City draper Robert Fabyan:

> ... the said earl [of Warwick] caused to be mustered his people in St John's Field, where unto that host were proclaimed and shewed certain articles and points that King Henry had offended in, whereupon it was demanded of the said people whether the said Henry were worthy to reign as king any longer or no. Whereunto the people cried hugely and said, Nay, Nay. And after it was asked of them whether they would have th'earl of March for their king and they cried with one voice, Yea, Yea. After the which admission thus by the commons assented, certain captains were assigned to bear report thereof unto the said earl of March, then being lodged at his place called Baynard's Castle. Of the which when he was by them

ascertained he thanked God and them. And how be it that like a wise prince he shewed by a convenient style that he was insufficient to occupy that great charge for sundry considerations by him then shewed, yet he lastly by the exhortation of the archbishop of Canterbury and the bishop of Exeter and other noble men then present took upon him that charge, and granted to their petition. . . . Then th'earl of March thus as is abovesaid being elected and admitted for king upon the morrow next ensuing rode unto Paul's and there rode in procession and offered, and there had Te Deum sungen with all solemnity. After which solemnisation finished he was with great royalty conveyed unto Westminster and there in the hall set in the king's see with St Edward's sceptre in his hand.

Edward was, however, careful to postpone his full coronation until he had dealt with Queen Margaret's army, still at large in Yorkshire. He did not want to owe his Crown entirely to the enthusiasm of the Londoners and the backing of the powerful Neville family. The Earl of Warwick, his uncle Lord Fauconberg and John Mowbray, Duke of Norfolk, left the capital first to muster recruits. Edward followed on 13 March. Two weeks later, on Palm Sunday, he led his army onto the field of Towton in a blinding snowstorm. In the longest and bloodiest engagement of the Wars of the Roses the Lancastrian army was completely destroyed. Warwick's brother, George Neville, Bishop of Exeter, reported that the battle 'began with the rising of the sun, and lasted until the tenth hour of the night'. The routed Lancastrians were ruthlessly hunted down and hacked to death until 'so many dead bodies were seen as to cover an area six miles long by three broad and about four furlongs . . . some 28,000 persons perished on one side and the other'.

'Our puppet', King Henry, accompanied by his wife and son, escaped the slaughter and was granted asylum by the Scots, in exchange for the surrender of the great frontier fortress of Berwick. After resting up for a few days at York, Edward returned to London to claim the Crown, already his by acclamation and by right of conquest.

2 The Kingmaker 1461-71

RIGHT Edward IV seated upon
the wheel of fortune,
flanked by members of the
Church and his army, including
his two brothers, Richard,
Duke of Gloucester and George,
Duke of Clarence.

BELOW Edward, as Earl of March,
fleeing to Calais with his
uncle, the Earl of Salisbury,
and his cousin, the Earl of
Warwick, in November 1459.
Henry VI is represented looking
on. These two illustrations
are taken from the
Chronicle of Edward IV.

PREVIOUS PAGES Richard Neville,
Earl of Warwick – popularly
known as 'the Kingmaker' –
and his wife, Anne Beauchamp:
illustrations from the
Rous Roll.

Nの EWS OF EDWARD'S GREAT VICTORY reached the Duchess of York and her younger sons two weeks later at Utrecht. While the fate of the House of York was in doubt, their welcome had been polite but reserved. Now Duke Philip of Burgundy visited the refugees in person and arranged for a magnificent send-off for them at Bruges. A few days later Richard and George were back in England at the royal manor of Sheen in Surrey.

Since he was only eight years old, it is unlikely that Richard was fully aware of the dizzying changes in his fortunes over the past two and a half years. The débâcle at Ludlow in 1460 left him in the custody of the House of Lancaster, the youngest son of an attainted rebel. A year later his father was Lord Protector and Richard stood fifth in line to the throne. At Wakefield he had lost a father, a brother and an uncle, and had to be smuggled abroad for his safety. Now he was back in England for the crowning of his universally popular brother. An Italian observer recorded that 'words fail me to relate how well the commons love and adore him, as if he were their God. The entire kingdom keeps holiday for the event'.

It was not long before Richard shared in his brother's good fortune. On the eve of Edward's coronation in June Richard and George acted out the elaborate ritual of induction as Knights of the Bath. Four months later, after George had been created Duke of Clarence, Richard in his turn became Duke of Gloucester, and was elected a Knight of the Garter. These titles had little bearing on his immediate future. It was the custom of the time that the sons of the nobility should be boarded out in the household of a family of equivalent rank, where they were known as henchmen. Foreign observers attributed this to the meanness of the English and their lack of affection; and it is probably true that the upper classes in the fifteenth century regarded their children as pawns to their social advancement. There was only one Yorkist lord in the England of 1461 of sufficient rank to take in the King's brother, and that was his cousin Richard Neville, Earl of Warwick.

The pre-eminence of the House of Neville was the supreme example of what inspired matchmaking could do for a family. Warwick's grandfather, Ralph Neville, married Joan Beaufort, bastard daughter of John of Gaunt. His father acquired the

ABOVE Illustrations from the *Chronicle of Alexander*, which was executed in Flanders in the late fifteenth century.
Left: Philip and Alexander outside Athens.
Right: The translator of the Chronicle presenting his book to Charles the Rash, Duke of Burgundy.
(Bodleian Ms Laud Misc 751, folios 32 and 17.)

earldom of Salisbury through his marriage to the former Earl's daughter, Alice. But the best catch of all was reserved for Warwick himself. He married Anne, the daughter of Richard Beauchamp, Earl of Warwick, owner of a vast inheritance in Wales, the West Country and the Midlands. When the senior branch of the Beauchamps became extinct in 1449 all this, along with the earldom of Warwick, was conferred in his wife's right on the twenty-one-year-old Richard Neville, whose possessions far exceeded those of his father and very nearly equalled those of York himself. The two families – Neville and York – were already closely linked. Richard, Duke of York had grown up

ABOVE Philip the Good, Duke of Burgundy, with his son Charles the Rash. Drawing from the *Recueil d'Arras*.

in the household of Warwick's grandfather, Ralph, and had later married Ralph's youngest daughter, Cicely. Marriage thus supplied the sinews of the tripartite alliance of Warwick, Salisbury and York which enabled those two Houses to take on the King and most of the older aristocracy.

Like all great landowners of the time Warwick had no permanent residence: but his favourite castle, and the home of his Countess, was at Middleham, capital of Wensleydale in the North Riding of Yorkshire. The massive keep, built by Robert Fitzralf in the 1170s and acquired by the Nevilles in the thirteenth century, still stands today, along with the gatehouse

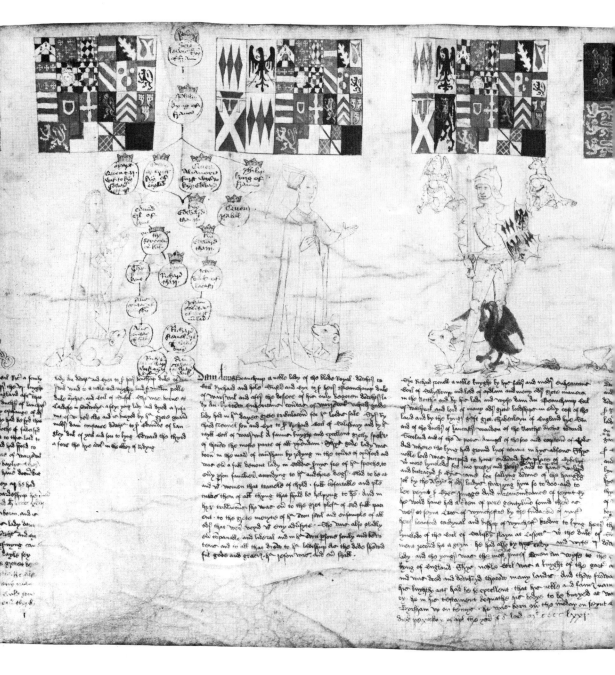

PREVIOUS PAGES Illustrations depicting the ceremony of initiation for the Order of the Bath. Left: The new knight being conducted by heralds and trumpeters to the Chapel of St John, to undergo his knightly vigil. Right: The following day, the new knight gives his old clothes to the heralds as their fee, and is dressed in a blue robe with a white hood and a token of white silk on the shoulder.

ABOVE The *Rous Roll*, an accoun of the Earls of Warwick written during Richard III's reign by John Rous, a chaplain at Guy's Cliff near Warwick. This section shows the Warwicks of

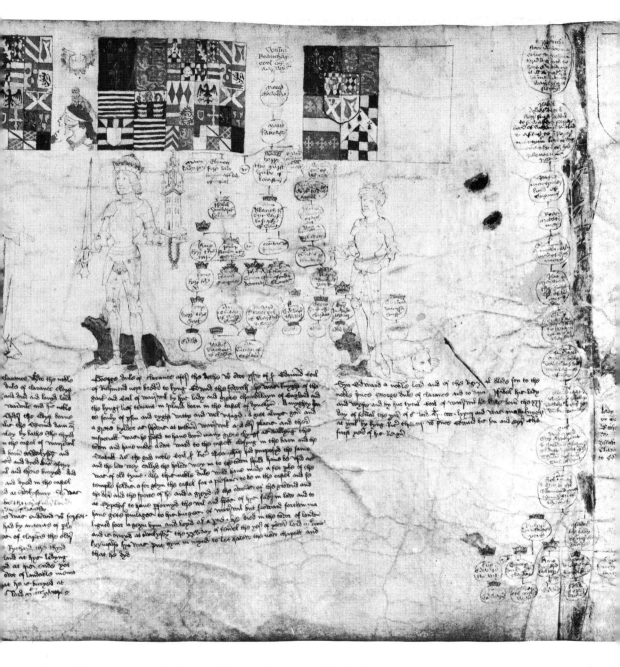

the later fifteenth century. Left to right, Lady Anne Beauchamp, daughter of the last Beauchamp Earl, Henry. She died in 1449. Anne Beauchamp, Countess of Warwick, the sister of Earl Henry, who married Richard Neville. Richard Neville, Earl of Warwick, 'the Kingmaker'. Isabel Neville, the elder daughter of Anne Beauchamp and Richard Neville. George, Duke of Clarence, who married Isabel Neville. Edward, Earl of Warwick, son of Isabel and George, who inherited the Warwick estates and title on his father's execution in 1478.

and the chapel. Here Richard was to spend the better part of the
next four years.

He and his fellow protégés were committed to the care of
Warwick's 'Master of Henxmen', a household official whose
duty it was to instil in Richard the rudiments of knightly conduct, described in the Household Book of Edward IV as 'the
schools of urbanity and nurture of England'. He taught the
henchmen to 'ride cleanly and surely; to draw them also to
jousts; to learn them to wear their harness and to have all courtesy in words, deeds, and degrees' and 'diligently to keep them
in the rules of goings and sittings'. The martial arts and good
conduct in the company of his peers formed the basis of
Richard's education but, like the traditional English public
school education, it was also tempered with book learning and
other liberal accomplishments. The Master of Henxmen would
teach his pupils 'sundry languages and other learning virtuous;
to harp, to pipe, sing, dance with other temperate behaving'.
The favourite popular reading of the time, prized for their
moral as well as entertainment value, were the traditional tales
of medieval chivalry. As William Caxton wrote later, 'read the
noble volumes of Saint Grail, of Lancelot, of Galahad, of
Tristram, of Perceforest, of Parseval, of Gawain and many
more. There ye shall see manhood, courtesy, gentleness.'
Richard never had the opportunity to read the greatest of all
these epics: Sir Thomas Mallory's *Morte d'Arthur* was published
three weeks before Bosworth.

When he was not out hunting with hawks and hounds in the
Yorkshire dales or practising with sword and lance in the tilt
yard, Richard's life centred around the communal routine of
the Great Hall, presided over by the Countess and supervised
by the Steward of the Household. Having risen shortly after
dawn, he would repair here for dinner, the main meal of the
day, at eleven. The whole of the 'standing' household – some
two hundred persons in the case of a great earl like Warwick –
would be present, seated at tables according to rank, and would
gnaw their way through six whole oxen in a single day.
Richard would again be on his best behaviour for 'this master
[of Henchmen] sitteth in the Hall, next unto these henchmen,
to have his respects unto their demeanings, how mannerly they
eat and drink and to their communication and other forms curial

2

ꝯ vius ... ꝗe noſtꝛe ſouuerain
ſeigneur ſꝫ eduuard le ꝗart
par la ꝗrace de dieu roy den
gleterre et de france / et ſeigne
dulande / departiſt du pais de zellande et

[courtly], after the book of urbanity'. Supper was at five, followed by a couple of hours of relaxation and then bed. In the winter months the servants would distribute a livery of candles and firewood to heat the upper chambers.

In common with most castles erected before the fifteenth century, Middleham was a cold and draughty place, built to withstand siege rather than to offer domestic comforts. Newly wealthy knights and barons might rebuild in brick or timber as at Hurstmonceux and Tattershall, Crowhurst Place and Ockwells, but the blue-blooded had to make do with modern improvements – painted glass in the windows, and tapestries richly emblazoned with hunting scenes or heraldic devices on the walls – to brighten the stone relics of their ancestors.

Richard's companions at this time included some who were to play important roles in his future. Two fellow henchmen – Francis Lovell and Robert Percy – would remain his friends for life. About the same age as Richard was the Countess's elder daughter, Isabel, who would marry his brother George of Clarence. The younger daughter, Anne, would one day sit at Richard's side as Queen of England.

During these four years of Richard's schooling the great Earl of Warwick was too busy fighting on the King's behalf to spend much time at Middleham. Steel-willed in adversity, Queen Margaret and her Scottish allies hammered repeatedly at Edward's northern frontiers. Warwick, with his brother John, Lord Montagu, was equally tireless in defence. Three times the Lancastrians invaded Northumberland and three times they were beaten back with heavy losses. The differences in character which finally destroyed the partnership between the Earl and the young King were already apparent in their methods. Where Warwick proffered a mailed fist, Edward held out a velvet glove. His willingness to forgive and forget, his attempts to charm his enemies into submission, were a powerful boost to his popularity. But the men who returned his generosity with treason paid for it with their lives. In February 1462 John de Vere, 12th Earl of Oxford and his eldest son, Aubrey, were executed after the discovery of a plot to assassinate the King.

A more potent menace was Henry Beaufort, Duke of Somerset – the eldest son and heir of York's great enemy – whom

OPPOSITE The great hall of Middleham Castle in Yorkshire, the favourite residence of Anne Beauchamp, Countess of Warwick. Middleham later became Richard's principal residence as Lieutenant of the North.

Edward singled out as a special target for his charm. In the autumn of 1463 Edward planned a visit to Yorkshire to 'see and understand the disposition of the people of the North'. He took with him the Duke of Somerset and a bodyguard of two hundred of Somerset's men 'well horsed and well harnessed'. On the way the citizens of Northampton, horrified to see their King apparently at the mercy of his hereditary foe, 'arose upon that false traitor the Duke of Somerset, and would have slain him within the King's palace. And then the King with fair speech and great difficulty saved his life for that time. . . . And the King full lovingly gave the Commons of Northampton a tun of wine that they should drink and make merry.' But the instincts of Edward's would-be rescuers proved correct. At the end of the year the Duke slipped away and organised a last ditch Lancastrian resistance from the Northumberland castle of Bamburgh. Again it was the Neville family who bailed Edward out from the consequences of his leniency. Outside Hexham on 14 May 1464, the Lancastrian rebels were soundly trounced by Lord Montagu. Somerset and his supporters were beheaded.

This battle virtually put an end to Lancastrian resistance. Shortly afterwards the Nevilles negotiated a fifteen-year-truce with the Scots and sealed the back door to Edward's kingdom. Warwick recaptured the three border strongholds of Alnwick, Dunstanburgh and Bamburgh – which had changed hands four times in as many years. Even Queen Margaret was momentarily subdued by this string of disasters; she retired at last to her father, René of Anjou's provincial Court at St Michel-sur-Bar. Sir John Fortescue described her little circle eking out a bitter Christmas in 1464: 'we beeth all in great poverty, but yet the Queen sustaineth us in meat and drink, so as we beeth not in extreme necessity . . . spend sparcely such money as ye have, for when ye come hither, ye shall have need of it'. Finally, in July 1465, Henry VI was tracked down to a Lancashire manor house and taken prisoner. With his feet tied to the stirrups, he rode through London as Warwick's captive to take up residence in the Tower.

If Edward's throne was now secure, he owed a heavy debt to his two cousins, the Earl of Warwick and his brother John, Lord Montagu. The victor of Mortimer's Cross and Towton had already shown signs of preferring the pleasures of food and

OPPOSITE Illustration from a law treatise of Henry VI's reign, showing the Court of the King's Bench at Westminster. At the top sit five presiding judges, and below them the King's Attorney, the Coroner and Masters of the Court, wearing party-coloured gowns of blue, and white, murrey and green. Standing on the green baized table are two ushers, one addressing the Court and the other administering an oath on the gospel to the jury. A prisoner stands in fetters at the bar in the custody of the marshall or tipstaff flanked by sergeants. Six more prisoners are shown in the foreground in the custody of tipstaffs.

49

The Schools of Urbanity and Nurture

Richard, Duke of Gloucester was taught the rudiments of knightly conduct in the Kingmaker's household at Middleham. Warwick's 'Master of Henxman' taught Richard and his friends to ride, to joust and to fight, and also supervised their book learning and reading.

RIGHT Chaucer's knight 'that from the time that he began to ride out, he loved chivalry, truth and honour', from the Prologue to the *Canterbury Tales*. This woodcut illustration is taken from Caxton's printed edition of the Tales.

LEFT Miniature from the *Ordinances of Chivalry*, which was written for Sir John Astley before 1486. This shows a knight donning his tilting armour in his 'hut', which has been specially erected close to the jousting arena.

RIGHT Illustration page from *Chemin de Vaillance*, a tale of medieval chivalry, produced for Edward IV. The miniature shows Nature appearing to the author in a dream and showing him the Lady Vaillance. The arms of Edward IV are held by a knight in armour at the bottom right-hand of the page, while the rest of the borders are decorated with various badges.

Cy commence le premier liure
de ce present volume intitule Le
chemin de vaillace ·
A glorieuse trinite
Trois persones en vnite
Pere filz et saint esprit
Qui humain lui
natre querit ·
Deternele dampnation

Par sa benoite passion
Ihe dpnst a mon commencement
Le don de sonarde ensement
Grace ponoir sens pour retaire
Vng compte que ie vous veul faire
Dune vision mermeilleuse
A comprendre moult perilleuse
Qui me adunt quant ionce estoie
Et la pres d · xx · ans auoie

drink and pretty girls to the rigours of a campaign in the saddle. The Bishop of St Andrews rightly referred to the all-powerful Earl as the 'conductor of the kingdom under King Edward'. While Edward was content to take the advice of his mentor, Warwick had no reason to complain. After his victory at Hexham Lord Montagu was invested with the rich earldom of Northumberland and Warwick's clerical brother George, already Chancellor of England, was elevated to the archbishopric of York.

However, by the time the twelve-year-old Richard had been reunited with his brother at Court in the spring of 1465, the seeds of discord had been sown. In the previous autumn, at a Great Council convened at Reading, Edward confronted a stunned assembly with the *fait accompli* of his secret marriage to Elizabeth Woodville. The circumstances in which this marriage took place were later recorded by Robert Fabyan:

> In such pass time, in most secret manner, upon the first day of May, King Edward spoused Elizabeth, late the wife of Sir John Grey, knight, which before time was slain at Towton or York Field, which spousals were solemnised early in the morning at a town named Grafton, near Stony Stratford; at which marriage was no persons present but the spouse, the spousess, the duchess of Bedford her mother, the priest, two gentlewomen, and a young man to help the priest sing. After which spousals ended, he went to bed, and so tarried there upon three or four hours. ...

Elizabeth, considering herself too good to become the King's whore, had the guts to turn down his advances and, like Anne Boleyn in the succeeding century, her scruples were rewarded with a Crown.

By any standards it was an amazingly tactless union. The Yorkist Queen was the widow of a Lancastrian knight, Sir John Grey, with two children of the same age as Edward's brothers. Far more important was the fact that it scotched the delicate negotiations that Warwick had set in motion for a marriage alliance with Europe's master diplomatist, King Louis XI of France. Such a match had obvious advantages for both parties. Edward's marriage to a French princess would knock away the last prop of Queen Margaret's hopes, and leave the King of France free to swallow up the two great ducal fiefs of Brittany and Burgundy. No family in England was more appreciative

OPPOSITE Elizabeth Woodville, the handsome widow who captured Edward IV's heart and almost lost him his kingdom. Elizabeth was one of the founders of Queens' College, Cambridge and this portrait hangs in the College Hall.

of the benefits of an advantageous match than the House of Neville, and Warwick rightly regarded the King's marriage as an affair of State rather than of the heart.

It rapidly became apparent that the Queen's relatives were no sluggards either when it came to playing the marriage game. Within fifteen months of Edward's revelation at Reading, the Earl of Arundel's heir, Lord Herbert's heir, and the twelve-year-old Duke of Buckingham were snapped up by three of the Queen's sisters, and one of her sons had taken the Duke of Exeter's heiress to the altar. The most notorious match was reserved for Elizabeth's brother John: in the words of a contemporary chronicler, 'Catherine, Duchess of Norfolk, a slip of a girl of about eighty years old, was married to John Wydeville, the Queen's brother, aged twenty years; a diabolical marriage.' To give Warwick his due, he was less upset by the advancement of the fecund Woodvilles than by the more basic differences in foreign policy which the marriage

The *Donne Triptych* by Hans Memling, painted for Sir John Donne of Kidwelly, who visited Flanders in 1468 for the marriage of Margaret of York to Charles the Rash. Sir John and his wife are portrayed kneeling before the Virgin, wearing collars of sunbursts, the personal badge of Edward IV.

revealed. He himself escorted Elizabeth into the abbey chapel at Reading for her ceremonial recognition as Queen of England, and, according to one source close to the Court, 'the Earl continued to show favour to the Queen's kindred, until he found that her relatives and connections … were using their utmost endeavours to promote the other marriage, which in conformity with the King's wishes eventually took place between Charles [of Burgundy] and the Lady Margaret [Edward's sister]'.

The Woodville affair could be pardoned as an indiscretion, but Edward's plan to ally England with Burgundy was in direct contradiction to his own plans for a *rapprochement* with France. It rapidly dawned on Warwick that Edward was no longer his protégé. Affable as ever, the King avoided a direct confrontation with the Earl, but while Warwick continued his negotiations with Louis, Edward calmly pressed on with his own plans. For a time it seemed as if England had two masters, each bent on his own course. In the spring of 1467 two rival embassies visited Westminster, headed by the Bastard of Bourbon for France, and the Bastard of Burgundy for his master, each dangling marriage treaties and trade agreements. Sir John Paston wagered three marks that Philip of Burgundy's son Charles would not marry Margaret within two years. But Edward had his way, and the marriage treaty was finally ratified in March 1468.

Edward's preference for Burgundy was not just a whim designed to show his independence of the Earl. Edward still called himself King of France. Memories of the Hundred Years' War were fresh in English minds and Louis had lent Margaret his most able general to reconquer the Crown for Lancaster. He had good reason to suspect that Louis's friendship could prove as dangerous as his enmity. Burgundy, on the other hand, was England's traditional ally and trading partner, and Duke Philip had shown his friendship in 1461 by sheltering the Yorkist refugees.

Warwick did not take his defeat lightly. In June 1468, as he rode with Edward, George of Clarence and Richard of Gloucester to escort the future Duchess of Burgundy on her bridal journey to Margate, a new scheme was already half formed in his mind. The Nevilles had made one King: why not another?

55

Edward had betrayed his trust, but his brother Clarence might prove more easily led – particularly if he was married to Warwick's nubile fifteen-year-old daughter Isabel. Edward had already incurred Clarence's resentment by vetoing this particular match, and other Yorkist magnates might well lend a hand if Warwick's *coup* promised an end to the ambitions of the voracious Woodvilles.

From the summer of 1468 to the spring of 1469 an uneasy truce prevailed as Warwick's plan matured. The country at large was well aware of the Earl's disaffection and particularly of his contempt for the Woodvilles. Robert Fabyan reported that

> ... many murmerous tales ran in the city atween th'earl of Warwick and the queen's blood, the which earl was ever had in great favour of the commons of this land, by reason of the exceeding household which he daily kept in all countries wherever he sojourned or lay, and when he came to London he held such an house that six oxen were eaten at breakfast, and every tavern was full of his meat, for who that had any acquaintance in that house, he should have had as much sodden and roast as he might carry upon a long dagger.

Edward's troubles began, early in 1469, with a series of mysterious risings in the North and Midlands, inspired by a rebel who called himself Robin of Redesdale. The size of Robin's army and the anti-Woodville slant of his proclamations were clear signs that he enjoyed the support of a more powerful backer. Somebody was also spreading the rumour that Edward was a bastard, in which event not he but George, Duke of Clarence, was rightfully King of England. In June Edward, accompanied by the Duke of Gloucester, set out to investigate the risings. Unaware that real danger threatened, he took with him only a small army and dawdled on the way. As soon as the King was safely out of reach, Warwick and Clarence slipped across the Channel to Calais and on 11 July George Neville, the Archbishop of York, officiated at Clarence's marriage to Isabel Neville. In the meantime Edward had realised that Robin of Redesdale's army was very much larger than his own and had fallen back on Nottingham. Warwick recrossed the Channel and marched north to join forces with Robin's men. Edward

Edward IV enthroned, surrounded by his courtiers. Sir William Herbert kneels before the King, dressed in armour with his coat of arms upon his surcoat. His wife is also portrayed, wearing her arms upon her dress and mantle. Miniature from John Lydgate's *Troy Book and Story of Thebes*.

sat tight waiting for a relieving force under William Herbert, Earl of Pembroke, to join him at Nottingham. On 26 July, however, Pembroke's troops were crushed between the two rebel armies of Robin and Warwick near Banbury and cut to pieces. After writing a farewell note to his Woodville wife, Pembroke himself was executed at Warwick's orders: 'wife, pray for me and take the said order [of widowhood] that ye promised me, as ye had in my life my heart and love'.

Edward was completely outmanœuvred. He now faced the choice of plunging the whole country into renewed anarchy or of total surrender. The course he took revealed him as a master of political strategy. He dispersed his army, allowed the Woodvilles to scatter for cover, and calmly awaited his captors. Gambling on the assumption that Warwick would not dare have him killed, he knew that public sympathy would rally to him as the news of Warwick's treachery spread through the country. Within a few months the kingmaking Earl found himself at an *impasse*. His rebellion had sparked off a chain of minor disturbances which he could not put down without the King's authority. Even Warwick's brother John, the newly created Earl of Northumberland, refused to co-operate. By the end of September Edward was in a position to summon his supporters to his prison at Pontefract, and return to London with George Neville, his episcopal gaoler, trailing disconsolately behind him, 'Peace and entire oblivion of all grievances upon both sides was agreed to. Still, however, there probably remained, on the one side, deeply seated in his mind, the injuries he had received and the contempt which had been shown to majesty, and on the other: "A mind too conscious of a daring deed"' (Croyland Chronicle).

'A mind too conscious of a daring deed'

Edward's bloodless counter-coup marks an important stage in the career of his youngest brother Richard, Duke of Gloucester, now just celebrating his seventeenth birthday. In the years between leaving Middleham and Warwick's rebellion, we catch only a few brief glimpses of him. In 1466 he attended the installation of George Neville as Archbishop of York, and sat at table with the ladies at the sumptuous banquet which followed. Warwick himself served as steward. The menu, which represented the labours of 62 cooks, included 104 oxen, 6 wild bulls, 4,000 sheep, calves and pigs, 500 stags and 400 swans, and was washed down with 300 tuns of ale and 100 of wine. As a *pièce de résistance* the guests demolished a marzipan sculpture of St George lancing the dragon.

In February of 1467 Richard's name was joined with Warwick's and Northumberland's in a legal commission to hear cases at York: in June 1468, he is mentioned again as a member of his sister Margaret's nuptial train on its way to Margate. But it was in 1469 that his adolescence ended, and he was called to take up offices which held more than mere ceremonial significance. The events of that summer showed that Richard, despite his close association with the Nevilles, was deaf to the blandishments that had seduced his brother Clarence. Shortly after Edward's return to London the seventeen-year-old Duke of Gloucester was appointed Constable of England, and received a generous grant of land, including the castle of Sudeley in Gloucestershire. An uprising in Wales provided him with his first independent military command. Under his leadership the rebel-held strongholds of Carmarthen and Cardigan were retaken before the year's end. In the spring of 1470 Richard was further rewarded with numerous grants and offices which conferred on him wide authority throughout Wales.

The Welsh rising, however, was a sideshow: in the early spring of 1470 it was still the Earl of Warwick who occupied the centre of the political stage. No one could seriously have expected his formal reconciliation with the King to offer anything more than a breathing space. During Edward's captivity he had put to death the Queen's father, Earl Rivers, and one of her brothers at Warwick Castle. This act, even more than his rebellion, committed him to try again, if only to save his own neck from Queen Elizabeth's vengeance.

In February rebellion raised its head again in Lincolnshire. Its leaders, Lord Welles and Sir Thomas Dymmock, were quickly brought to heel by promises of a royal pardon, but Welles's son, Sir Robert, remained at large, defying the King in the name of the Duke of Clarence and the Earl of Warwick. By 12 March Edward's army was at Stamford, only a few miles from Sir Robert's forces. Warwick and Clarence were on their way from Coventry, ostensibly to help the King. But, before Warwick could join his forces to either side, the Lincolnshire rebels were put to flight at the battle known as Lose-Coat Field, and Sir Robert was a prisoner in Edward's hands. Sir Robert's confession confirmed the King's suspicions: the rising had been Warwick's work.

His treason unmasked and his Lincolnshire allies routed, Warwick cast about for other allies, first his own brother the Earl of Northumberland, then the Lancashire magnate Lord Stanley. Both turned a deaf ear. With the wretched Clarence still in tow, he fled south to the Devon coast and there boarded a ship for France. It was time to cash in on his friendship with King Louis. Embarrassed at first by the arrival of these uninvited guests, Louis soon rallied to evolve a scheme worthy of his diplomatic talents. If he could team up the fugitive Yorkist Earl with the exiled Lancastrian Queen in a successful bid to unseat

RIGHT Philip de
Commynes, Seigneur
d'Argentan, chronicler and
councillor to Louis XI of
France. From a drawing in
the *Recueil d'Arras*.

FAR RIGHT Henry VI
enthroned, from an
English psalter of 1460.

King Edward, he would not only have his peace with England
but also sever the English alliance with Burgundy. The reconciliation of two such bitter enemies was a formidable challenge
to Louis's powers of persuasion: 'the queen was right difficile
and showed to the King of France ... that with the honour of
her and her son, he nor she might not, nor could not pardon the
said Earl, which hath been the greatest causes of the fall of
King Henry'. Nevertheless, Margaret's thirst for revenge on
the House of York overcame her loathing for Warwick and on
22 July 1470, she formally accepted his submission at the
cathedral of Angers. Three days later the pact was sealed with

60

ominus illumi
naco mer 7 falus
mea quem timebo
ominus pro
rector vice mee a quo
trepidabo.

the betrothal of the Queen's sixteen-year-old son, Edward, to Warwick's younger daughter, the fifteen-year-old Anne Neville. The Duke of Clarence, a willing enough stooge in his time, was quietly jettisoned with the promise that he would succeed to the throne if Edward and Anne failed to produce an heir.

Warwick's landing in Devon on 13 September was well timed, since it caught Edward in the north of his kingdom. Already accompanied by John de Vere, 13th Earl of Oxford and by Jasper Tudor, the Kingmaker was soon joined by John Talbot, 3rd Earl of Shrewsbury and Lord Stanley. But once again there was to be no battle, thanks to another important defection from Edward's camp. Earlier in the year the King had tried to reconcile the powerful Lancastrian Percy family by restoring to it the earldom of Northumberland, which he had earlier bestowed on John Neville. In return John was asked to make do with the marquisate of Montagu. In response to this imagined slight the Marquess now decided to throw his lot in with his brother Warwick and almost succeeded in capturing the King at Doncaster. In the nick of time Edward rode away with a small band that included his brother Richard, his brother-in-law Anthony, Earl Rivers, and his Chamberlain, Lord Hastings. He commandeered a flotilla of fishing boats at the East Anglian port of Lynn and sailed for Burgundy. In London King Henry VI was hastily released from the Tower – 'not so cleanly kept as should seem such a Prince' – and dressed up in a blue velvet gown to receive the Kingmaker's homage. In the following month Edward's Queen Elizabeth gave birth to her first baby boy, Edward, in the Sanctuary of Westminster Abbey, where her husband's flight had compelled her to take refuge.

Edward and Richard were now the guests of Charles the Rash – ruler of Burgundy since Duke Philip's death in 1467 – and his Duchess, their sister Margaret. Charles was at first reluctant to become embroiled in the dynastic politics of his wife's family, but underwent a rapid conversion when King Louis declared war on him at Christmas. He realised that his duchy would not long survive an alliance between the French King and England's new master, the Earl of Warwick. On 11 March 1471 the Yorkists sailed from Flushing with a mixed

LEFT Hanseatic merchants in the port of Hamburg, from a fifteenth-century miniature.

OVERLEAF Miniatures from *Les Œuvres de Miséricorde,* showing the charitable acts of Margaret of York, Duchess of Burgundy.

Le prologue du liure qui senfieut Jntitule
xnois feront les miferico2dieuv.

lonneur et reuerence donneu
et pour le falut dunchafeun
¶ Chofe falutaire et moult
p2o2uffitable eft de ftauoir.

64

De saint augustin en ung sermon.

Comme on ne peut nettoier
ne curer les pechies par si
ne mais ce fait on bien
par aumosne Jasoit ce q

Dꝛes touttes ces choses ainsy
aduenues le sezieme iour du
dit mois le roy eut nouuelles
que marguerite soy disant roy
ne ꝺ sa tresmauluaise pretente et vsurpatiõ

Two of the miniatures decorating the chapter headings of the French version of the *Historie of the Arrivall of Edward IV*.

LEFT The Battle of Tewkesbury, 4 May 1471, when Edward IV crushed the Lancastrian forces of Margaret of Anjou. Many leading Lancastrians were killed in the battle, including the only son and heir of Margaret and Henry VI, Edward Prince of Wales.

RIGHT Several Lancastrians escaped the field and sought refuge in Tewkesbury Abbey, but Edward IV demanded that the Abbot should hand them over to him. Amongst these was Edmund Beaufort, 3rd Duke of Somerset, whose execution on 6 May is portrayed here. To the right of the illustration, John Langstrother, Prior of the Hospital of St John at Jerusalem, awaits execution.

army of Burgundians and Englishmen in a fleet of fourteen ships provided by the German merchants of the Hanse towns. Rebuffed in Norfolk and scattered by a storm off the Yorkshire coast, Edward's fleet at last made landfall on the Humber estuary. At this stage his meagre force of sixteen hundred men lay at the mercy of the Marquess Montagu and the Earl of Northumberland who each commanded superior forces in the vicinity. But both held back, content for the moment to let others decide the issue. Edward marched south unmolested, gathering recruits to his standard at Nottingham and Leicester. By 29 March he was outside Coventry, offering battle to his arch-enemy the Earl of Warwick. The Kingmaker refused to leave the shelter of the city walls until he could be reinforced by the three converging armies of Montagu, Oxford and Clarence. It seemed as if his brash Yorkist cousin would soon be overwhelmed by superior numbers or sent packing back to Burgundy.

But Edward had an ace up his sleeve. During the winter of his exile 'great and diligent labour, with all effect, was continually made by the high and mighty princess, the duchess of Burgogne, which at no season ceased to send her servants, and messengers, to the king, where he was, and to my said Lord of Clarence, into England'; through the good offices of his sister Margaret, Clarence was duly persuaded to return to the fold. On 4 April the three brothers met outside Warwick. Clarence went down on his knees and made a formal submission to the King. A more tangible asset was the force of four thousand men that Clarence brought with him to swell the Yorkist army.

With Warwick still bottled up in Coventry refusing to come out and fight, Edward decided to march on London. The defence of the capital had been entrusted to George Neville, the Archbishop of York, who also had charge of Henry VI. Robert Fabyan described his futile attempts to rally support in the solidly Yorkist city:

> And for to cause the citizens to bear their more favour unto King Henry, the said King Henry was conveyed from the palace of Paul's through Cheap and Cornhill, and so about to his said lodging again by Candlewick Street and Watling Street, being accompanied with the archbishop of York which held him all that way by the hand ... the which was more liker a play than the showing

of a prince to win men's hearts, for by this mean he lost many and won none or right few, and ever he was shewed in a long blue gown of velvet as though he had no moo to change with.

On 11 April Edward and Richard entered London to rapturous applause.

Edward's hold on London was one of the keys to his ultimate triumph over the House of Lancaster. Louis XI's adviser, Philip de Commynes, rather frivolously suggested that he owed his support to the gratitude of the burghers' wives whom he had selected to share his bed. But apart from his emotional appeal, Edward had always fostered the interest of the merchant community, even to the extent of undertaking a number of commercial ventures on his own account. Unlike Henry VI in his single blue velvet gown, Edward was a big spender with a lot of unsettled bills to his name.

After a brief reunion with his wife and mother at Baynard's Castle and a first glimpse of his six-month-old son, Edward led his army out of London on the road to Barnet. For on Easter Saturday he heard the welcome news that Warwick had just passed through St Albans. Why was he now ready to give battle when he had refused Edward's challenge at Coventry? Queen Margaret was expected to land any day in Devon where John Courtenay, Earl of Devon and Edmund Beaufort, Duke of Somerset, were already levying troops in her name. Most probably he felt that his own position, already jeopardised by Clarence's defection, must be retrieved by a glorious victory won without the Queen's assistance.

Edward's outriders galloped into Barnet village that same afternoon, putting Warwick's scouts to flight. Half a mile beyond, they collided with the Earl's front line drawn up across a low ridge well shielded by hedgerows. Richard, who led the Yorkist van, conferred with his brother and despite the failing light they decided to press on beyond the village and take up their positions right under Warwick's nose. All night long Warwick's cannon pounded into the darkness. 'But', recorded an eye witness, 'thanked be God! it so fortuned that they alway overshot the King's host, and hurted them nothing.'

At daybreak on Easter Sunday both armies were obscured

69

Illustration from the French version of the *Historie of the Arrivall of Edward IV* showing the Bastard of Fauconberg, Margaret of Anjou's ally, laying siege to London with a force of Kentishmen. This was raised when news came through that Margaret of Anjou had been captured after the Battle of Tewkesbury.

from each other's sight by a thick fog. Unbeknown to Edward the two lines of battle overlapped; his left, under Lord Hastings, was outflanked by Warwick's right under the Earl of Oxford, while the Yorkist right, commanded by Richard, outflanked the Duke of Exeter's men on the Lancastrian left. As soon as the fighting began, Hastings was in trouble. Under heavy pressure both from the front and on the flank his troops wavered, fell back and finally broke. With Oxford's men at their heels, they abandoned the field and streamed back down the road towards London. By mid-morning the streets of the capital were alive with rumours that 'the King was distressed and his field lost'. At the same time Richard was taking advantage of his corresponding overlap on the right, so weakening Exeter's flank that Warwick had to commit the Lancastrian reserves.

Edward, commanding the Yorkist centre, was now in great danger from Oxford's victorious troops. Returning from the rout of Hastings' men, Oxford intended to attack the King from the rear. But by now the line of battle had swung around from an east-west to a north-south axis, and the Earl of Oxford's men collided not with Edward's troops, but with Montagu's. Met by a volley of arrows from Montagu's archers, Oxford's men panicked and fell back. The Earl of Oxford himself fled from the field, convinced that Montagu had turned his coat again.

The ensuing confusion decided the day. By 7 am the Lancastrian front was broken, and Montagu was dead. Warwick was overtaken in flight by the King's men and put to death on the spot. As proof of his decisive victory, Edward had the two Neville corpses exposed to public view at St Paul's.

On that same Easter Sunday, Queen Margaret landed at Weymouth with her son, Prince Edward. Bottled up by head winds at Honfleur for three weeks, she came too late to save the House of Neville. But the Duke of Somerset was quick to point out that Edward's army too had been badly mauled; in Wales and Lancashire, the traditional strongholds of her House, she could still bring enough men to her banners to reverse the verdict of Barnet. Speed was all important, for if Edward could hold or destroy the bridges on the River Severn before she could cross, Margaret would be cut off. On 3 May she reached the first crossing-point at Gloucester after an all-night march: but the gates were closed and Edward was by now too close behind to let her risk an assault on the town. Without pause she drove on to the next passage at Tewkesbury. Here, at four in the afternoon, she was compelled to rest. Her foot soldiers were exhausted and even the horses were flagging. Camping in a field outside the town that night, Margaret realised that she must now turn and fight.

On Saturday, 4 May 1471, it was Richard, Duke of Gloucester who led the Yorkist van on the road from Cheltenham to Tewkesbury. This time he faced the Lancastrian left, commanded by Edmund Beaufort, Duke of Somerset, the third to bear that title in a cause which had already carried off his father and his elder brother. The ground between the two armies was a patchwork of 'foul lanes and deep dykes, and many hedges',

well reconnoitred by Somerset's scouts but unfamiliar to Richard. Perceiving his advantage, Somerset marched his men swiftly round to Richard's flank and launched his attack.

It was a well-judged move, but Somerset knew nothing of the company of spearmen Edward had stationed in a wood a few hundred yards to the left of Richard's position. Those '200 spears' now found themselves ideally placed at Somerset's rear. Seizing their opportunity they 'came and brake on, all at once upon the Duke of Somerset and his vanguard ... whereof they were greatly dismayed and abashed, and so took them to flight into the park, and into the meadow that was near, and into lanes and dykes, where they best hoped to escape the danger'. Richard's men surged forward and the pursuit became a rout. Somerset's retreat was cut off by the River Avon and the field across which he fled earned the name of Bloody Meadow.

Richard's success proved decisive. While Edward pressed the attack on the Lancastrian centre, Richard's men rounded on their unprotected flank. The entire Lancastrian line crumbled and fled. Prince Edward was overtaken by a detachment of Clarence's men and butchered. The rebel leaders who had taken sanctuary in Tewkesbury Abbey were dragged out, condemned and beheaded in the market place. A few days later Queen Margaret was taken prisoner and the last Lancastrian force in England – the Kentishmen raised by the Bastard of Fauconberg – retired from an abortive siege of London.

One last grisly act sealed the triumph of the House of York. In the words of the chronicler John Warkworth:

> And the same night that King Edward came to London, King Henry, being inward in prison in the Tower of London, was put to death, the 21st day of May, on a Tuesday night, between eleven and twelve of the clock, being then at the Tower the duke of Gloucester, brother to King Edward, and many other; and on the morrow he was chested and brought to Paul's, and his face was open that every man might see him; and in his lying he bled on the pavement there; and afterward at the Black Friars was brought, and there he bled new and fresh; and from thence he was carried to Chertsey Abbey in a boat, and buried there in our Lady Chapel.

OPPOSITE On 21 May 1471, Henry VI was murdered in the Wakefield Tower. His body was taken to Blackfriars Priory, and thence to Chertsey Abbey for burial. This miniature from a manuscript belonging to Margaret de Foix, Duchess of Burgundy, shows a fifteenth-century burial scene.

3
'Loyalty binds me'
1471-83

E DWARD'S MURDER of the harmless, kindly and befogged King Henry shocked many of his contemporaries. In the words of the author of the Great Chronicle of London, Henry cared 'little or nothing of the pomp or vanities of this world, wherefore after my mind he might say, as Christ said to Pilate, "my kingdom is not of this world" for God had endowed him with such grace that he chose the life contemplative, the which he forsook not from his tender age unto the last day of his life'. Of his many acts of kindness, none is more poignant than the concern he showed for Edward's wife during her confinement in Westminster Abbey, when he sent her food and wine.

Yet Henry was the victim not of Edward's cruelty, but of his own saintly indifference to worldly affairs. He lost his throne because England needed a king, not a monk – a strong king who could restore order, dispense justice and promote trade. He lost his life because the magic of his name could still inspire the respect and loyalty that men like Warwick needed to mask their cynical ambitions. With Henry as a focus for the plots, uprisings and invasions that blighted the early promise of Edward's reign, the monarchy tumbled into disrespect and the Crown became no more than first prize in an aristocratic power game. As the chronicler John Warkworth shrewdly noted 'When King Edward reigned, the people looked after all the aforesaid prosperities and peace, but it came not; but one battle after another, and much trouble and great loss of goods among the common people.' Henry, the guiltless cause of so much trouble, had to die so that the king could be king.

A later generation of Tudor historians, brought up on tales of Richard's villainy, could not resist the imputation that Richard was personally responsible for the deaths of both Henry VI and his son Edward. According to Edward Hall, who wrote in Henry VIII's reign, Prince Edward was not slain at the battle of Tewkesbury but taken prisoner and brought before the King, 'being a goodly feminine and well featured young gentleman'. Whereupon the King:

> ... demanded of him, how he durst so presumptuously enter into his Realm with banner displayed. The prince, being bold of stomach and of a good courage, answered saying: to recover my father's kingdom and inheritance. ... At which words King Edward said nothing, but with his hand thrust him from him (or, as some

PREVIOUS PAGE Edward IV, portrait by an unknown artist.

76

say, stroke him with his gauntlet), whom incontinent, they that stood about which were George, Duke of Clarence, Richard, Duke of Gloucester, Thomas, Marquess Dorset and William, Lord Hastings, suddenly murdered and piteously manquelled.

Of Henry VI's death the same author writes: 'Poor King Henry the Sixth, a little before deprived of his realm and imperial crown was now in the Tower of London spoiled of his life ... by Richard Duke of Gloucester (as the constant fame ran) which to the intent that King Edward his brother should be clear of all secret suspicion of sudden invasion, murdered the said king with a dagger.' In fact, there is no foundation for either of these stories. All the contemporary accounts of Tewkesbury, Lancastrian and Yorkist, simply state that Prince Edward was slain on the battlefield. Likewise, all that is known of Henry's murder is the bald fact of his death, along with Warkworth's statement that Richard accompanied his brothers 'and many others' to the Tower on the fatal night.

The Duke of Gloucester was, however, to play a vital part in restoring the majesty of the Crown. In July 1471 – only a few weeks after the exhausting ordeal of the Tewkesbury campaign – he was on his way north to deal with a new rash of border incidents on the Scottish Marches. This was no temporary commission. Edward had decided to invest the eighteen-year-old veteran of his two great victories with the spoils – and the responsibilities – of the conquered Earl of Warwick.

In the northern counties and the Scottish Marches a strong tradition of lawlessness and independence defied the efforts of the distant Council at Westminster to impose order and justice. The rugged and backward North had long enjoyed a political complexion different from that of the South. In order to protect the border against Scottish incursions, successive English kings had invested great families, such as the Nevilles and the Percies, with huge estates and semi-regal powers to raise private armies as Wardens of the Marches. For fifteen years, the open warfare between the Nevilles and Percies had promoted local feuds and invited the depredations of the Scots.

With the extinction of the House of Lancaster and the disgrace of the Nevilles, only one great magnate was left in the North. Edward had restored Henry Percy, barely in his twenties, to the earldom of Northumberland in 1470. The last

ABOVE Stained-glass window from Canterbury Cathedral, portraying the family of Edward IV. Left to right, Richard Duke of York, Edward Prince of Wales, Edward IV, Elizabeth Woodville, Princesses Elizabeth, Cecilia, Anne, Catherine and Mary.

LEFT Marginal illustration of a tournament from a Book of Hours produced at Ghent in about 1480. The arms of William Lord Hastings appear in the book, but it was probably executed for Edward V when Prince of Wales. RIGHT Anthony Woodville, Earl Rivers, presenting the *Dictes and Saying of the Philosophers* to his brother-in-law, Edward IV. Rivers had translated the Dictes from a French manuscript given to him during a pilgrimage to St James of Compostella. This was one of the first books printed by William Caxton at his press near Westminster Abbey. Elizabeth Woodville stands to the far right with Edward Prince of Wales in front.

four generations of Percies had died in civil wars, the last two in the Lancastrian cause. Clearly the time had come to appoint a strong man who could both fill the vacuum left by the Nevilles, and balance the dubious loyalty of the young Earl of Northumberland. Richard's headquarters were to be at the familiar castle of Middleham, which was granted to him along with the former Neville lordships of Sheriff Hutton and Penrith, and the whole of Warwick's holdings in Yorkshire and Cumberland. Two important offices further buttressed his power: the stewardship of the duchy of Lancaster beyond the Trent, and the wardenship of the West Marches towards Scotland, with final authority over Henry Percy, who was Warden of the Middle and Eastern Marches. His former Welsh offices were, in the meantime, transferred to the young William Herbert, Earl of Pembroke (later Earl of Huntingdon).

The summer months passed as Richard reviewed his new estates and conducted a short foray against the Scottish border raiders, but in the autumn he hurried back to London on family business. Prior to his departure Richard had sought and obtained the King's permission to marry Anne Neville. Only sixteen years old, the Kingmaker's daugher was already the fatherless widow of a Prince, although it is unlikely that the marriage was ever consummated. From Richard's point of view the young cousin who had watched him learn to hunt and joust at Middleham was an ideal bride. The marriage would discharge a debt of honour to the family which had taken him into

Miniature from the *Book of Hours* of Isabel Neville, Duchess of Clarence.

Anne Neville, younger
daughter of the
Kingmaker, who was first
married to Henry VI's son
Edward, and then in 1472
married Richard,
Duke of Gloucester.

their household. On a material level, it would confirm him in
his title to Warwick's northern possessions, and bring him a
share of the even more extensive Beauchamp estates which
Warwick had held in his wife's right.

It was the question of Anne's inheritance which now sparked
off an ugly quarrel with Clarence. As the husband of Warwick's
elder daughter, Isabel, Clarence had hoped to appropriate the
whole of the Beauchamp lands which belonged properly to his
mother-in-law, Anne Beauchamp. Even this princely inheritance – more than one hundred and fifty manors scattered
throughout the country from Devon to Durham – was a
meagre consolation for the crown Clarence dreamed of wearing, and he did not intend to share it with his younger brother.

When Richard arrived at Clarence's lodgings to claim his
prospective bride, he was told to keep his hands off her. Richard
appealed to the King, who ordered Clarence not to interfere
with the proposed marriage. Clarence retaliated by persuading
Anne to dress up as a kitchen maid, and concealed her in the
household of a friend. Like most of Clarence's schemes, the ruse
was soon uncovered, and Richard had her removed to the
sanctuary of St Martin's. At this point the King intervened to
mediate between the brothers before the affair got out of hand.
Both put their case at a Council meeting, where even the
lawyers were surprised by the subtlety of their arguments. In
point of fact, Clarence had no case at all: he was not Anne's
guardian in any legal sense, and the girl's mother was still alive,
immured in the sanctuary of Beaulieu Abbey since the battle of
Tewkesbury. Nevertheless, Edward found it politic to soothe
Clarence's ruffled feathers and a compromise was reached.
Richard's marriage was to go ahead, but he was to receive only
a part of Warwick's personal holdings, while the rest, including
the Countess's inheritance and the earldoms of Warwick and
Salisbury, was reserved for Clarence. In addition, Richard was
induced to give up to Clarence his office of Great Chamberlain.

Although Anne and Richard were cousins, the marriage was
quickly celebrated without the formality of a papal dispensation, and the couple retired to Yorkshire. Early in 1473 the
Duchess of Gloucester gave birth to a son who was christened
Edward. Four months later Richard persuaded the King – despite vehement protests from Clarence – to allow his mother-in-

law to leave Sanctuary unharmed and to join the household at Middleham.

The Clarence-Gloucester quarrel exhibits all the worst features of a private baronial feud blown up into a threat to public order by the irresponsible behaviour of those involved. Richard's considerate treatment of the Countess of Warwick and his subsequent attempts to obtain a pardon for George Neville, the Archbishop of York, show that his motives, at least, were tempered by some concern for the family under whose roof he had grown up at Middleham. But it is hard to find any redeeming features in Clarence's behaviour. He was bent on making trouble, even though he had acquired the lion's share of the Warwick inheritance. In 1472 and 1473 rumours again linked his name with Louis XI, who sponsored an unsuccessful invasion led by that most tenacious of all Lancastrian supporters, the Earl of Oxford. When the Earl landed at St Michael's Mount in late September 1473, Clarence was breathing dark hints of treason and vengeance. In London Sir John Paston reported that the King's entourage sent for their harness to prepare for the worst: 'the Duke of Clarence maketh himself big in that he can, showing as he would but deal with the Duke of Gloucester. But the King intendeth to be as big as they both and to be a stifler between them. And some think that under this there be some other thing intended, and some treason conspired.'

The crisis was happily averted – or at least postponed – by the failure of Oxford's attempted invasion. He never got further than St Michael's Mount, where he was bottled up until Edward induced him to surrender in February 1474. Clarence was not called to account for his treasonable posturings: the King patiently agreed to look into his grievances, and a fresh division of the Warwick estates was submitted to Parliament for approval.

The long-term consequences of this episode were by no means exhausted, but towards the end of 1474 a more important enterprise overshadowed the affairs of the kingdom. Edward IV had decided to settle accounts with Louis XI, and was preparing to lead an invasion of France in the following spring. Since 1461 Louis had sanctioned one attempt after another against the Yorkist throne: first, Margaret of Anjou's, then Warwick's and

now Oxford's. Edward did not seriously contemplate the re-conquest of a kingdom at least four times as populous as his own: but in concert with Louis's arch enemy, Charles, Duke of Burgundy, he could inflict a punishing blow which would restore England's initiative in foreign policy and avenge the endless humiliations of Henry VI's reign.

Edward's enterprise was first mooted in 1472, and Parliament

Miniature from *Quinte Curse Ruffe des fais du Grand Alexandre*, translated by Vasco de Luceña. The translator is portrayed presenting his book to Edward IV.

had already voted a special tax to pay the wages of thirteen thousand archers. Efforts to collect this tax foundered on the stubborn resistance of 'the generality of his said commons', and the King was compelled to resort to the equally unpopular but more effective practice of raising benevolences. These loans-on-demand, voluntary in theory but difficult to refuse in practice, were begged or bullied from all men of substance – £30 from the Mayor of London, £10-£20 from the Aldermen and £4 11s 3d, 'the wages of half a soldier for a year', from the head commoners. One merry widow from Suffolk was rewarded for her £10 by a royal kiss, and promptly doubled her contribution.

Summons issued by Edward IV in 1475 to indent the leading men of his kingdom to supply men for the war against Louis. The heraldic symbols of the principals are drawn next to their names: thus Clarence heads the list with a black bull, Richard is represented by his boar badge, the Duke of Norfolk by a white lion, the Duke of Suffolk by a gold lion with a forked tail, and the Duke of Buckingham by the Stafford knot.

84

The army was raised by means of indenture – a contract whereby the principals bound themselves to supply an agreed number of men at an agreed fee. Richard, as the second man in the kingdom, indented for one hundred and twenty mounted lances and one thousand archers – about one-tenth of the host that embarked for Calais in June 1475. Louis's adviser, Philip de Commynes, described it as 'the most numerous, the best disciplined, the best mounted and the best armed that ever any king of that nation invaded France withal'. The French Court was close to panic: an Italian envoy reported that 'his Majesty is more discomposed than words can describe and has almost lost his wits. In his desperation and bitterness he uttered the following precise words, among others, Ah Holy Mary, even now when I have given thee 1,400 crowns, thou dost not help me one whit.'

Nevertheless, divine intervention was at hand. Twelve months previously the Duke of Burgundy had bound himself to join Edward with a force of ten thousand men not later than 1 July 1475. But for months past he had been embroiled in the schemes of his eastern neighbour, the Holy Roman Emperor, and when he finally presented himself on 14 July, his promised army was busy pillaging Lorraine. 'God,' as Commynes remarked, 'had troubled his sense and his understanding.'

Prospects of a second Agincourt were receding fast, and on 11 August they were blighted by a second disappointment. The Count of St Pol, who had promised Charles and Edward the important town of St Quentin, closed the gates and fired on the English as they advanced to take possession. On the same day the Duke of Burgundy took his leave, ostensibly to collect his army for an assault on Champagne. For Edward this was the last straw: the following day he opened negotiations with Louis. Too much of a realist to hope for the reconquest of Normandy and Guienne, Edward was quite prepared to let the threat of force extract concessions as favourable as any he might obtain on the battlefield. Louis also was a realist, and it took only three days to hammer out the main heads of agreement. For a down payment of seventy-five thousand crowns and an annual subsidy of fifty thousand, Edward would take his army home again. English and French merchants were freed from trade restrictions in each other's countries. The five-year-old Dauphin

The Treaty of Picquigny,
concluded by Edward IV
and Louis XI on
29 August 1475.

was betrothed to Edward's ten-year-old-daughter Elizabeth. Margaret of Anjou, a prisoner since Tewkesbury, would be ransomed for a further fifty thousand crowns. And both Kings promised to aid each other against rebellious subjects. Before the treaty was formally concluded on 29 August 1475 by the two sovereigns in person at Picquigny, Louis organised a gigantic alcoholic party for the entire English army at Amiens: it lasted three days.

There was, however, a minority who felt that Edward's peace treaty was no cause for celebration – among them the Duke of Gloucester. Richard was conspicuously absent from the signing ceremony: his sympathies were with the Gascon knight who told Commynes that Picquigny was a disgrace outweighing all King Edward's battle honours. Or, as Louis himself put it, 'I have chased the English out of France more easily than my father ever did; for my father drove them out by force of arms, whereas I have driven them out with venison pies and good wine.'

Who, in fact, gained most from the Peace of Picquigny? The speed with which terms were arranged suggests that both sides got what they wanted. Edward had made his point about Louis's meddling in English affairs, and received a handsome tribute for the privilege. Louis was left free to plot the destruction of Burgundy, and he could call the King of England his pensioner.

On 21 August Edward's army re-embarked for England and early in September Richard was back in Wensleydale. Here he spent the best part of the next two years. When he returned to the Court in February 1477 it was to face a new crisis in foreign policy – and the last act in the pitiful career of George, Duke of Clarence. The crisis arose from the death in the battle of Nancy of Charles, Duke of Burgundy, at the hands of Swiss pikemen, on 1 January 1477. With him were slaughtered the remains of the Burgundian army which had already sustained a crushing defeat at the battle of Morat six months previously. King Louis, wrote Commynes, 'was so overjoyed he scarcely knew how to react'. This was an overstatement. Since Charles left no male heir, Louis immediately claimed that the duchy of Burgundy, along with the northern counties of Artois, Picardy and Flanders reverted to the French Crown. His opponents

Maximilian, only son of Frederick III, Duke of Austria and Holy Roman Emperor. He was a handsome, chivalrous youth who quickly won the admiration of the Burgundian Court, and in particular that of Mary of Burgundy and her stepmother, Margaret of York. Maximilian and Mary were married in 1478.

were Charles's twenty-year-old daughter Mary, and her child-less step-mother, Margaret of York.

Margaret naturally turned to her brother Edward for help. But Edward could not make up his mind. There was a strong case for propping up the shaky Burgundian régime which had, in the past, provided a useful check to Louis's more extravagant ambitions. Should the Burgundian possessions in Flanders fall to the French Crown, England's Continental foothold at Calais would be entirely surrounded by Louis's domains. But if Edward declared openly in favour of Charles's heiress, he would have to forego his French pension and disburse the

Marie
de
Bourgogne
1457·1482

Mary of Burgundy, only daughter of Charles the Bold. Charles agreed unconditionally to Mary's betrothal to Maximilian before his sudden death in battle at Nancy in 1477.

considerable treasure he had amassed since 1475 on an expeditionary force. In the end he made a few ineffectual protests and did nothing. Despairing of Edward's help, Mary's advisers scoured the Courts of Europe for a rich and war-like husband to come to her rescue. An atmosphere of gloomy foreboding dominated the English Court. 'It seemeth that the world is all quavering', wrote John Paston, 'It will reboil somewhere, so that I deem young men shall be cherished.'

The young man the Dowager Duchess Margaret cherished was George, Duke of Clarence. Here was a golden chance to bestow on her favourite brother, whose wife had just died in childbirth, the hand of the greatest heiress in Europe. However, it was hardly surprising, as the Croyland Chronicler put it, that:

> ... so great a contemplated exaltation of his ungrateful brother displeased the King. He consequently threw all possible impediments in the way, in order that the match before-mentioned might not be carried into effect, and exerted all his influence that the heiress might be given in marriage to Maximilian [of Austria], the son of the [Holy Roman] Emperor; which was afterwards effected. The indignation of the Duke was probably still further increased by this; and now each began to look upon the other with no very fraternal eyes. You might then have seen (as such men are generally to be found in the courts of all princes), flatterers running to and fro, from the one side to the other, and carrying backwards and forwards the words which had fallen from the two brothers, even if they had happened to be spoken in the most secret closet.

Clarence's paranoid feelings were further inflamed by the news that Edward had proposed as his candidate for Mary's husband a member of the despised Woodville clan, the Queen's brother Anthony, Earl Rivers. This time Edward was not prepared to turn a deaf ear to his brother's threats of treason and revenge. After a final warning Clarence was to be struck down. The warning took the form of a death sentence on one of the Duke's retainers, one Thomas Burdett, who was condemned on charges of treasonable writing and necromancy. Ignoring the danger signal Clarence interrupted a Council meeting at Westminster to protest Burdett's innocence. Even more recklessly he began to spread the old story that Edward was a bastard, armed his retainers and managed to engineer riots in Cambridgeshire and Huntingdonshire. In the meantime, King Louis, ever anxious to keep his English cousins at each other's throats while he completed the dismemberment of Burgundy, sent word of further treasonable gossip. Edward summoned Clarence to Westminster and had him confined to the Tower.

There is no record that Richard had any part in these proceedings, and it seems likely that the summer months kept him busy in Yorkshire. When he rejoined the Court in the late autumn Clarence's life hung by a thread. The Woodvilles, who still regarded him as Warwick's accomplice in the murder of two of their kin, were baying for his blood, and the story of the King's bastardy was one that snapped even Edward's patience.

Richard was the only member of the royal family to speak up for his brother: Clarence was a nuisance, but since Warwick's defeat he had never been a threat. Moreover, he was loath to see the Woodvilles manœuvring one of his brothers into killing the other.

But Edward was determined to go through with it. On 16 January 1478, the Lords assembled in Parliament before the King to try Clarence on charges of high treason. In a hushed chamber none of them dared utter a word in accusation or defence. Only the King could prosecute the King's brother. The verdict was 'guilty', and the Duke of Buckingham, as Steward of England, pronounced the sentence of death. When Edward hesitated to set a date for the execution, the Commons presented a petition that it should be carried out swiftly. A few days later the Duke of Clarence at last earned in his death the fame that had eluded him in his lifetime, when he was drowned in a butt of Malmsey wine. Contemporary accounts record that Edward offered Clarence a choice of death, and that he elected to be drowned in a butt of wine. This has led later historians to declare that Clarence was a drunkard, but others have suggested that the butt of Malmsey held a symbolic significance as a reminder of the presents of tuns of wine sent to Clarence by Edward in happier days. Margaret Pole, Clarence's daughter, certainly wore a model of a wine cask on her wrist in remembrance of her father's death.

Dominic Mancini, the Italian cleric who in 1483 wrote an invaluable account of his stay in England, states that Richard was 'overcome with grief for his brother'. He also provides the clue to the origins of Richard's bitter antagonism towards the Woodvilles:

> Thenceforth [Mancini continues] Richard came very rarely to court. He kept himself within his own lands and set out to acquire the loyalty of his people through favours and justice. The good reputation of his private life and public activities powerfully attracted the esteem of strangers. . . . Such was his renown in warfare, that whenever a difficult and dangerous policy had to be undertaken, it would be entrusted to his discretion and his generalship. By these arts Richard acquired the favour of the people, and avoided the jealousy of the Queen, from whom he lived far separated.

'He kept himself within his own lands and set out to acquire the loyalty of his people through favours and justice'

Clarence's death clearly left scars on Richard's memory. Three days after the execution he procured a licence to set up two religious foundations to pray for the royal family and for his dead brothers and sisters. It is equally clear that he blamed the Woodville Queen for what had happened. But his estrangement from the Court went deeper than this. The reference to 'the good reputation of his private life' hints at a contrast between Richard's asceticism and the frivolity, the gormandising and the freewheeling sexual antics of Edward's entourage. The differences between the two surviving sons of York are so strong as to prompt the thought that there may have been some foundation for the tale of Edward's bastardy. Richard, short, frailly built, intense and rather straight-laced, and ill at ease in company; Edward, a fat, pleasure-loving giant with easy manners and extravagant tastes. Mancini paints a striking portrait of Edward in his later years:

> In food and drink he was most immoderate: it was his habit, so I have learned, to take an emetic for the delight of gorging his stomach once more. For this reason and for the ease, which was especially dear to him after his recovery of the crown, he had grown fat in the loins, whereas previously he had been not only tall but rather lean and very active. He was licentious in the extreme: moreover it was said that he had been most insolent to numerous women after he had seduced them, for, as soon as he grew weary of dalliance, he gave up the ladies much against their will to the other courtiers. He pursued with no discrimination the married and unmarried, the noble and lowly: however he took none by force. He overcame all by money and promises, and having conquered them, he dismissed them. Although he had many promoters and companions of his vices, the more important and especial were three of the aforementioned relatives of the queen, her two sons and one of her brothers.

As Mancini points out, it was in the North, far removed from the Court's politics and pleasures, that Richard's talents were most fruitfully employed. *'Loyauté me lie'* – 'loyalty binds me' – was the motto Richard adopted, and for thirteen years he effectively ruled the northern counties as Edward's deputy in war and peace. His first task was to establish a working relationship with the Earl of Northumberland. Generations of Percies had been lords of the North, and much depended on Richard's

OPPOSITE Although York Minster was commenced in the thirteenth century, it was not completed until the mid-fifteenth, when the western towers and central tower were added in the Perpendicular style.

93

tactful handling of the young Earl. In May 1473 the two men entered into a formal agreement, whereby Henry Percy recognised Richard's ultimate authority, while Richard promised to uphold the Earl's rights. In the East Riding and in Northumberland Percy's authority continued unchallenged: Westmorland, Cumberland and the West Riding were Richard's preserve.

The key to the North was York itself, a city of more than twelve thousand inhabitants, and headquarters of a prosperous merchant community. The Merchant Adventurers of York, incorporated more than a century before, carried on a brisk trade with the Hanse towns and supplied the city with its municipal officers. More than once discontented factions appealed to the Earl of Northumberland over Richard's head, but the city's records show that the great majority of the citizens regarded the Duke of Gloucester as their special friend and protector. The details of his administration confirm the importance that the Yorkist rulers attached to their relationships with the major cities of the realm – a fact often obscured by the battles, executions, feuds and intrigues that monopolised the attentions of the chroniclers. Authorising the destruction of illegal fish traps on the Humber and the Ouse, arbitrating in disputed municipal elections, quelling riots and commuting taxes in times of need, Richard worked hard to earn the title of 'our full tender and especial good lord'. A typical entry in the civic minutes records the decision that 'the Duke of Gloucester shall, for his great labour now late made unto the King's good grace for the confirmation of the liberties of this City be presented, at his coming to the City, with six swans and six pikes'. When the traditional spring pageant was celebrated in 1477 Richard and Anne marked their special bond with the city by joining the Corpus Christi Guild, a religious fraternity closely associated with the powerful Merchant Adventurers.

It was an active life which left Richard little time to enjoy the comforts of his Duchess's household at Middleham. When in York he generally stayed at the house of the Augustinian friars at Lendal. His estates at Sheriff Hutton, about ten miles north-east of the city, were also conveniently close and bordered on some of Henry Percy's chief manors. The castle of Pontefract, twenty-two miles to the south-west, was his official residence as Steward of the Duchy of Lancaster beyond Trent, while

94

Ryght hygh & myghti prince and our full gude & gracious
lord we your humble servantz humbly recomandes us to
your gude grace with all our servicis and thankes your of your gude
& gracious lordshyp to be shewyd us afore this in especiall
of that at whan we were afore committed to our most dradd
soverayne lord the kyng the nombyr of [ ] bj archers
to this sidge now to be had in to Skotland that is lyst
your gude grace of your benevolence to conceyve the poynt
of this wynd tre to yow us to the nombyr of b skor
archers & a capitayn the wich nombyr we have sent
at this tym with our gentilman servant John [ ]
& Thomas Dabyson to abyde apon your nobill person to
whom & to be we beseke you to be as ye have beyn at
all tymes gude & gracious lord. And to doo your gracious
commandment bothe we and thei at all tymes shalbe
redy.
[ ] to our power to the grace of god whom we beseke
to preserve your full nobill person in this your nobill journey
& all odyr. At york the xxiij day of July

To the ryght hygh & myghti prince & our
full gude & gracious lord the dukis grace
of Glowceter grete chamberlayn constabill
admirall of yngland & wardeyn of the
west marches of yngland agaynst Skotland

By your humble servantz the
mayre & your brodyr knyghttz
& all the gude counsell of
the city of york

James III of Scotland with his son, Prince James, and St Andrew, the patron saint of Scotland. The painting forms one panel from an organ case formerly kept at Holyroodhouse Palace. These panels were painted for Canon Edward Bonkil by Hugo van der Goes, when the Canon visited Flanders with Prince James to attend the wedding of Margaret of York and Charles the Rash of Burgundy.

Barnard Castle, some fifty miles to the north-west, was his chief seat in the county of Durham. Richard's normal administrative duties were frequently supplemented by legal commissions that toured the countryside hearing pleas, initiating inquiries and settling disputes. As Richard's reputation spread, the personal following who comprised his Council took on increasingly the functions of a court of law, offering 'good and indifferent justice to all who sought it, were they rich or poor, gentle or simple'.

Richard's other great office, the wardenship of the West March, did not seriously occupy his attention until the spring of 1480. Persuading James III of Scotland to break his truce and authorise large-scale border raids was one of Louis's many ploys to keep the English busy while he tidied up his Burgundian conquests. In May Richard's military powers were augmented by the office of Lieutenant General in the North, and in the autumn of 1480 he launched a border raid of his own into Scottish territory. This was to be the curtain-raiser to a full scale invasion planned for the summer of 1481. King Edward was to command in person. With Northumberland as his deputy, Richard spent the winter inspecting the border garrisons, repairing the fortifications of Carlisle and conducting a military census. Late in March 1481 he was with Edward in London, putting the finishing touches to their plan of campaign.

But the campaign never materialised. Although a fleet under Lord Howard devastated Scottish shipping in the Firth of Forth, Edward never stirred from his capital, immobilised by financial worries and failing health. Richard and Northumberland were left to conduct a border raid on a scale no greater than that of the previous autumn. By the spring of 1482 a significant victory over the Scots had become a political as well as a military necessity. The exceptionally bad harvest of 1481 was causing severe disturbances in several counties; Edward's attempts to levy a tax, commuted on his return from the inglorious French campaign of 1475, proved as unpopular as benevolences; and there were rumours that Burgundy, despairing of armed support from England, was about to come to terms with King Louis. In that event England would be isolated without a Continental ally, and Edward could kiss goodbye to his annual French pension.

In 1482 the sole command of the Scottish expedition was vested in the Duke of Gloucester. The two brothers met at

Fotheringhay in June, and Richard was furnished with an unexpected ally in the person of James III's younger brother, the Duke of Albany – a 'Clarence in kilt' – whom the brothers promised to seat on James's throne. Early in July Richard and Northumberland marshalled their forces under the battlements of Alnwick Castle in Northumberland. The army was estimated at twenty thousand men, backed by a formidable siege train of artillery. Their first objective was the town of Berwick, in Scottish hands since Margaret had surrendered it two decades before. The town itself capitulated at once but the citadel, commanded by the Earl of Bothwell, held out. Detaching Lord Stanley and his contingent from Lancashire and Cheshire to press the siege, Richard drove on to meet the Scottish army. After all the efforts and expense that had gone into the campaign, it must have come as something of a disappointment to hear, at the end of July, that James III was the victim of a *coup* organised by his own barons. Disillusioned by their sovereign's foolhardy sabre-rattling, the Scottish lords refused to risk their lives in a pitched battle, and Richard entered Edinburgh unopposed. At Albany's request Richard's soldiers were forbidden even their traditional right to pillage the conquered city. Negotiations for a peace settlement proved equally fruitless: no treaty would long survive the political upheavals of James's Court. Mindful of the crippling costs of keeping his army in the field indefinitely, Richard had no alternative but to march back the way he had come, determined at least to salvage his and the nation's pride by completing the reduction of Berwick Castle. Albany, who had made his peace with the Scottish lords, remained behind, promising to secure a lasting truce for his English allies. On 24 August the Scots at last agreed to the permanent cession of Berwick to the English Crown, and the citadel was delivered to Lord Stanley. The news was trumpeted in London as if Richard had won a second Agincourt, and Edward was lavish in his praises. In a sour and more realistic vein, the Croyland Chronicler noted that 'this trifling, I know not whether to call it "gain" or "loss" (for the safekeeping of Berwick each year swallows up ten thousand marks) at this period diminished the resources of the king and kingdom by more than a hundred thousand pounds'.

The man who benefited most from Richard's martial exploits

Louis XI of France, the 'universal spider'. Portrait attributed to Colin d'Amiens.

was undoubtedly 'the universal spider', Louis XI. For, shortly after Christmas, the Court learned that Maximilian and Mary of Burgundy had signed a treaty with the King of France. Their daughter Margaret was to marry the Dauphin, in flagrant disregard of the Dauphin's previous betrothal to Edward's daughter Elizabeth.

The collapse of Edward's diplomacy abroad did not touch Richard's reputation. In recognition of ten years and more of service in the North, capped by the subjection of Edinburgh and the recapture of Berwick, Parliament bestowed on him in February 1483 the permanent and hereditary wardenship of the West Marches towards Scotland. This plum was sugared with a further grant of the castle and city of Carlisle, and all the King's manors and revenues in the county of Cumberland. To these would be added any further conquests won from the Scots. At the age of thirty Richard could look forward to the undisputed possession of his own palatinate, and many years of active service in which to give rein to his proven talents.

Henricus septimus   Edward quartus

Ante pie dño Oliuero kyng · Juris vtri-
Edwardi quinti · et Henrici septimi

asque professor · ac illustris Edward
principali secretario · dignissimo ordu

4 The Usurper April-July 1483

PREVIOUS PAGES Painted wooden panels from St George's Chapel Windsor, portraying, left to right, Henry VII, Edward V (who was never crowned and therefore his crown is shown suspended above his head) and Edward IV. This panel was commissioned by Oliver King, one of Henry VII's most loyal servants, who therefore wished to emphasise the legitimacy of Henry VII's claim: Richard III is not included.

RICHARD'S SOJOURN as Lieutenant of the North was brought to an abrupt end by the death of Edward IV on 9 April 1483. Overweight and oversexed, his indulgence of these two appetites had undermined his health, but it was a chill caught on a fishing trip which was reported to have killed him. He left his kingdom and his Crown to his twelve-year-old son Edward, Prince of Wales, who kept his own Court at Ludlow Castle under the care of his uncle Anthony, Earl Rivers.

England had known relative peace for twelve years; but a royal minority threatened to unleash all the tensions created by Edward's patronage of the Woodville family and inflamed by Clarence's execution. On his deathbed Edward had foreseen the worst, and striven to prevent it. He entrusted his son not to the Queen but to his brother Richard, who was named Protector. Richard could command the obedience of older nobility who despised the Queen and the swarm of relatives whom the King had endowed with high office, titled husbands and wealthy heiresses. As a further insurance he persuaded two particular rivals, Lord Hastings and the Queen's eldest son by her first marriage, Thomas Grey, Marquess of Dorset, to shake hands in a formal gesture of reconciliation.

But these hatreds were more than skin deep. While preparations were still in hand for Edward's lavish funeral, the Queen's party took action to protect themselves against the reprisals they considered inevitable if the King's will were allowed to take effect. Their principal asset was time. Until Richard and the rest of the peers of the realm reached London, they commanded a slender majority in the Council. Besides her son Dorset and her two brothers Lionel and Edward, the Queen could count on the support of two important clerics – Thomas Rotherham, Chancellor and Archbishop of York, and John Morton, Bishop of Ely. With these allies, the Woodvilles passed a resolution that Richard's protectorship should be replaced by a Regency Council headed, but not dominated, by the Duke of Gloucester. 'By this means', Mancini later reported with the benefit of hindsight, 'the Duke would be given due honour and the royal authority greater security. ... If the government were committed to one man he might easily usurp the sovereignty.' Mancini also reminds us of the Woodvilles' motives when he adds that 'all who favoured the Queen's family voted for this

Petri Carmeliani Brixiensis Poete Laureati
ad Edwardum clarissimū Anglie Principe
De Vere Carmen.

Cogitanti mihi iandudu Illustrissie
princeps quo nam pacto Sublˈˈ tue
me notum facere possem . id tadem
mihi fieri posse arbitratus sum si qppiam meoꝝ
carminum ad te dedissem quod tibi uel ex eoꝛ
sententia uel fortassis compositione aliqua ex
parte placere posset . Qocirca noua materia
aggressus ueris silicet prime anni ptis descp
tionem / quam a quoquam maiorū nostroꝛ
diffuse scriptam adhuc non legi : no dubitaui
opusculum hoc pbreue qdem celsitudini tue
dicare · quod in hac Redemptoris nostri re
surectione muneris Loco susaperes · potissi
mum hoc egi cu tali te ingenio predítu esse
intelligerem ut spectaculu quoddam no púuq̃

Easter verses dedicated to Edward v, when Prince of Wales, by Petrus Carmelanus of Brescia, the Court poet.

proposal, as they were afraid that if Richard took the crown, or even governed alone, they who bore the blame of Clarence's death would suffer death or at least be ejected from their high estate'.

To give legal and military sanction to their *coup* the Woodvilles further proposed to bring the young King to Westminster for his coronation as soon as possible with as many armed men as Earl Rivers could summon on the road from Ludlow. Under the dire precedent of Henry vi's reign, Edward's minority would end with his crowning and the boy would be free to choose his own advisers. But the thought of Edward arriving with a Woodville army at his back alarmed even the Queen's supporters. The majority bowed to Lord Hastings' threat to

St George's Chapel, Windsor

The magnificent Perpendicular Chapel dedicated to St George in Windsor Castle was begun by Edward IV, and work progressed constantly up to Richard III's death. On Edward's death in April 1483, his body was taken first to Westminster Abbey for the funeral service. It was then buried at Windsor. Richard erected a two-storeyed chantry chapel to his brother in the north choir aisle. The chapel remains very much a monument to Edward, as it is full of his personal badges on the stonework and carved in wood.

LEFT Frieze of angels with sunbursts – the symbol of Edward IV – in their crowns and in the stonework below. This forms part of the Rutland Chantry set up in memory of the eldest sister of Edward IV and Richard III, Anne, Duchess of Exeter.

LEFT The exquisite iron grill which surrounds the tomb of Edward IV in the lower part of his Chantry Chapel. This was made by the King's blacksmith, John Tresilian.
RIGHT Roof boss from the north choir aisle, showing Edward IV and Bishop Beauchamp, Master of the Works at Windsor, kneeling before the Cross of Gneth, a palladium seized from the Welsh by Edward III during his campaigns, and originally housed in the Chapel.

retire like Warwick to Calais, of which he was Governor. The size of Edward's escort was fixed at two thousand men.

Richard was kept fully informed of these developments by couriers from Lord Hastings, who urged the Protector to put himself at the head of an army and race to London before Rivers arrived from Ludlow. But Richard was unwilling to risk a head-on collision with the Woodvilles. For the moment he contented himself with a polite but firm letter to the Council, stressing his devotion to his nephews and warning them not to enact anything contrary to his brother's will.

He then proceeded to York, according to the Croyland Chronicler, 'with a becoming retinue, each person being arrayed in mourning'. Here, 'he performed a solemn funeral service for the King, the same being accompanied with plenteous tears. Constraining all the nobility of these parts to take the oath of fealty to the late King's son, he himself was the first to take the oath.' Richard's letter made a favourable impression in London, and won over a number of waverers to his cause. Nevertheless the Council fixed the coronation date for 4 May, and instructed Rivers to make sure that the King arrived not later than 1 May. Overriding all objections with calculated arrogance, the Marquess of Dorset is said to have told Lord Hastings and his supporters, 'We are so important that even without the King's uncle we can make and enforce these decisions.'

Shortly after Edward IV had been laid to rest in St George's Chapel at Windsor on 20 April, Richard left York for Northampton with a retinue of about six hundred men. At Northampton he was to join Rivers and the King for the final stage of their progress to London. Clearly neither party expected violence from the other, since Richard arrived with a retinue he knew to be outnumbered, and Rivers was under no compulsion to consent to the meeting in the first place. When Richard arrived on 29 April, as arranged, he learned that the King's escort had already passed through the town and were now quartered twelve miles closer to London at Stony Stratford. Shortly before supper Earl Rivers rode back to Northampton with a small following and presented Edward's greetings to his uncle. He explained the King's removal to Stony Stratford by pointing out that Northampton was too small for both their retinues. Richard politely invited the Earl to stay to supper. They could ride together to join the King in the morning.

During the meal Richard received a second visitor in the person of Henry Stafford, Duke of Buckingham. 'Harre Bokingham', as he signed himself, was the joker in the royal pack who played out the tragedy of Richard III. Lineal descendant of Thomas of Woodstock, Duke of Gloucester, fifth son of Edward III, he ranked as the first peer of England after Richard and the King's nine-year-old brother Richard Duke of York. He also harboured a deep-seated grudge against the Queen, for after his father was killed fighting for the House of Lancaster in 1455, he became a royal ward and was saddled with a Woodville wife. Ever anxious to feather the family nest, Queen Elizabeth had bestowed on him the hand of her younger sister Catherine 'whom', according to Mancini, 'he scorned to wed on account of her humble origins'. No doubt he saw in Richard the instrument of his revenge.

A piece of parchment bearing at the top the signature *Edwardus Quintus,* with below Richard's motto, *Loyaulté me lie,* and his signature; and at the bottom *Souvente me souvene* and 'Harre Bokingham', the motto and signature of Buckingham. This was probably written at St Albans, on 3 May, when the young King halted overnight with Richard and Buckingham on their journey to London.

When Rivers and his companions had retired to bed, Buckingham, Richard and their advisers settled down to a midnight conference. Clearly they had met at Northampton by design: but it is doubtful whether they could have arranged in advance the plan that was now proposed for the following morning. Buckingham's later career will show that he was ambitious, conceited and reckless. He was also an accomplished and persuasive speaker. He must now have pointed out to Richard the danger of pursuing the prudent course he had so far undertaken. Once Rivers had delivered the King to his mother in London and set a crown on his head, only a civil war could unseat the Woodvilles. They were outnumbered – even with the three hundred men that Buckingham had brought from London – but in London the odds would be even longer. If they were to act, it must be now.

At dawn on 30 April Richard ordered the arrest of Rivers, and

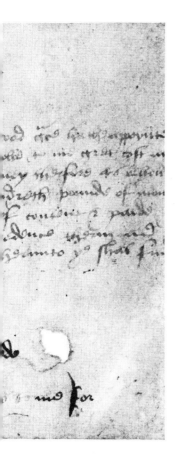

Application made by
Richard to his nephew,
Edward v for £100, signed
by Richard as
Duke of Gloucester.

posted guards on the road to prevent the news from reaching Stony Stratford. Accompanied by a troop of soldiers, the two Dukes galloped the twelve miles to Stratford and requested an audience with the King. The interview was brief and rather stilted. Richard began by offering his condolences on the death of the King's father, which he blamed on his ministers and their encouragement of his vices. The same men were guilty of conspiring to ambush the Protector on the road to London. Edward objected that he had every confidence in his father's ministers and intended to entrust the government to the peers of the realm and the Queen, upon which Buckingham broke in to say that women had no business in the government of a kingdom. If Mancini's account is to be believed, Edward must have been a precocious child and well-rehearsed in his role – an important point in the light of later events. Nevertheless, the interview ended, in Thomas More's account, with the King in tears. His half-brother Lord Richard Grey and his Chamberlain, Sir Thomas Vaughan, were placed under arrest. The King's Welsh escort, with no word from its leaders, was told to go home, and the Dukes returned to Northampton with their captives.

The news reached London at midnight and sent the Queen scurrying with her remaining children to take Sanctuary in Westminster Abbey. By the morning of 1 May the city was in uproar. The Marquess of Dorset tried to raise an army to re-capture the King, but gave up to join the Queen in Sanctuary when he saw that public opinion sided with the Protector. The Thames was swarming with boatloads of Richard's supporters who had come out to cut the Queen's communications with the city. Archbishop Rotherham of York, who had rashly delivered the Chancellor's seal to the Queen, now sent a messenger to reclaim it. Lord Hastings did his best to lower the political temperature by calling a meeting of the remaining lords at St Paul's and explaining, in Thomas More's words, that 'the Duke of Gloucester was sure and fastly faithful to his prince and that the Lord Rivers and Lord Richard [Grey] were, for matters attempted by them against the Dukes of Gloucester and Buck-ingham, put under arrest for their surety, not for the King's jeopardy'. The city authorities were also soothed by a letter from Richard, promising an early date for the coronation.

The King and the two Dukes made their entry into London on 4 May. As proof of the villainy of the Queen's family, the procession was headed by four horse-drawn cartloads of weapons embellished with the Woodville insignia, and a group of street-criers who proclaimed that these arms had been placed in secret *caches* on the city outskirts. This gambit rather back-fired since a number of the onlookers knew that the armouries had been established by Edward IV for use against the Scots. The procession made its way to the Bishop of London's Palace at St Paul's, where the King was safely lodged. On the same day the Lords, Bishops, Mayor and Aldermen were invited to take the oath of allegiance.

For the moment the future seemed secure. The non-aligned members of the Council, whose prime concern was not to side with Richard or the Queen but to prevent an outbreak of violence, were relieved to find that the transfer of power had been achieved without bloodshed. 'With the consent and good-will of all the Lords', the Croyland Chonicle reports, 'the Duke of Gloucester was invested with power to order and forbid in every matter, just like another king.' The coronation was now to take place on 24 June, and on the following day the Lords and Commons assembled in Parliament would be asked to ratify the protectorate. At Buckingham's suggestion the King was moved to the more spacious royal apartments in the Tower.

Richard was happy to leave the membership of the Council virtually unchanged. Even Rotherham kept his seat, although his indiscretion with the seal lost him the chancellorship. The new Chancellor was John Russell, Bishop of Lincoln – an appointment which earned the approval even of Richard's enemies. If the absence of Woodvilles left a vacuum, it was filled by the Duke of Buckingham who was also rewarded with wide grants of authority in Wales and the West Country.

The Woodvilles were not forgotten. One member of the family – Sir Edward Woodville – was still at large in the Channel with a fleet that had sailed on 29 April to clear the seas of French and Breton pirates. To persuade the sailors to return to port, Richard offered a free pardon to all but the leaders. Thanks to the ingenuity of two Genoese sea-captains who persuaded Sir Edward's men to drink themselves insensible and then tied them up, the ruse was successful. Sir Edward himself managed to escape to Brittany with only two ships.

Although Rivers, Grey and Vaughan were safely in custody in Richard's northern strongholds, the Protector felt the need to justify his actions at Stony Stratford by bringing charges of treason against them. In this instance the bishops – civil servants who formed the backbone of the neutral peace party in the Council – overrode him. Clearly the tale of the intended ambush cut little ice in government circles. The Council were also keen to reach some arrangement with the Queen who was still cooped up in Sanctuary. If she could be persuaded to come out with her children and accept an honourable retirement as Queen Dowager, all rifts would be healed. Negotiations dragged on until the first week in June, but Elizabeth made no move, reluctant either to accept defeat or to trust her brother-in-law's assurances.

Shortly after 5 June, when Anne arrived from Middleham to join her husband, a new crisis erupted suddenly. On 10 and 11 June Richard fired off a series of letters to his friends and supporters in the North. 'We heartily pray you', he wrote to the Corporation of York, 'to come unto us to London in all the diligence ye can possible ... with as many as ye can make defensibly arrayed, there to aid and assist us against the Queen, her bloody adherents and affinity, which have intended and daily doth intend to murder and utterly destroy us and our cousin the Duke of Buckingham and the royal blood of this realm.'

'Aid and assist us against the Queen, her bloody adherents and affinity'

The urgency of the letters makes little sense unless the ranks of the Queen's 'bloody adherents' had been swelled by a new recruit of some importance. This was none other than Lord Hastings. Towards the end of May, apparently, he and Archbishop Rotherham, Lord Stanley and Bishop Morton had fallen into the habit of holding their own informal meetings in the Tower while Richard's intimates gathered around him at his house of Crosby's Place. The grouping of these four was in itself a danger signal, since it signified a rift between the Protector's personal supporters and the men who had formed the inner circle of Edward IV's advisers. But Richard did not feel unduly threatened until he caught wind of a *rapprochement* between Hastings and the Queen.

What could have persuaded Hastings to turn against the man

whose interests he had defended so vigorously in the weeks of crisis following the death of Edward IV? Sir Thomas More and Tudor historians readily persuaded themselves that Hastings bitterly regretted his support when he learned of Richard's intention to usurp the Crown. It was his loyalty to Edward V and the memory of his father that caused Hastings to repent.

This notion cannot be disproved, but it seems unlikely on two counts. Family loyalty is hardly the dominant motif of the Wars of the Roses: uncles, cousins and brothers had been fighting and killing each other since 1455 and traded their allegiance whenever it suited their interests. Hastings had never turned his coat on Edward IV but there is no reason to suppose that he would have risked his life for Edward V and the hated Woodvilles unless loyalty was cemented with self-interest. In the second place, there is no evidence that at this time Richard had made up his mind to disinherit his nephews. The draft of Chancellor Russell's speech for the opening of Parliament has survived, and it states clearly that the first business of the Parliament was to confirm Richard's title as Protector.

Hastings turned to the Woodvilles in June for precisely the same reason as he turned to Richard in April – because his interests were threatened from another quarter. By upholding Richard's claims during the Protector's absence in the North, he doubtless hoped to be rewarded with the lion's share of the spoils and the most important voice in his Council. However, he soon realised that it was Buckingham who had adopted the role of Kingmaker. Buckingham rode beside Richard when the Protector entered London, and Buckingham was rewarded with almost vice-regal powers in Wales and the West. As Lord Chamberlain to Edward V, Hastings could still hope to recoup his position after the coronation. But here again he was disappointed, when Richard proposed to extend his authority until the King came of age.

The remedy that Richard applied to Hastings' disaffection was drastic and quick. On 13 June he struck, without waiting for his reinforcements from Yorkshire. While the official side of the Council was in session at Westminster, Richard summoned the four offenders, Buckingham, Howard and a number of his personal staff to a meeting at the Tower. What followed is vividly described by Sir Thomas More, who derived his

OPPOSITE Marginal illustration of a royal barge from a Flemish Book of Hours, which was probably produced for Edward V when Prince of Wales.

D

lo nonam
Eus in ad
iutorium
meum in
tende. Do
mine ad
adiuuandum me festina.
loria patri et filio. Vni
ein arator spē mentes
tuozum visita imple
suprna gracia quetu crastī
pctoza Memento salutis
auctor quod nostrquondā
corporis ex illibata virgīne
nascendo formam sumpsi
stis. Maria mater gracie

William, Lord Hastings
was summarily executed
on 12 June 1483 on Tower
Green. His body was taken
to St George's Chapel,
Windsor, where he was
buried close to Edward IV,
who had requested in his
will that his closest friend
should lie near him.
A chantry chapel was set
up for Hastings, and is
decorated by an unknown
English artist with wall-
paintings of the life of
St Stephen. Hastings'
badge of a *manche*, or
sleeve, can be seen in the
right-hand corner.

information from one of those present – John Morton, Bishop
of Ely. The Protector entered the Council Chamber at nine
o'clock, 'excusing himself that he had been from them so long,
saying merely that he had been asleep that day. And after a little
talking unto them, he said unto the Bishop of Ely: "My Lord,
you have very good strawberries at your garden in Holborn, I
require you let us have a mess of them."' Shortly after opening
the meeting Richard asked the Councillors to excuse him for a
moment and left the room. Between 10 and 11 am, 'he returned
into the chamber among them, all changed, with a wonder-
fully sour angry countenance, knitting the brows, frowning
and fretting and gnawing on his lips'. The Council sat stunned
by this sudden change. Then Richard asked them, '"What
were they worthy to have, that compass and imagine the destruction of me, being so near of blood unto the King and Protector of his royal person and realm?"' To this Hastings
replied '"that they were worthy to be punished as heinous
traitors, whatsoever they were". "That is yonder sorceress, my
brother's wife", cried Richard, "and others with her."'

Still unaware of what lay in store for him, Hastings was
relieved to hear that Richard had cast those familiar bogeymen,
the Woodvilles, as the villains of his little drama. But the alarm
was clearly sounded when the Protector went on to accuse Jane
Shore of abetting the Queen in her sorcery. For Jane, once
Edward's favourite mistress, now shared the Lord Chamberlain's bed. Nevertheless Hastings repeated that any such traitors
deserved punishment, if they could be proved guilty. '"What,"
exclaimed Richard, "thou servest me, I wean, with ifs and with
ands, I tell thee they have so done, and that I will make good on
thy body, traitor." And therewith as in a great anger, he
clapped his fist upon the board a great rap. At which token
given, someone cried "Treason!" without. Therewith a door
clapped, and in come there rushing men in harness, as many as
the chamber might hold.' Hastings, Stanley, Rotherham and
Morton were promptly arrested. A priest was brought so that
Hastings could make his peace with God. Minutes later he was
'brought forth into the green beside the Chapel within the
Tower, and his head laid down upon a log of timber and there
striken off'.

Richard promptly sent for a number of important citizens,

114

Seynt Edward

England

Fraunce

Ireland

Irlond of Gran

Walys

The most noblest lady & prynces bone of the roall blode of thre
realmes lengally descending fro pryncess kynges ... ...
... glorious spouse dam Anne by the grace ... ...   The most worthy prynce Rychard by the grace of god kynge
of England and of fraunce and lord of Ireland by verey mary
... to dert by constellacions ... and descending on the ladie   The noble and mighty prynce Edward prynce of walys d...
of cornewaile and erle of chestre son & eire to the most
excelent prynce kynge Rychard the third And hys most...

dressed himself up in rusty armour and explained to them that his strange attire was due to the discovery that Hastings and others had planned to assassinate himself and Buckingham at the Council table. A proclamation to this effect was immediately published to forestall another panic in the city.

Hastings' execution was characteristic of Richard's response to a crisis. The remedy was impulsive, direct and quick. If More's narrative is at least half-way accurate, it was also badly staged and politically inept. By taking the short cut, without regard for legal forms, and dressing the affair in a cloak of crude melodrama, he can only have undermined the confidence of the great men on whom his political future depended. The Woodvilles could be roughly dealt with because the baronial class were only too glad to be rid of them; but Hastings was one of them, a popular man and important office-holder, and long a close friend of the late King.

With Hastings dead, Richard felt he had little to fear from the other three conspirators. Perhaps as a gesture to quiet the fears of the nobility, Lord Stanley was restored to the Council almost immediately. Rotherham, who had once before given proof of his ineffectiveness as an opponent, was released after a short imprisonment. Only John Morton, an altogether more subtle and dangerous enemy, was to be kept out of circulation under Buckingham's custody in the Welsh stronghold of Brecon Castle.

Hastings's conspiracy now led Richard to make the most important decision of his life. Hastings's death had narrowed the base of his support to a point where not even the office of Protector, extended until Edward v's majority, seemed a sufficient guarantee for the future. To survive, he must rule, and to rule he must be King. Perhaps the decisive factor, after Hastings' removal, was the personality of the young King. Already at Stony Stratford Edward had shown he was capable of standing up to his uncle in defence of his mother and her family. Dominic Mancini gives further evidence of his precocity: 'In word and deed he gave so many proofs of his liberal education, of polite, nay rather scholarly, attainments far beyond his age.' Most remarkable was 'his special knowledge of literature which enabled him to discourse elegantly, to understand fully, and to declaim most excellently from any work, verse or prose, that

OPPOSITE ABOVE Part of the *Rous Roll,* showing Richard III flanked by his wife Anne Neville, and his son Edward, who died at Middleham in 1484 at the age of nine.
BELOW Details from a military roll, painted in 1480 for Sir Thomas Holme, Clarenceux King of Arms. Altogether the arms of 248 knights are depicted, from the counties of Suffolk, Essex and Kent.

came into his hands, unless it were from among the more abstruse authors'. With his character and intellect already cast to this degree, Edward could hardly be expected to cherish the man who had imprisoned his favourite uncle, Earl Rivers, sent his mother and brother into Sanctuary and now beheaded his Lord Chamberlain not a stone's throw from the royal apartments.

Any doubts that Richard was now committed to obtaining the Crown for himself were dispelled three days later on Monday, 16 June when the Council met to discuss the removal of Edward's younger brother, Richard, Duke of York, from the Sanctuary of Westminster Abbey to the Tower. The two Dukes, accompanied by the Archbishop of Canterbury, Cardinal Bourchier, and a retinue of armed men, proceeded to Westminster by barge. Richard was prepared to use force if necessary, but in order to avoid a violation of Sanctuary the Archbishop went in to persuade the Queen to surrender her son voluntarily. Elizabeth was probably not deceived by Bourchier's promise that the boy would be restored after his brother's coronation, but she bowed to the threat of force. The Protector embraced his nephew affectionately at the door of the Painted Chamber and accompanied him to the Tower.

With the Princes in his power and his northern followers expected in London within the week, Richard lacked only a legal fiction to justify his claim to the throne. For this purpose he dredged up the story of Edward's marriage contract with Lady Eleanor Butler – a daughter of Old Talbot, the 'Terror of the French'. If true, this story is another example of Edward's disastrous passion for older women. Lady Eleanor was the widow of Sir Thomas Butler and died in 1468. Had the engagement taken place, it would have invalidated his subsequent marriage to Elizabeth Woodville and made bastards of her children. There is in fact no reason to suppose that the story was not true; Edward could never resist a pretty face and troth plight was a common device for coaxing reluctant virgins into bed. Clarence had cast the same aspersions on Edward's marriage six years before, and Robert Stillington, the Bishop of Bath and Wells, claimed to have acted as Edward's go-between in the affair. The news was broken to the people of London on 22 June in a carefully staged sermon at Paul's Cross.

OPPOSITE A page from Anthony Woodville's translation of the *Dictes and Saying of the Philosphers,* which was printed by William Caxton on his newly-erected press at Westminster in 1477. This is the first printed book in England to bear a date, 18 November of that year.

Here it is so that every humayn Creature by the
suffrance of our lord god is born & ordeigned to
be subgette and thral vnto the stormes of fortune
And so in diuerse & many sondry Wyses man is perpley-
id With Worldly aduersitees/Of the Whiche J Antoine
Wydeuille Erle Ryuyeres/lord Scales &c haue largely &
in many different maners haue had my parte And of hem
releued by thynfynyte grace & goodnes of our said lord
thurgh the meane of the Mediatrice of Mercy/Whiche gce
euidently to me knowen & Vnderstonde hath compelled me
to sette a parte alle ingratitude/And droof me by reson &
conscience as fer as my Wreechednes Wold suffyse to gyue
therfore synguler louynges & thankes/And exorted me to
dispose my recouerd lyf to his seruyce/in folowing his lawes
and commandemets/And in satisfaccon & recompence of myn
Inyquytees & fawtes before don/to seke & execute y Werkes
that myght be most acceptable to hym/And as fer as myn
fraylnes Wold suffre me J rested in that Wyll & purpose
Duryng that season J Vnderstode the Jubylee & pardon to
be at the holy Apostle Seynt James in Spayne Whiche
Was the yere of grace a thousand.CCCC.lxxiij.Thenne
J determyned me to take that Voyage & shipped from Southampton in the moneth of Juyll the said yere/And so
sayled from thens til J come in to the Spaynyssh see there
lackyng syght of alle londes/the Wynde beyng good and
the Weder fayr/Thenne for a recreacon & a passyng of tyme
J had delyte & axed to rede some good historye And amõg
other ther Was that season in my copanye a Worshipful gen-
tylman callid lowys de Bretaylles/Whiche gretly delited

Richard selected as his mouthpiece the Lord Mayor's brother, Dr Ralph Shaa, who took as his text the Old Testament quotation *'Spuria vitulamina non agent radices altas'* – 'Bastard slips shall not take deep root'.

In the meantime, the Lords and Commons, originally summoned in May to ratify Richard's protectorate in Parliament, were beginning to arrive in London. Richard, Buckingham and their agents were kept feverishly busy, sounding out opinions and canvassing for support. Richard exchanged the black cloth of mourning he had worn since his brother's death for an outfit of purple velvet, and paraded through the streets of the capital with an army of retainers. The great hall at Crosby's Place was thronged every day at dinner-time with the Protector's guests. On 24 June the Duke of Buckingham enlarged on the theme of Dr Shaa's sermon with an appeal to the Mayor and leading citizens at the Guildhall. He laid great stress on the abuses of government and the financial exactions which had marked the Woodville ascendancy. Under Richard's rule he offered them, 'the surety of your own bodies, the quiet of your wives and your daughters, the safeguard of your goods; of all which things in times past ye stood evermore in need'. Who had been able to count himself master of his own possessions 'amoung so much pilling and polling, amoung so many taxes and tallages, of which there was never end and often time no need?'. Reiterating Richard's rightful claim to the throne 'which ye well remember substantially declared unto you at Paul's Cross on Sunday', Buckingham reminded them that the title of King was no child's office. 'And that great wise man well perceived when he said: woe is that Realm, that hath a child to their King.' The Duke, according to Sir Thomas More, was 'marvellously well spoken'; and one eye witness was much impressed by the fact that he did not even pause to spit between sentences. Nevertheless, the speech had a cool reception until the Duke's servants, at the back of the Hall, threw their caps into the air with shouts of 'King Richard, King Richard'.

Even if the people of London still had their reservations, the Parliament which met at Westminster on Wednesday, 25 June, was not disposed to argue. The majority were probably content with any arrangement that promised an end to civil strife. Others who still nursed private grudges against the Woodvilles

Drawing of Simon Eyre, a London alderman in the mid-fifteenth century, taken from the *Wriothesley Manuscript* in the Guildhall Library.

gladly assented to a measure which ensured their eclipse. And Richard's opponents were prepared to bide their time, cowed for the moment by Hastings' fate and the presence in the capital of so many northerners. Unanimously, the Parliament assented to a document which followed much the same lines as Buckingham's speech in the Guildhall and was couched in the form of a petition to the Duke of Gloucester to take the Crown. On the following day a deputation, headed by none other than the Duke of Buckingham, made its way to the Protector at Baynard's Castle and presented their petition. In keeping with his taste for amateur dramatics, Richard feigned surprise and

Illustration from a law treatise of Henry VI's reign (see also p. 48), showing the Court of the Exchequer at Westminster. The Court is presided over by the Lord High Treasurer – possibly John Tiptoft, Earl of Worcester – dressed in red robes with a turban, and four other judges in mustard-coloured robes. Around the table are clerks and officers of the Court, two counting gold coin. In the foreground are two prisoners in a shuttered enclosure, and two ironbound chests. The table is not chequered, but probably this illustration represents functions of the Court for which a plain cloth was used.

reluctance before he acceded to more shouts of 'King Richard, King Richard'. The nobility pressed forward to take the oath of allegiance, and King Richard rode in state to Westminster Hall. Here he laid formal claim to his title by seating himself on the marble chair of King's Bench.

While the Lords and Commons were listening to the petition at Westminster, a more melancholy scene was enacted in Yorkshire. Under the supervision of the Earl of Northumberland and Sir Richard Ratcliffe, Anthony Earl Rivers, Lord Richard Grey and Sir Thomas Vaughan were executed at Pontefract. Witnesses were surprised to learn that the magnificent and talented Earl wore a hair shirt next to his body. Thus Richard signified his triumph over the Woodvilles by killing the one member of the family whose talents and popularity might have redeemed the greed and cruelty of his kin and threatened the ascendancy of his executioner.

In London arrangements were in hand for the most magnificent coronation of the century. Rich ermines, velvets and cloth-of-gold, so lately intended for Edward v's enthronement were made to serve the occasion of Richard's. While the Master of the Wardrobe laboured to fulfill his contract, Lord John Howard prevailed on the King to confer on him the dukedom of Norfolk and the right to bear the crown to Westminster Abbey as High Steward of England. At the beginning of July, the King held a review of the five thousand men of Yorkshire, Northumberland, and Westmorland who had at last arrived under the command of the Earl of Northumberland. The review took place at Moor Fields and provoked some disparaging comments from Londoners who noted their rusty gear and bedraggled appearance.

On the 6 July 1483, the King and Queen, preceded by heralds and trumpeters, walked barefoot in procession to the Abbey. Behind the bishops and Cardinal Bourchier came Northumberland with the Sword of Mercy, Lord Stanley with the Constable's mace, Richard's brother-in-law John de la Pole, Duke of Suffolk with the sceptre and Suffolk's eldest son John, Earl of Lincoln with the orb. These were followed by the newly-created Duke of Norfolk who carried the crown, and his son, Thomas Howard, Earl of Surrey, with the Sword of State. The King himself was flanked by Viscount Lovell and the Earl of

Kent bearing the Swords of Justice. Buckingham held Richard's train, and behind him walked the remaining earls and barons of the realm. After the King's procession came the Queen's, her regalia borne by two earls and a viscount. At the high altar Richard and Anne stripped to the waist and were anointed with the chrism. They then changed into cloth-of-gold and Cardinal Bourchier set the crowns on their heads. A *Te Deum* was sung and the royal couple received communion, before they returned to the dais at Westminster Hall for the coronation banquet.

For King Richard III the coronation was a triumph. Not only had it set a new precedent in splendour, but it had also been attended by virtually the entire peerage of England, including Henry Tudor's mother, Margaret Beaufort, Countess of Richmond, who had carried Anne's train, and the Queen Dowager's brother-in-law, Viscount Lisle. And all this had been achieved at the cost of only four lives.

Looking back over the crowded months of April, May and June 1483, it is easy to see how the Tudor historians, reading history backwards, came to the conclusion that Richard's path to the throne was carefully planned from the moment he left York. The clockwork sequence of events from the seizing of Edward V, the execution of Hastings, the abduction of the Duke of York, Dr Shaa's sermon, to the mummery of the petition – hint at a cold-blooded and cynical intelligence systematically removing the obstacles that lay between Richard and the inheritance of his nephew. Even Dominic Mancini, who wrote his account only six months later and drew no pension from the Tudors, saw Richard's usurpation in this light.

Yet this portrait is too glib to be convincing. It does not mesh with what is known of Richard in previous years – the years of service as a soldier and an administrator with a distaste for courtly intrigues and political in-fighting. The portrait makes better sense if Richard is seen as a man whose eyes were only by degrees opened to the logical consequences of his own actions. His reaction to each succeeding crisis bears the mark of an impulsive man of action taking the short cut to his immediate objective without pausing to work out the long term effects. If Richard is to be judged, then he must be accused not of too much guile, but of too little.

Crosby Place was built in 1466 by John Crosby, a rich London merchant. Originally it stood in Bishopsgate Street, set in a courtyard, with the great hall flanked by a solar and great chamber range to the north and to the south by a chapel. The house passed to Richard, who used it as his London residence and probably held Court there in the brief period of Edward v's reign.

ABOVE The timber ceiling of the great hall, which is richly gilded and decorated.

RIGHT The oriel window of the great hall. The whole building was transferred from the City to Chelsea in 1908.

5 'The Most Untrue Creature Living' August–November 1483

RICARDVS · III · ANG · REX ·

LORD HASTINGS DEAD, the Queen Dowager in Sanctuary, the boy King in the Tower, the capital invaded by wild northerners, the Duke of Gloucester King. ... News travelled slowly in fifteenth-century England, and the revolutionary events of the past two months had set the whole country buzzing with wild rumours and unsubstantiated gossip. The new King must therefore show himself to his subjects, dispense justice and favours with an open hand, and promise to be every man's good lord. Two weeks after his coronation Richard set out on a royal progress through the West Country and the Midlands to Yorkshire and the North.

But first the three men who had made his usurpation possible received their rewards. Buckingham had the lion's share: he was appointed Constable and Great Chamberlain of England. In addition Richard recognised his long-standing claim to a huge part of the de Bohun inheritance, with an annual income of over £700. To the Earl of Northumberland went the wardenship of the West March and Richard's palatinate in Cumberland. John Howard, the newly-created Duke of Norfolk, received Crown lands worth about £1,000 a year in Suffolk, Essex, Kent and Cambridgeshire. The princely extent of these grants, which virtually created three principalities in Wales and the West Country, in the North, and in East Anglia, show how desperately narrow had become the clique on which Richard's power rested.

On about 20 July the royal cortège set out from Windsor. Anxious to impress on his subjects that he ruled not by force but by consent, Richard dispensed with an armed escort and was accompanied instead by a magnificent retinue of the principal officers, lay and clerical, of his kingdom. By 23 July they were at Reading. At Oxford the King was entertained by Magdalen's founder, William Waynflete, Bishop of Winchester, and attended two scholarly debates on moral philosophy and theology. At nearby Woodstock he restored to the inhabitants some lands which Edward had annexed to the forest of Whichwood. To the city of Gloucester he granted a new charter of liberties. The abbot of Tewkesbury, whose abbey housed the bones of Clarence and of Henry VI's son, Prince Edward, received a donation of £300. At Warwick early in August, Richard was joined by his Queen. And so, by way of

Coventry, Leicester and Nottingham, the procession came to Pontefract where Richard paused to prepare for the climax of his triumphant progress – the State entry into York and the investiture of his son Edward as Prince of Wales.

The King's secretary, John Kendal, had written in advance to the Mayor, Recorder, Aldermen and Sheriffs of York instructing them 'to receive His· Highness and the Queen as laudably as their wisdom can imagine'. The city streets were to be hung 'with cloth of arras, tapestry-work and other; for that there come many southern Lords and men of worship with them which will mark greatly your receiving Their Graces'. On 29 August the Mayor and other local dignitaries duly turned out in scarlet and red gowns to greet their Sovereign outside the city walls. His retinue included six bishops; five earls; Lord Stanley, the Steward of the Household; Viscount Lovell, the Lord Chamberlain; Sir William Hussey, the Chief Justice; Alexander, Duke of Albany; the Spanish Ambassador, de Sasiola; and a great train of royal household officials.

An even more magnificent spectacle took place on Sunday, 7 September, after a week of plays, banquets, speeches and pageants. This was the day selected for the ten-year-old Earl of Salisbury's investiture as Prince of Wales. The survival of a letter dated 30 August to the Master of King's Wardrobe, requisitioning large quantities of satins, silks, velvet and cloth-of-gold, suggests that the investiture may have been a last-minute addition to Richard's programme. The order included no less than thirteen thousand fustian badges emblazoned with his device of the silver boar and 'three coats of arms beaten with fine gold for our own person'. Forty trumpeters heralded the arrival of the royal party at York Minster, where the Prince was invested with a plain gold coronet and a golden rod. In honour of the occasion de Sasiola was knighted and received a collar of gold. It was, as Henry VII's official historian, Polydore Vergil, testified, 'a day of great state for York ... there being three princes wearing crowns – the King, the Queen and the Prince of Wales'.

While Richard was busy impressing his subjects with the majesty of his office, powerful forces were conspiring in the South to deprive him of it. Once the initial shock of the usurpation had worn off, some form of reaction on the part of the

THE DUKE OF NORFOLKE KILLED AT BOSWORTH FEILD

Jockey of norfolk For Dickon thy

be not too bold master is bought and sold

John Howard, 1st Duke of Norfolk. He was Admiral of England, Ireland and Aquitaine, served as High Steward at Richard's coronation, and was killed at Bosworth. This portrait, by an unknown artist, was probably painted in the sixteenth century, and inscribed with the message given to Howard before Bosworth – 'Jockey of Norfolk be not too bold, For Dickon thy master is bought and sold.'

dispossessed was only to be expected. Most prominent among the dispossessed were, of course, the Woodvilles. The ex-Queen's relatives – the Marquess of Dorset, Sir Richard Woodville and Lionel Woodville, Bishop of Salisbury – formed the sinews of a plot which bound together the chronic discontent of the Kentishmen, the outrage felt by the old guard of Edward IV's personal friends and retainers, and the traditional outposts of Lancastrian loyalism in the south-west. The Wars of the Roses had a habit of uniting strange bed-fellows in a common aim: to these was now added the alliance of Woodville and Lancaster, created by the pervasive rumour that Edward IV's

William of Wykeham, Bishop of Winchester, founded a grammar school at Winchester and New College at Oxford, in the late fourteenth century. These drawings are taken from a life of William of Wykeham, produced after 1464.
LEFT Portrait group with William in the centre, seated, holding a model of New College Chapel.
RIGHT The warden and scholars of New College, with the college buildings behind them. (Chandler Ms, New College, 288, folios 4 and 8).

sons had been quietly murdered in the Tower, or spirited away to some northern fortress whence they would never emerge.

These rumours transformed the prospects of a penniless young exile at the Court of Francis, Duke of Brittany. For Henry Tudor, now in his twenty-seventh year, was the sole surviving heir to the claims of the House of Lancaster. On the side of his mother, Margaret Beaufort, he traced his descent from John of Gaunt's extra-marital liaison with Catherine Swynford. The four children of this union, who took the name of Beaufort, were later declared legitimate through the favour of their half-brother, Henry IV, although barred from the royal succession by Act of Parliament. But Acts of Parliament could be repealed as readily as they were made. On his father's side Henry's lineage was equally distinguished and equally tainted with the bar sinister of bastardy. Edmund Tudor, Earl of Richmond was the son of an obscure Welsh gentleman, Owen Tudor, who had found his way into the bed of Henry V's

widow, Queen Catherine. Owen claimed to have married the Queen, but the only proof that was ever forthcoming was the three children she bore him. Henry's double illegitimacy offered him some protection during the early years of Yorkist rule and until 1470 he grew up quietly in the household of the Yorkist Earl of Pembroke, William Herbert. But after the battle of Tewkesbury in 1471 had put paid to Lancastrian hopes and to the last two legitimate Lancastrian claimants, the fourteen-year-old boy became a valuable dynastic chess piece and was smuggled to Duke Francis's Court in Brittany by his uncle, Jasper Tudor. But with the disaffection of the Woodvilles and the old guard of Edward's supporters, the pawn began to assume the stature of a king.

The chief danger to Richard's régime lay in the possibility of a marriage alliance between Henry and one of Edward IV's daughters. In his absence, Richard's Council had already taken steps to guard against this unwelcome prospect by making sure

Magdalen College, Oxford was founded by William of Waynflete, Bishop of Winchester and Lord Chancellor of England, in the mid-fifteenth century. Waynflete had been Master of Winchester from 1429 to 1442, and thus knew well William of Wykeham's educational ideas, which he developed at Magdalen. BELOW The cloisters at Magdalen, which were built in the late fifteenth century. Surmounting the buttresses are various mythical beasts.

Ricardus Dei gracia Rex [...]

nos de gracia nostra speciali ac ex certa sciencia et [...]
nobis est Dilectis nobis Johem Wrathe alias dicto Garter rex armor[um] parium bonorum Reg[is] Cha[...]
[...] successores suos scilicet se Garter rex armor[um] Anglis
[...]tores sine persenand[...] armor[um] qui pro tempore fuint impetiunt sint vniun corp[or]
sis cordem her[e] et exerceret valeant impetinin Ac q[uo]d ipi et successores sui per no[m]i[n]
Wraff et alior[um] Heraldor[um] prosecutor[um] siue persenand[er] armor[um] impetin iniucipeitin[...]
Et q[uo]d ydeni Garter rex armor[um] Anglicor[um] rex armor[um] parium Austral[ium] inui rex ar[mor]
humsmodi nomen terras tenementa Hereditamenta et possessiones ac bona et catalla
atingi in quibuscu[m]q[ue] acionib[us] causis demandis querelis et plitis tam realib[us] et p[er]so[n]
trialib[us] vel scealaub[us] plitare et implitari ac respondere et respondri valeant impetin
potuunt et consueuerunt q[uo]d in p[re]dict[o] Garter rex armor[um] Anglion rex armor[um] par[i]
cor[um] successores ad cor libitum muicem comorētur ac assies loci et tempora conuenia et
et Aiusamento pro bono statu eius divoue et [...]minite facultatis sue sciate contentin
nouti nostro deduimus et concessimus eisdem Garter rex armor[um] Anglior[um] rex armor[um]
armorum vnum mesuagium cum p[er]tinencis in soudou in parochia omnium san[ctorum]
parium Austral[ium] rex armor[um] parium bonalium rex armor[um] Wraff et Herald[or]
tempore existencium impetinin Absq[ue] compoto seu aliquo alio inde nobis vel Heire[...]
niis p[re]dicis quantum in nob[is] est p[re]fatis Garter rex armor[um] Anglicorum rex armor[um]
armorum et successorib[us] suis q[uo]d ipi terras tenementa redditus et possessiones que d[...]
a quibuscu[m]q[ue] p[er]sonis scealaub[us] vel regularib[us] adquirere possint her[e] et tenere eis
armo p[re]dicto vel extra ad libitum kerrun Armor[um] p[re]dictor[um] pro salub[er] statuiro et Anne Co[m]
Ac pro bono statu omnium Benefactor[um] kerrun Armor[um] supranominator[um] suis viuenti
naciones p[re]dict Garter kerrun armor[um] Anglicor[um] kerrun armor[um] parium Austral[ium]
suor Et her omnia absq[ue] impetiaoue impedimento p[er]turbaoue aut grauamine ipi[...]
aliquibus aliis his kerrun patentib[us] seu aliquibus inquisicionib[us] seu aliquo hac de ac
Et absq[ue] sine seu feod[o] inde nobis vel heiraub[us] nostris fiens seu soluens Statuto
p[re]dicm aut cetior[um] finisfor[um] siue cor[um] aliquius vel de aliis donis siue concessionib[us] p[er] n[ost]ra
[...]io Champneys aut eor[um] alian ante hec tempora fact[o] in p[re]sentib[us] minime sat[...]
vel materia quacu[m]q[ue] non obstant[e]. **In cuius** rei testimonium has litteras n[ost]r[as] [...]

... grauie et ... omnibus ... ibme ... omnibus ad quos presentes litere puenerint salutem. Sciatis qd ...

... neccon certis consideracionibz nos specialiter mouentibz concessimus pro nobis z heredibz nostris quantum in ...
... Anglicorum Thome Holme alias dicto Clarenceu regi armorum partium Austrialium Johi More alias dicto ...
... dicto Glouceste' regi armorum partium Wall' z omnibus alijs Heraldis psecutoribz siue purseuans armorum qd ...
... partium Austrialium rex armorum partium Borealium rex armorum partium Wall' ac omnes alij Heraldi prose ...
... re z nomine Heant qz successionem petuam necnon quosdam sigillum comune pro negocijs z alijs agen ...
... regis armorum Anglicorum regis armorum partium Austrialium regis armorum partium Borealium regis armorum ...
... successores p eadem nomina sint psone habiles z capaces in lege ac nomen illis Heant z gerant imppm ...
... Borealium rex armorum partium Wall' ac alij Heraldi prosecutores siue pursenandi armorum z successores sui p ...
... z here possint Ac pro terris tenementis redditibz z possessionibz nullisque rebus bonis z catallis quibus ...
... amississentque generis siunt vel nature in quibuscumque Cui' coram quibuscumque Justiciar' aut Judicibz ...
... eodem modo quo ceteri liberi nostri psone habiles z capaces in lege pl'itare z impl'itari respondere z respond'i ...
... rex armorum partium Borealium rex armorum Wall' z alij Heraldi prosecutores siue pursenandi armorum z ...
... z quaud eis placet ad tractand' comunicand' z concordand' inter se ipos vnacum alijs p consilio ...
... ut ipi quendam locum siue mansionem congruum in ea parte Heant **Dedimus** nostra speciali et ex mero ...
... regi armorum partium Borealium ... armorum Wall' z alijs Heraldis prosecutoribz siue pursenandi ...
... Colde ... Heus z tenenda nostis ... illas ad ptem eisdem Garter' regi armorum Anglicorum regi armor ...
... siue pursenandi armorum z successoribus suis ad vsum suodam principalium z proborum eorundem pro ...
... seud' vel facend' **Et vlterius** de vberiori gra nostra concessimus z licenciam dedimus pro nobis z herede ...
... regi armorum partium Borealium regi armorum Wall' et alijs Heraldis prosecutoribz siue pursenandi ...
... ceantur in capite ad valorem viginti libras p annum vltra repusis z vltra nesuatium p'dictum cum ptinentis ...
... suis impetrandi ad intencionem inueniend' vnum Capellanum p'ditem ad celebrand' singulis diebz in me'ou ...
... vxoris principis Wall' primogeniti nostri quum vixerimus z pro animabz nostris cum ab hac luce migrauerim' ...
... nabz suis cum ab hac luce migrauerint ac pro animabz omnium fidelium defunctor' iuxta districciones z ordi ...
... partium Borealium regis armorum Wall' et aliorum Heraldorum prosecutor' siue pursenandi Armorum z successorum ...
... Justiciar'or' Vicecomitum Esclaetor' Coronator' ballinor' seu ministror' nostror' quorumcumque Et absqz ...
... aut aliquo alio mandato regio in ea parte quoismodo psequend' Heus facend' capiend' seu retornand' ...
... venientia ad manum mortuam non potenid' edit aut eo qd expressa mencio de vero valore annuo mesuagii ...
... psensor' siue p'decessor' nostror' tempore Anglie pfatis Johanni Writhe Thome Holme Johi More et ...
... quo statuto actu ordinacone siue restriccione incontrarium fact' edit siue ordinat' aut aliqua alia re causa ...
... litteras patentes Teste me ipo apud Westmonasterium secundo die Januarij Anno regni nostri primo. **Carolus**
      p bre de priuato sigillo z de dat' predicta auctoritate parliamenti.

that Edward's daughters remained cooped up at Westminster. The Croyland Chronicle tells us that 'the noble Church of the monks at Westminster, and all the neighbouring parts, assumed the character of a castle and fortress while men of the greatest austerity were appointed to act as keepers thereof'. But the actual link between the rebels at home and the Lancastrian Court in exile was supplied by a new defector who now ranked as the second man in the kingdom.

The King was at Lincoln on 11 October when he heard the astounding news that Buckingham had joined the other conspirators already identified by his informers. Buckingham's rebellion makes no sense unless it is assumed that his earlier support of Richard's cause was, all along, part of a grand design to clear his own path to the throne. Tudor historians later concocted a variety of fables to account for this breathtaking *volte-face* – a quarrel over the de Bohun lands, remorse over the death of the Princes, the pervasive wiles of Buckingham's prisoner Bishop Morton – but only Polydore Vergil plumbs the Duke's motives when he reports the rumour that 'the Duke did the less dissuade King Richard from usurping the kingdom by means of so many mischievous deeds that he afterward, being hated both of God and man, might be expelled from the same, and so himself called by the commons to that dignity'. The scheme was not as hare-brained as its ultimate failure made it appear. For Buckingham bore the unquartered arms of Thomas of Woodstock, youngest son of Edward III, and his lineage was untainted by the bastardy that blemished Henry Tudor's Beaufort claims. Certainly the Yorkists, who had killed his father at St Albans in 1455 and his grandfather at Northampton in 1460, had no claims on his loyalty. Having used Richard to eliminate the senior branch of the Yorkist line he now planned to use the Lancastrian Tudor to unseat the junior branch. The tale of his repentance would in the meantime reconcile the Woodville rebels to co-operating with the late instrument of their downfall.

John Morton, Bishop of Ely, a prisoner at Brecon Castle since Hastings' execution, put Buckingham in touch with Henry Tudor's mother, Margaret Beaufort, Countess of Richmond, and she in turn contacted her son in Brittany. Other couriers linked the Brecon conspirators with the Woodvilles. By these

covert means the substance of a tripartite agreement between Henry, Buckingham and the Woodvilles was hammered out. Buckingham pledged his support to Henry's claims; Henry promised to marry the Queen Dowager's eldest daughter, Elizabeth of York. By the end of September all the rebel groups had co-ordinated their plans for a simultaneous rising on 18 October, and Henry Tudor had secured the Duke of Brittany's financial backing for an invasion by sea. Morton was doubtless astute enough to realise that Buckingham the Kingmaker had himself in mind for the throne rather than Henry Tudor, but that was an issue which could wait on Richard's destruction.

In the event Richard was saved by good intelligence, prompt action and foul weather. With so many different factions involved in the plot, it comes as no surprise that a few stool pigeons came to roost in Richard's camp. Within twenty-four hours of hearing the news, the King had sent out the summonses for a royal army to assemble at Leicester by 21 October. Here is the letter he addressed to the Mayor of York:

BY THE KING

Trusty and well-beloved: we greet you well, and let ye wit that the Duke of Buckingham traitorously has turned upon us, contrary to the duty of his allegiance, and entendeth the utter destruction of us, you and all other our true subjects that have taken our part; whose traitorous intent we with God's grace intend briefly to resist and subdue. We desire and pray you in our hearty wise that ye will send unto us as many men defensibly arrayed on horseback as ye may goodly make to our town of Leicester the 21st day of this present month without fail as ye will tender our honour and your own weal, and we will see you so paid for your reward as ye shall hold ye well content. Give further credence to our trusty pursuivant this bearer. Given under our signet at our city of Lincoln the 11th day of October.

By the time that he and Northumberland were reviewing their troops at Leicester on the 21st, Richard was cheered to hear of the swift measures taken by his lieutenant in the South, the Duke of Norfolk, for the defence of London. Finding their way to the capital blocked by Norfolk's men at Gravesend, the Kent and Surrey rebels led by Sir John and Richard Guildford were compelled to withdraw and await the promised arrival of the Duke of Buckingham.

Thanks to the King's effective early warning system and to an exceptional bout of heavy rains which deluged Wales at this moment, the rebel Duke had sufficient troubles of his own.

> In no drowsy manner [reports the Croyland Chronicle] King Richard contrived that, throughout Wales, as well as in all parts of the marches thereof, armed men should be set in readiness around the said Duke, as soon as ever he had set a foot from his home, to pounce upon all his property; who, accordingly, encouraged by the prospect of the Duke's wealth, which the King had, for that purpose, bestowed upon them were in every way to obstruct his progress. The result was, that, on the side of the castle of Brecknock [Brecon], which looks towards the interior of Wales, Thomas, the son of the late Sir Roger Vaughan, with the aid of his brethren and kinsmen, most carefully watched the whole of the surrounding country; while Humphrey Stafford partly destroyed the bridges and passes by which England was entered, and kept the other part closed by means of a strong force set there to guard the same.

Drenched by the rains and harassed by the guerillas, Buckingham's retainers lost heart and melted away as they struggled across the Welsh borders into Herefordshire. At Lord Ferrers' manor of Webley the Duke was abandoned even by Bishop Morton, who fled first to the Fen Country, then to Flanders. Sick with fear, the Duke himself deserted what was left of his following. He disguised himself as a commoner and took refuge in the Shropshire cottage of one of his servants, Ralph Bannaster of Wem. For Master Ralph the chief attraction of his guest lay in the £1,000 reward the King had set on his head, and he promptly betrayed the Duke to the local sheriff.

With London in safe hands and Buckingham washed out, Richard was able to concentrate his entire army on the western rebels – Sir Richard Woodville at Newbury, Bishop Lionel Woodville, Sir John Cheyney and Walter Hungerford at Salisbury, and Dorset, the Courtenays and Thomas St Leger at Exeter – whose only hope now lay in Henry Tudor's fleet. But Henry did not even set out until 31 October, and as Richard's army marched south into Wiltshire, the rebels scattered into Sanctuary or sought shelter abroad. When the King entered Salisbury unopposed on 28 October, the great rebellion was over. Buckingham, tried and sentenced by the Vice-

The Bloody Tower, known in the fifteenth century as the Garden Tower, because it stood next to the Constable's Garden. It is believed that Richard lodged his young nephews in this tower, and that they were murdered in the bedchamber.

Constable, Sir Ralph Assheton, was beheaded in Salisbury market place on Sunday, 2 November.

At Exeter on 8 November Richard at last had news of Tudor's ships. Sailing from the Breton port of Paimpol on 31 October with fifteen ships and five thousand men, the fleet had been scattered at sea by a storm. When he hove to outside Poole Harbour in Dorset with his two remaining ships, the shore was lined with armed men. They were Buckingham's men, they shouted, come to escort him to the Duke. Henry was undeceived. Sailing on to Plymouth he learned that the whole of the West Country lay in Richard's power, and hoisted sail for the return voyage to Brittany.

One great question still overshadows the episode of Buckingham's rebellion. What *had* happened to the late King's children, Edward and Richard, the Princes in the Tower?

The few surviving scraps of contemporary evidence offer

only rumour and hearsay. Dominic Mancini unfortunately left England early in July 1483, shortly after Richard's coronation, and does not even mention Buckingham's revolt. Of the Princes he tells us only that, after Hastings' execution,

> ... he [Edward] and his brother were withdrawn into the inner apartments of the Tower proper, and day by day began to be seen more rarely behind the bars and windows, till at length they ceased to appear altogether. A Strasbourg doctor, the last of his attendants whose services the King enjoyed, reported that the young King, like a victim prepared for sacrifice, sought remission of his sins by daily confession and penance, because he believed that death was facing him.

Mancini goes on to say that 'already there was a suspicion he had been done away with. Whether, however, he has been done away with, and by what manner of death, so far I have not at all discovered.'

The other contemporary English source – the Croyland Chronicle – confirms that these rumours, reported by Mancini as early as July, were also current on the eve of Buckingham's rebellion in September. 'A rumour', it states, 'was spread that the sons of King Edward had died a violent death, but it was uncertain how.' However, the wording here implies that the rumour may well have been spread by the rebels with malice aforethought.

The only outright accusation of murder that dates from this time appears in a speech made before the Estates General by the French Chancellor at Tours in January 1484. The Chancellor invited the assembled delegates to spare a thought for the children of Edward IV 'whose massacre went unpunished, while the assassin was crowned by popular assent'. But the French, who had only a few months before torn up the Treaty of Picquigny, were obviously eager to clutch at any straw which would promote the civil discords of their enemies, and this 'evidence' must be taken with a pinch of salt. De Rochford most probably heard the rumours from Mancini and translated them for propaganda purposes from suspicion into fact.

Stricter confinement, suspicion and propaganda ... that is as far as the literary evidence goes. But the dearth of these contemporary sources contrasts strangely with the long and involved story given by Sir Thomas More in his unfinished fragment *The History of King Richard III*. More's account, written forty years later, had such a decisive influence on subsequent versions that it is worth quoting in full:

King Richard, after his coronation, taking his way to Gloucester to visit in his new honour the town of which he bare the name of his old, devised as he rode to fulfil that thing which he before had intended. And forasmuch as his mind gave him that, his nephews living, men would not reckon that he could have right to the realm, he thought therefore without delay to rid them, as though the killing of his kinsmen could amend his cause and make him a kindly King. Whereupon he sent one John Green, whom he specially trusted, unto Sir Robert Brackenbury, constable of the Tower, with a letter and credence also that the same Sir Robert should in any wise put the two children to death. This John Green did his errand unto Brackenbury, kneeling before our Lady in the Tower, who plainly answered that he would never put them to death, to die therefore; with which answer John Green, returning, recounted the same to King Richard at Warwick, yet in his way. Wherewith he took such displeasure and thought that the same night he said unto a secret page of his. 'Ah, whom shall a man trust? Those that I have brought up myself, those that I had weaned would most surely serve me, even those fail me and at my commandment will do nothing for me.'

'Sir,' quoth his page, 'there lieth one on your pallet without, that I dare well say, to do your Grace pleasure, the thing were right hard that he would refuse', meaning by this Sir James Tyrell, which was a man of right goodly personage and for nature's gifts worthy to have served a much better prince, if he had well served God and by grace obtained as much truth and good will as he had strength and wit. The man had an high heart and sore longed upward, not rising yet so fast as he had hoped, being hindered and kept under by the means of Sir Richard Ratcliffe and Sir William Catesby, which longing for no more partners of the prince's favour, and namely not for him whose pride they wist would bear no peer, kept him by secret drifts out of all secret trust. Which thing this page well had marked and known. Wherefore, this occasion offered, of very special friendship he took his time to put him forward and by such wise do him good that all the enemies he had, except the devil, could never have done him so much hurt. For upon this page's words King Richard arose (for this communication had he sitting at the draught [privy], a convenient carpet for such a counsel) and came out into the pallet chamber, on which he found in bed Sir James and Sir Thomas Tyrell, of person like and brethren of blood, but nothing of kin in conditions. Then said the King merrily to them: 'What, Sirs, be ye in bed so soon!' and calling up Sir James, broke to him secretly his mind in this mischievous matter; in which he found him nothing strange. Wherefore, on the morrow, he sent him to Brackenbury with a letter, by which he was commanded to deliver Sir James all the keys of the Tower for one night, to the end he might there accomplish the King's pleasure in such thing as he had given him commandment. After which letter delivered and the keys received, Sir James appointed the night next ensuing to destroy them, devising before and preparing the means. The prince, as soon as the protector left that name and took himself as King, had it showed unto him that he should not reign, but his uncle should have the crown. At which word the prince, sore abashed, began to sigh and said: 'Alas, I would my uncle would let me have my life yet, though I lose my kingdom.' Then he that told him the tale used him with good words and put him in the best comfort he could. But forthwith was the prince and his brother both shut up: and all others removed from them, only one called Black Will or William Slaughter except, set to serve them and see them sure. After which time the prince never tied his points, nor aught wraught of himself, but with that young babe his brother lingered in thought and heaviness till this traitorous death delivered them of that wretchedness. [An examination of the remains generally held to be those of the Princes shows that Edward V was suffering from a bone disease of the lower jaw and his state of depression may well have been due to ill health rather than any premonition of his fate.] For Sir James Tyrell devised that they should be murdered in their beds. To the execution whereof, he appointed Miles Forest, one of the four that kept them, a fellow fleshed in murder beforetime. To him he joined one John Dighton, his own horsekeeper, a big broad, square, strong knave. Then, all the others being removed from them, this Miles Forest and John Dighton, about midnight (the silly [innocent] children lying in their beds) came into the chamber and suddenly lapped them up among the clothes, so bewrapped them and entangled them, keeping down by force the feather bed and pillows hard unto their mouths, that within a while, smothered and stifled, their breath failing, they gave up to God their innocent souls into the joys of heaven, leaving to the tormentors their bodies dead in the bed. Which after that the wretches perceived, first by the struggling with the pains of death, and after lying still, to be

'Alas, I would my uncle would let me have my life yet, though I lose my kingdom'

143

William Caxton: the First English Printer

Caxton was originally a mercer, spending much of his time in Bruges, the central foreign market of the Anglo-Flemish trade. By 1463 he was Acting Governor of the Merchant Adventurers' Company in the Low Countries. When Margaret of York married Charles the Rash, Caxton entered her household as a commercial adviser.

In 1471 Caxton went to Cologne, and there learned the art of printing. He first set up his press in Bruges, and then in 1476 returned to England and established his press at Westminster. He was patronised by many of Edward IV's leading courtiers, including Anthony Woodville, Earl Rivers, whose work was printed on Caxton's presses.

ABOVE RIGHT Caxton's advertisement announcing that he had set up his printing press at the sign of the red pale in the almonry of Westminster Abbey, 1476.

RIGHT William Caxton presenting his translation of the popular romance *The Recuyell of the Historyes of Troye,* to his patroness, Margaret of York. He printed the *Recuyell* at Bruges in 1474–5, in partnership with Colard Mansion.

If it plese ony man spirituel or temporel to bye ony pyes of two and thre comemoracions of salisburi vse enpryntid after the forme of this preset lettre whiche ben wel and truly correct, late hym come to westmonester in to the almonesrye at the reed pale and he shal haue them good chepe

Supplico stet cedula

Woodcut of a blacksmith from Caxton's *Game and Play of the Chess*, which was probably printed in 1483.

Page from Caxton's edition of Chaucer's Prologue to the *Canterbury Tales*, which he printed in 1483. This depicts the pilgrims feasting on boar's head.

Prologus

Gret chere made our ost to vs everychon
And to souper sette he vs anon
He serued vs wyth vytayll at the beste
Stronge was the wyne & wel drynke vs lyste

A semely man our oste was wyth alle
Forto be a marchal in a lordes halle
A large man he was wyth eyen stepe
A feyrer burgeys is ther non in chepe
Bold of hys speche and wel was y taught
And of manhood lacked he right nought
Eke therto was he right a mery man
And aftir souper to pleyen he begon
And spak of myrthe among other thynges
Whan that we hadde made our rekenynges
He sayd thus now lordynges truely
Ye be to me right welcome hertly
For by my trowthe yf I shal not lye
I saw not thys yeer so mery a companye

t iiij

thoroughly dead: they laid their bodies naked out upon the bed, and fetched Sir James to see them. Which, upon the sight of them, caused those murderers to bury them at the stair foot, meetly deep in the ground, under a great heap of stones.

Then rode Sir James in great haste to King Richard, and showed him all the manner of the murder, who give him great thanks and, as some say, there made him knight. But he allowed not, as I have heard, the burying in so vile a corner, saying he would have them buried in a better place, because they were a King's sons. Lo the honourable courage of a King! Whereupon they say that a priest of Sir Robert Brackenbury took up the bodies again, and secretly entered them in such place, as by the occasion of his death, which only knew it, could never since come to light. Very truth is it and well known, that at such times as Sir James Tyrell was in the Tower, for treason committed against the most famous prince King Henry the Seventh, both Dighton and he were examined, and confessed the murder in manner above written, but whither the bodies were removed they could nothing tell. And thus have I learned of them that much knew and little cause had to lie, were these two noble princes, these innocent tender children, born of most royal blood, brought up in great wealth, likely long to live to reign and rule in the realm, by traitorous tyranny taken, deprived of their estate, shortly shut up in prison, and privily slain and murdered their bodies cast God knows where by the cruel ambition of their unnatural uncle and his dispiteous tormentors.

More's account, written in 1513, carries a certain glib conviction, because he claims as his source the confession of the alleged assassin, Sir James Tyrell, who was executed for treason in 1502. But to accept it at its face value raises a number of unanswerable questions: why would Sir James make such a damaging confession? Why did Henry VII never have it taken down in writing and circulated? Why does his official historian, Polydore Vergil, omit all mention of the confession?

The lack of incriminating evidence against Richard and the obvious holes in More's testimony have led to some ingenious theorising about Henry VII as the possible assassin. In the summer of 1486 – one year after Bosworth – Henry VII issued not one but two royal pardons in the name of Sir James Tyrell. Using this fact in conjunction with More's narrative, it has been argued that Tyrell did indeed murder the Princes, not at Richard's bidding but at Henry's. Added to this there is

'Lo the honourable courage of a King!'

146

Henry's rather puzzling failure to make use of Richard's alleged murder of the Princes as a weapon in the propaganda war, either before or after Bosworth. Although it would have made sense to publish the Princes' death as a means of strengthening his wife Elizabeth's claims to be Edward IV's heiress, there is only a single, indirect reference to the 'shedding of infants' blood' tucked away in the Act of Attainder which he presented to his Parliament in October 1485. Finally, there is the evidence of Henry's shabby treatment of his mother-in-law, the Dowager Queen Elizabeth Woodville. In February 1487 he abruptly had her stripped of her possessions and shut up in a nunnery. This has been taken as evidence of the fact that the Queen Dowager had learned of Henry's guilt in the disposal of her sons, and had to be locked up to prevent her causing a scandal.

The most effective rebuttal of Henry's guilt lies in the only piece of hard evidence we possess. In 1674 workmen demolishing a staircase outside the White Tower discovered a wooden chest containing the skeletons of two children. From both their location and their approximate ages it was immediately assumed that these were the mortal remains of the murdered Princes, concealed where More indicated they were buried, but not removed for reburial elsewhere as he further stated. In 1933 these skeletons were submitted to a medical examination. From the bone formation and the structure of the teeth it was concluded that the skeletons were those of two children aged about twelve and ten respectively. This tallies with the ages of the two Princes in the early autumn of 1483; if these are the skeletons of the Princes, and their ages have been accurately assessed, it can be argued that Henry VII is exonerated from any part in their deaths.

By the same logic, if the Princes died in the autumn of 1483, there are only two men who could conceivably have been responsible – Richard and Buckingham. Both had the same motive. While Edward IV's children were alive they would provide a focus for legitimist conspiracies. There were numerous precedents for doing away with embarrassing prisoners of royal blood – from King John's nephew Arthur to King Henry VI – to persuade their gaolers that reasons of State overrode the dictates of private conscience.

On two counts Buckingham makes a more plausible villain than Richard. First, his motive was stronger than the King's. By 6 July Richard had already cleared the hurdle of winning the consent of the people who mattered to his usurpation of the Crown. By the simple device of proclaiming his nephews to be bastards he also had a theoretical justification for his successful *coup*. Although the Princes would be an embarrassment, they were no longer an obstacle. But if Buckingham was aiming to depose Richard in his turn, he would have to enlist the support of men who were loyal to the memory of Edward IV – men who would not subscribe to the theory of his children's bastardy. It was thus essential to make sure the Princes were dead before he made his bid – and to put the blame on Richard.

This interpretation would help to explain the agreement which Richard reached with the Queen Dowager in February 1484. In return for a guarantee of her daughters' safety, Elizabeth agreed that they should leave the Sanctuary of Westminster Abbey and place themselves in Richard's care. This would seem to be an extraordinary stupid thing to do if she knew – or even suspected – that Richard had already murdered her two sons.

However, the Buckingham theory is snagged by one fatal flaw. If Buckingham was guilty, Richard could have saved himself a lot of trouble by saying so. 'The most untrue creature living' had a lot of crimes laid at his door, but never the murder of the Princes. At the risk of complicating the issue still further, we could go on to ask, why did Richard not avail himself of the opportunity to accuse Buckingham, even if he was guilty himself? The simplest answer would be that they were still alive when the Woodville daughters emerged from Sanctuary and met their death shortly afterwards. This would be within an acceptable margin of error as far as medical evidence on the skeletons is concerned. It would also tally with the statement in the Great Chronicle of London that the rumours of the Princes' deaths were current after Easter 1484.

On balance this too is improbable, for there are more powerful reasons to support the conclusion that the Princes were already dead when Richard heard the news of Buckingham's treachery. First of all, the marriage between Elizabeth of York and Henry Tudor, which was negotiated in September 1483,

Elizabeth of York, Edward IV's eldest daughter, who was to marry Henry Tudor. Portrait by an unknown artist.

would not have gained the Queen Dowager's assent if she still had reasonable hopes of seeing her two boys alive. Secondly, Richard never made any attempt to quash the rumours circulating in the autumn of 1483 by parading Edward and Richard in public. Finally, there is no mention of any guarantees for their safety in the pact which brought their sisters out of Sanctuary on 1 March 1484.

As the alternative suspects are eliminated and the time-scale of the murders narrows, Richard's defence begins to appear more and more shaky. It is therefore worth taking a second look

at the most convincing circumstantial evidence in his favour –
the fact that on 1 March 1484, the Queen Dowager permitted
her daughters to leave the Sanctuary of Westminster Abbey.
Elizabeth Woodville was no fool. The former widow of a
Lancastrian knight, she was canny enough to become the wife
of a Yorkist king. She was also hardy enough to have given
birth to her elder son twelve years before in the same Sanctuary. If she knowingly delivered her daughters to the man who
had done away with her sons, she must have been prompted
by something more than naïvety or claustrophobia.

Sanctuary, she knew, was not an inviolable privilege. After
the battle of Tewkesbury in 1471, Edward IV gave orders for
the Lancastrian rebels who had taken refuge in the Abbey to
be dragged out and executed. If Richard was determined to get
her and her daughters out, she had no reason to suppose his
scruples would be any stronger than his brother's. This much is
hinted in Croyland Chronicle: 'After frequent entreaties *as well
as threats* had been used, Queen Elizabeth, being strongly
solicited to do so, sent her daughters from the Sanctuary at
Westminster to King Richard.' If Sanctuary was unsafe, was
there any greater certainty that Richard would respect his
promise not to harm her daughters? The wording of his oath
provides the clue:

> Memorandum that I, Richard ... in the presence of my Lords
> spiritual and temporal, of you, Mayor and Aldermen of my City
> of London, promise and swear *verbo regio* and upon these Holy
> Evangiles of God by me personally touched, that if the daughters
> of Dame Elizabeth Grey, late calling herself Queen of England,
> that is to wit Elizabeth, Cecily, Anne, Katherine and Bridget, will
> come out into me of the Sanctuary of Westminster, and be guided,
> ruled and demeaned after me, I shall see that they be in surety of
> their lives, and also do not suffer any manner of hurt ... in their
> body and persons by way of ravishment or defouling contrary to
> their wills. ...

The terms are what we might expect: it is the witnesses who
are the key. Richard's private word of honour was reinforced
by a public undertaking, witnessed by Lords, Bishops, Mayor
and Aldermen. If the King broke his oath, the whole kingdom
would know of it. Every public act that Richard undertook in

1483 – the heralds announcing the discovery of the Woodville arms caches, the staging of Dr Shaa's sermon, the royal progress of July and August, the magnificent investiture of the Prince of Wales – witnesses how sensitive he was to public opinion. The Princes might be done away with in secret, but their five sisters would find no safer refuge than in the limelight of Richard's Court.

We have thus come in a full circle back to Richard as the prime suspect and the early autumn of 1483 as the most likely date. The evidence is not conclusive in a legal sense, and never will be. Richard stands convicted not so much by the evidence against him as by the lack of evidence against anybody else.

The murders leave an ineradicable stain on Richard's character. Despite the long list of precedents the act was as shocking then as it appears today. But it does not prove that his nature was warped by a vein of deliberate cruelty. His treatment of the vanquished Nevilles and his defence of Clarence show Richard in a kinder light. It is also more than likely that Buckingham egged him on to the murder as persuasively as he propelled him towards the throne.

More important than the moral issue were the political consequences. The murder of the Princes has often been described as a Renaissance solution in the manner later prescribed by Macchiavelli. In fact it was a colossal blunder. Nothing else could have prompted the deflated Woodvilles to hitch themselves to Henry Tudor's bandwagon. In October Richard was rescued from the consequences by the storm that scattered Henry's Breton fleet. But the menace remained and would cast its shadow over the brief twilight of Richard's reign. At the cathedral of Rennes on Christmas Day 1483, Henry Tudor swore a solemn oath in the presence of the Lancastrian Court in exile that he would marry Elizabeth of York. It was both a promise and a warning.

6
The King
1483-4

RETURNING TO HIS CAPITAL on 25 November 1483, Richard received a heartening welcome at Kennington from the Mayor and Aldermen in their scarlet robes, and was escorted to Blackfriars by a troop of horsemen clad in violet. He had survived the first real crisis of his reign with surprisingly little effort. His army had been sent home without striking a blow. The overwhelming majority of the gentry, the cities and even the barons had ignored the rebel call to arms, and signified their consent to his usurpation. The storm clouds gathering in Brittany were not allowed to disturb the magnificent Christmas festivities, which prompted Commynes to declare that Richard 'was reigning in greater splendour and authority than any king of England for the last hundred years'. With one London mercer alone he ran up a bill for £1,200.

Richard was not the sort of man to indulge himself for long in the sybaritic pleasures of the Court. Early in the New Year he was back in the saddle, on a progress through Kent. Unlike the ceremonial tour of the previous summer, this was a strictly business-like affair. During the late rebellion Kent had once again lived up to its reputation as the most troublesome shire

Miniature depicting the craft guild examination of a carpenter.

in his kingdom. A special oath of allegiance was now administered to the men of Kent by commissioners appointed for that purpose, and one of Richard's most trusted household knights, Sir Marmaduke Constable, was installed at Penshurst to put down the evils of livery and maintenance. The royal proclamation which followed on the heels of the oath is interesting because it puts Richard's political philosophy in a nutshell. Any man who found himself 'grieved, oppressed or unlawfully wronged' was invited to 'make a bill of complaint and put it to his highness, for his grace is utterly determined that all his subjects shall live in rest and quiet, and peaceably enjoy their lands, livelihoods and goods, according to the laws of this his land, which they were naturally born to inherit'. It was a clear recognition that a king must earn his subjects' loyalty with firm, effective government and speedy, impartial justice.

The tragedy of Richard III was that he had so little time to put his good intentions into effect. Nevertheless, at the first and only Parliament of his reign, which opened on 23 January, he made an impressive beginning.

Unlike the tyrant of legend, Richard had a healthy respect for the assembly of Lords and Commons who met together in the Painted Chamber at Westminster to hear the Chancellor's opening address. Parliament was the highest court of the realm, with a special competence in the larger political issues of the succession, the disinheritance of traitors by act of attainder, the imposition of taxes, the overhaul of the machinery of justice and other great issues touching the welfare of the community as a whole. Over the last two centuries, the knights and burgesses who represented the shires and the towns had won many important privileges, including the right to hold their own deliberations in the refectory of Westminster Abbey under a Speaker of their choice, to put forward collective requests of their own devising, known as common petitions, and to make all Parliamentary legislation conditional on their assent. During the troubled years of Henry VI's reign the Commons had shown themselves particularly aggressive, forcing on the King's Council their proposals for the reform of his slipshod finances, and even impeaching Queen Margaret's favourite minister, the Duke of Suffolk. In Edward IV's capable hands the situation was quickly reversed. Far from resisting reform, it was the King's Council which most actively promoted it, and entered into a fruitful partnership with the Commons. This was the precedent that Richard determined to follow.

John Russell's opening speech was originally intended for Edward V's first Parliament, but it would serve as well for Richard's. It was an appeal to the Lords to forget their private quarrels and 'each amiably hearken upon the other, so that they might attend to the welfare of the body politic'. A postscript on the Duke of Buckingham – 'a rotten member of the body' – was added, to drive the lesson home. Business began in earnest on the following Monday, when the Commons paid their King the compliment of choosing his personal confidant, William Catesby, as Speaker. Their first priority was the confirmation of Richard's title: the Act reiterated the story of Edward's pre-contract with Eleanor Butler, accused Elizabeth Woodville of witchcraft and sorcery, and attributed all the subsequent 'destruction of the noble blood of this land' to her 'ungracious

Richard: Rex fitius.

pretensed marriage' to the King. Since Edward's children were bastards and Clarence's had been attainted, Richard was king by right of inheritance, as well as by the election of the three estates assembled in Parliament. Prince Edward, his son, was declared heir apparent.

The attainders came next. Ninety-five men had been singled out as the leaders of the rebellion and had their lands confiscated – twenty-eight from Kent and Surrey, fourteen from Berkshire, thirty-three from Wiltshire and eighteen from the Exeter clique. These measures were not unduly harsh: at least a third of the attainders were subsequently revoked and many of those named had already found refuge at Henry's Court in exile. The two women most closely implicated were treated with generosity. The Duchess of Buckingham, *née* Catherine Woodville, received an annuity. The much more deeply implicated Countess of Richmond suffered no further punishment than having to place her lands in the keeping of her husband, Lord Stanley. Without a doubt, she owed her survival to Stanley who, with his unusually sensitive nose for picking the winner, had remained loyally at Richard's side throughout the crisis.

The remainder of the session was devoted to more constructive work. The Commons approved a whole sheaf of government-sponsored statutes aimed at stopping legal loop-holes and sharp practices. One ensured that juries should be properly qualified and free from intimidation. Another provided that bail should be allowed to men arrested on suspicion of felony. A third put a stop to fraudulent property transfers which concealed from the buyer that a part of the property in question had already been sold to somebody else. These were clearly aimed at local dignitaries who used their position to exploit less powerful neighbours, and they show that Richard was not afraid of causing offence among his more influential subjects in the name of better justice.

In drafting these reforms Richard employed the help of some of the most able and learned men in the kingdom, for apart from his personal confidants, the backbone of Richard's Council were the churchmen who traditionally staffed the upper echelons of the civil service in the Middle Ages. All of them were professionals with years of service under Edward IV to their names. The Chancellor, John Russell, was an experienced diplomat, as was Thomas Langton, Bishop of St David's, whom Richard would shortly send on a mission to the Pope. Thomas Rotherham, Archbishop of York and Robert Stillington, Bishop of Bath and Wells, were both Cambridge academics and former Chancellors. John Alcock, Bishop of Worcester, became the founder of Jesus College, Cambridge. John Gunthorp, Dean of Wells, was Keeper of the Privy Seal and the royal chaplain, Edmund Chatterton, held a key financial post as Treasurer of the Chamber. These men not only brought a wealth of experience to the Council table, but also provided the vital element of continuity with the previous régime.

If the Commons were impressed by Richard's conscientious programme of legal reforms, they were probably even more gratified by his failure to ask for a Parliamentary subsidy. The military expenses of the previous autumn had proved a heavy drain on his resources and the substantial treasure hoard bequeathed to him by Edward IV was almost depleted. Furthermore, he knew that Henry Tudor would soon try his luck again. To meet the threat more troops would have to be paid, ships fitted out, battlements repaired and garrisons provisioned. His reticence in asking the Commons for money must therefore have been a political gesture. Unless some grandiose chauvinistic venture like the conquest of France was in the offing, the increasingly prosperous middle classes were particularly resentful of direct taxation, and expected the king to maintain his household and meet the day-to-day expenses of government from his own resources. In his earnest effort to win their approval Richard went one step further: he renounced in advance the fund-raising device of voluntary loans or benevolences which had caused so much unfavourable comment during his brother's reign. On 20 February, the last day of Parliament's sitting, the Commons granted him in return the customs revenues, known as tonnage and poundage.

Richard's greatest source of power and wealth lay, in fact, in the Crown lands. At his accession in 1483, these included not only the combined possessions of the Lancastrian and Yorkist kings, but also vast forfeitures of dead or attainted Lancastrian magnates, which Edward had granted to Clarence and to Richard himself, as Duke of Gloucester. This accumulation of manors, castles and townships yielded an annual revenue of nearly £25,000. Even after the salaries of a small army of royal officials had been paid, estate management could be made to show a handsome profit and more than covered the £11,000 needed to support Richard's perambulatory household. For the organisation that administered the Crown lands Richard was again indebted to his profit-conscious brother. Edward IV had been very professional about estate management, appointing men with legal training rather than local squires or knights as his stewards and surveyors, conducting regular audits, and controlling the whole operation through the Treasurer and clerks of his Chamber.

As a usurper Richard was inevitably committed to handing out a fair chunk of his estates as rewards for his supporters. At the time of his coronation a golden shower of grants fell on the not unexpectant trinity of Norfolk, Buckingham and Northumberland. But these grants were only a curtain raiser for those that followed at the end of the year. The confiscations and attainders visited on the rebels of Buckingham's rebellion gave Richard the opportunity to create a whole class of men with a vested interest in his political survival. Buckingham himself was the greatest landowner in England after the King, and the annual value of the lands Richard bestowed on his loyal followers totalled £12,000. It was this redistribution of property – the greatest since Richard II despoiled his opponents in 1398 – that prompted Sir Thomas More's acid comment: 'with large gifts he got him unsteadfast friendship, for which he was fain to pillage and spoil in other places, and got him steadfast hatred'.

The list of recipients again contains the names of the small nucleus of barons who were neither dead nor exiled. Northumberland was granted the extensive holdings of his mother's family, the Poynings, in Surrey, Sussex and the West Country. Lord Stanley and his brother, Sir William, shared in the spoils of Buckingham's Welsh holdings. Other rewards were parcelled out to Norfolk and his son, Thomas Howard, Earl of Surrey, to Richard's nephew, John de la Pole, Earl of Lincoln, and to William Herbert, Earl of Huntingdon, who had married the King's bastard daughter, Catherine. But the largest group were men with a more direct stake in Richard's future, his personal following of knights and esquires, whose rewards

Queens' College, Cambridge was founded by Queen Margaret of Anjou in 1448, and later patronised by Queen Elizabeth Woodville, hence the plural designation. Right: False hammerbeam carved as an angel, from the timber roof of the college hall. The angel carries a crowned shield with the initial letter of Margaret of Anjou.

were coupled with responsibilities as sheriffs, keepers of castles or guardians of the royal estates. The harsh lessons of the careers of Warwick and Montagu, Clarence and Buckingham had taught Richard not to build his fortunes solely on the shifting sands of baronial loyalty.

The King's preference for men of middle rank, especially for the associates of his lieutenancy in the North, did not pass without comment. The Croyland Chronicler reported that 'the immense estates and patrimonies' collected by attainder were all 'distributed among his northern adherents whom he planted in every spot throughout his dominions, to the disgrace and lasting and loudly expressed sorrow of all the people in the south'.

Of Richard's three closest advisers, two – Francis, Viscount Lovell and Sir Richard Ratcliffe – were former members of his Council in the North. The third, William Catesby, came from the Midlands and was a comparatively recent discovery. This trio was commemorated in the famous rhyme nailed to the door of St Paul's later that year in July:

> 'The Cat, the Rat and Lovell our dog
> Rulen all England under an Hog.'

The King's secretary, John Kendal, had previously served as the Duke of Gloucester's secretary, and was rewarded with the lucrative office of Controller of the Mint. Lord Scrope of Bolton, another of Richard's Northern Council, also belonged to the inner circle of the King's Council. Further down the scale were a number of other northern knights, including James Tyrell; Robert Brackenbury, the Constable of the Tower and Sheriff of Kent; Robert Percy, the King's boyhood friend and Controller of the Household; and Ralph Assheton, the Vice-Constable of England. Richard's trust in these northerners was not misplaced: with one exception all of them would ride with him to Bosworth.

As soon as Parliament had concluded its business Richard was chafing to resume his travels. Two final precautions – both of them reminders that he still had powerful enemies – detained him until the first week of March 1484. One was the agreement negotiated for the release of the Queen Dowager's daughters from Sanctuary. The other was a solemn ceremony described by the Croyland Chronicler:

Shortly after mid-day nearly all the lords of the realm, both spiritual and temporal, together with the higher knights and esquires of the king's household, met together at the special command of the king in a certain lower room near the passage which leads to the Queen's apartments; and here each subscribed his name to a kind of new oath … of adherence to Edward, the king's only son, as their supreme lord, in case anything should happen to his father.

Then he was away, with Queen Anne at his side, heading for the cloisters of Cambridge University, and what was to be the last interlude of peace in his short, unhappy reign. During the week they spent at Cambridge, Richard and Anne made generous endowments to King's and the Queens' Colleges, which the University promised to remember in a special Mass to be celebrated on 2 May. As the royal cortège left Cambridge, Richard's thoughts turned to the challenges that the new campaigning season would bring: French and Breton ships were preying on English merchantmen; the Scots were stirring on his northern borders; and in Brittany Henry Tudor was gathering his resources for a fresh invasion. On 20 March Richard established his military headquarters behind the massive battlements of Nottingham Castle. Here, poised at the heart of the kingdom, he would be ready to strike wherever danger threatened.

Here too, in the middle of April, he received the news that must have affected him more deeply than any of the bereavements and betrayals which already crowded his life. Edward, Prince of Wales, was dead. A note of emotion is visible even in the terse report of the Croyland Chronicle: 'this only son of his, in whom all the hopes of the royal succession, fortified with so many oaths, were centred, was seized with an illness of but short duration and died at Middleham Castle in the year of our Lord, 1484. … You might have seen his father and mother in a state almost bordering on madness, by reason of their sudden grief.'

The public impact went further than the private grief. Throughout the Wars of the Roses the uncertainty of the succession was at the root of the conflict and invited the aristocracy to further mischief in their own interests. Prince Edward's death now invited the surviving magnates – Norfolk, the Stanleys and Northumberland – to reconsider their allegiance

'You might have seen his father and mother in a state almost bordering on madness, by reason of their sudden grief'

163

FAR LEFT Effigy of Edward Prince of Wales, Richard's only legitimate son and heir, who died in 1484 aged nine. He was buried in the parish church at Sheriff Hutton.

LEFT Ruins of Sheriff Hutton Castle, Yorkshire, one of Richard's principal residences in the North. After the death of his son, Richard created a royal household at Sheriff Hutton for his nephews, Edward, Earl of Warwick, and John de la Pole, Earl of Lincoln, whom he made his heir.

to Richard. Equally important was the psychological effect on the gentry, the merchants and the yeoman classes – men whose tacit consent was vital in turning a successful *coup d'état* into enduring government. They might well reflect that the little known Lancastrian claimant, allied to a Yorkist bride, was better placed to outlaw faction at home and piracy at sea than a childless usurper.

As the war of nerves mounted in the spring and summer, Richard pondered on the choice of his successor. Queen Anne, barren for ten years since Edward's birth, could bear him no more children. The King inclined at first to Clarence's son, Edward, Earl of Warwick. This ten-year-old boy was eventually passed over, not so much because he was Clarence's son but because he was too young and showed signs of being mentally retarded. Edward of Warwick is one of the most pitiable victims of dynastic politics: kept in solitary confinement from the age of five he grew up, according to one report, unable to 'tell a goose from a capon'. Richard did something to alleviate his condition by establishing him with a household in the oak-lined park of Sheriff Hutton, but under Henry VII he was returned to the Tower and eked out his imprisonment until he was executed on a fabricated charge of treason.

Richard's final choice fell on John de la Pole, Earl of Lincoln, eldest son of the Duke of Suffolk and Richard's sister Elizabeth. The young Earl of Warwick was too risky a candidate at this time of crisis, while Lincoln was a grown man, already identified with Richard's government. On 21 August Richard followed Yorkist tradition by appointing the heir apparent Lord Lieutenant of Ireland.

In the meantime Richard laboured to put his kingdom in readiness for war. On 1 May he sent commissions of array to his chief lieutenants, empowering them to call men to his standards at short notice. A network of couriers was set up to link him with his Chancellor's Council in London and with his sentinels on the coasts. However, Richard was not content to wait for Henry to come to him: he was also engaged in organising a diplomatic *coup* whose success would render his military preparations unnecessary.

Relations with Brittany had been fouled from the start by Duke Francis's attempt to blackmail Richard. In exchange for keeping his guest Henry Tudor on a tight leash, Francis demanded four thousand English archers to help him in his quarrels with the King of France. Richard refused. Francis responded with generous loans to the Lancastrian exiles and loosed his Breton corsairs on English merchantmen. A vigorous naval campaign undertaken in the winter of 1483–4 led to the conclusion of a truce in April 1484. Since Francis was suffering from some form of mental illness, the government of the duchy was by now in the hands of his more amenable treasurer, Pierre Landois, and when the truce was ratified at Pontefract on 8 June, it contained an additional secret clause. Richard would supply the Bretons with one thousand archers, provided that the self-styled Earl of Richmond was kept in custody. This accord was apparently followed by further overtures, during which Landois was offered the revenues of the earldom of Richmond if he would deliver Henry Tudor to Richard's agents. Rumours of these proposals came to the attentive ears of John Morton in Flanders. He promptly despatched a warning message to Henry at Vannes. The messenger – a priest named Christopher Urswick – was instructed to continue his journey to the French Court and ask for political asylum on behalf of the Earl of Richmond and his followers. Permission was eagerly granted. The French were in some disarray since the recent death of Louis XI: but Charles VIII's Council were agreed that King Richard was no friend of France. Had he not led the hard-liners who spoke out against the Treaty of Picquigny in 1475, and given fresh proof of his enmity by seeking an alliance with Brittany?

Richmond's next problem was to elude the vigilance of Landois' men and slip over the duchy's borders into France. With only five followers he rode out of Vannes under the pretext of visiting a neighbour. As soon as he was clear of the town, he exchanged clothes with a servant and rode hell for leather towards the frontier. As he crossed into Anjou, those whom Landois sent in pursuit were only an hour's ride behind him.

It was a near miss. But the restless summer brought other achievements to set against this diplomatic failure. Richard's punishing itinerary bears witness to the energy with which he tackled the perennial problems of the Scottish border and the administration of the northern counties. Early in May he visited York, Middleham and Durham. Naval preparations kept him at Scarborough until the second week of June, when he received the Breton embassy at Pontefract. By mid-June he was in York, then on to Scarborough again, and back to York late in July. Haunted by the spectre of Henry Tudor's invasion, Richard was determined to step up the military and diplomatic pressures on the Scots until James III came to his senses and sought a permanent peace. Details of the campaigns he set in motion have not survived, but the Croyland Chronicle reports that the Scots 'sustained a great defeat from our people by land' followed by an equally significant naval victory for the Scarborough squadron. These measures achieved precisely the effect Richard had in mind, for in July James III sent Lord Lisle to open negotiations. Once he had assured himself that the Scots were in earnest, the King gave safe conducts for a formal embassy to attend on him at Nottingham in September.

Equally important was the form of government that Richard established for the North at York on 21 July. A formal Council, under the lieutenancy of the Earl of Lincoln, was to supervise the keeping of the King's peace throughout the counties of Yorkshire, Westmorland and Cumberland. Although Lincoln was appointed Lieutenant in the North, the Council derived

FAR LEFT Watercolour of the stained glass in the hall of Ockwells, a fine fifteenth-century manor house near Maidenhead. This detail shows the arms of John de la Pole, Duke of Suffolk, who married Richard's sister, Anne.

its authority from the King, and the household he maintained at Sheriff Hutton was designated the King's household in the North. The detailed instructions Richard dictated for his Council's operation emphasised that 'all letters and writings ... be made in our name, and the names to be endorsed with the hand of our nephew of Lincoln below with the words *"per consilium regis"'*.

In effect the Council served as a junior branch of Richard's Council at Westminster. It was to meet every quarter at York to 'hear, examine and order all bills and complaints and other there before them to be served', and was vested with complete authority to cope with public disorder. The military duty of defending the border lay outside its functions and was retained by the Warden General. The Councillors included both local magnates and professional lawyers. Few of their names are known to us. Northumberland, certainly, was a member of the Council, as was Lincoln's brother-in-law, Lord Morley. The retarded Earl of Warwick, who was entrusted to Lincoln's care at Sheriff Hutton, was given a nominal role by merit of his royal blood. Richard's innovation clearly grew out of his own Council during the last decade of Edward's reign. But in another sense it represented a significant break with the past. The Duke of Gloucester's authority sprang from the fact that he was a great landowner in the North, while Lincoln was a royal official, appointed to serve at the King's pleasure.

With the North in safe hands Richard found time in August to spend a few weeks in London which he had not visited since he left the capital in March. During this stay, he had the bones of Henry VI transferred from Chertsey to their final resting place in St George's Chapel at Windsor. Some said that this was a spiteful move to put an end to the pilgrimages made to his tomb. But it was more likely an act of conventional piety and even his enemy John Rous conceded that the ceremony was conducted with the greatest solemnity.

By 11 September the King had returned to Nottingham, where he received the Scottish ambassadors in great state. The embassy included the Earl of Argyll, Chancellor of Scotland, the Bishop of Aberdeen, Lord Lisle and a train of clerics, heralds and attendants. In the great hall of Nottingham Castle, they were greeted by Richard and his Chancellor, the Duke of

Charles VIII of France, who
succeeded to the throne
in 1483.

Norfolk, the Earl of Northumberland, Lord Stanley, the two
Chief Justices and the principal officers of the royal household.
Before the commissioners got down to business the Archdeacon
of Lothian, who was also James III's secretary, delivered a
lengthy panegyric in Latin on Richard's virtues. Never, according to the Archdeacon, had nature endowed a small frame with
so great a soul and such strength of mind. Ten days later, the
negotiators had completed their discussion. There was to be a
three-year truce, and James's heir, the Duke of Rothesay, was
to marry Richard's niece, Anne de la Pole. With the back door
to his kingdom sealed by a treaty of friendship and marriage,

FAR LEFT Part of the beautiful angel roof in the church of St Wendreda at March, Cambridgeshire.

LEFT The de Vere porch at Lavenham Church, Suffolk, which was built in the late fifteenth century, by John de Vere, 13th Earl of Oxford.

Richard was free at last to concentrate his efforts on Henry Tudor.

The threat of invasion was, in fact, receding. October was too late to contemplate a military campaign, and the realm was safe until the following spring. Nevertheless, Richard sat out the whole of the month of October on the black rock of Nottingham, before returning to his capital. 'On the eleventh

day of November', recorded Robert Fabyan, 'the mayor and his brethren, being clad in scarlet, and the citizens to the number of five hundred or more, in violet, met the King beyond Kingston in Southwark and so brought him to the Wardrobe, beside the Black Friars.'

Since his surrender at St Michael's Mount nearly ten years previously, John de Vere, Earl of Oxford, had been imprisoned in the great fortress of Hammes which guarded Calais. But with Henry Tudor at the French Court, Richard had taken the precaution of ordering Oxford's transfer to an English prison. His suspicions were only too well-founded, for now he learned that Oxford had persuaded his gaoler, James Blount, to turn his coat, and the pair of them had fled to Paris. Some of the smaller fry were less fortunate. Late in November Richard laid his hands on William Colyngbourne, a former servant of Cicely Neville, the King's mother, who had been sending messages to Henry Tudor. Evidently he had a sense of humour too, for it was he who penned the rhyme about the Cat, the Rat, the Dog and the Hog. Richard determined to make an example of the rhymester, who was tried at the Guildhall early in December and condemned to a traitor's death. 'For the which he was drawn unto the Tower Hill and there full cruelly put to death, at first hanged and straight cut down and ripped, and his bowels cast into a fire. The which torment was so speedily done that when the butcher pulled out his heart he spake and said JESUS, JESUS.'

Treason was in the air. In an atmosphere of deepening mistrust and suspicion Richard gave out fresh proclamations against his rival's claims, renewed the commissions of array first issued in May, and authorised the commissioners to summon 'the knights, squires and gentlemen within the said counties, and know from them what number of people, defensibly arrayed, every of them severally will bring at half a day's warning, if any sudden arrival fortune of the King's rebels and traitors'. Harwich was reinforced with a strong royal garrison, and the faithful Sir James Tyrell was sent across the Channel to assume command of the castle of Guisnes. To preserve an outward façade of strength and confidence, Christmas was celebrated at Westminster with the magnificence of a second coronation. But behind the show of 'dancing and gaiety and many vain

OPPOSITE Monumental brass to Sir John Reytout and his two wives, 1485, from Isleham Church, Cambridgeshire.

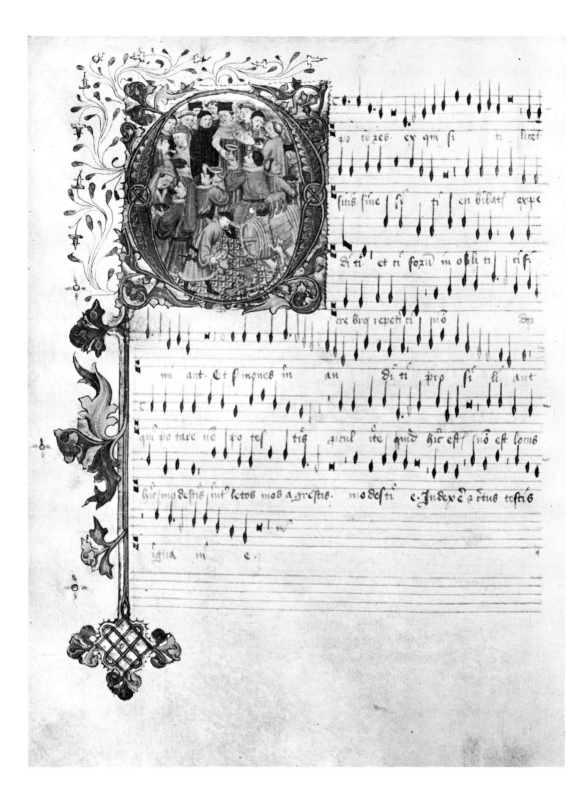

changes of apparel', Richard was champing for action. The strain of waiting was beginning to affect his purse as well as his nerve. The careful administration of the royal estates covered the normal expenses of his household in peace time: but it could not generate the huge sums of ready cash needed to maintain a permanent state of military alert.

The best news that reached Richard at Christmas 1484, came from his agents in France: the Lancastrian invasion was definitely scheduled for the following summer. At last the issue would be decided one way or the other.

Early in March 1485 another personal tragedy put a potent psychological weapon into Henry Tudor's hands. Queen Anne was dying, wasted by a disease her doctors declared to be mortal and highly infectious. On the 16th, 'upon the day of the great eclipse of the sun, Queen Anne departed this life and was buried at Westminster with no less honours than befitted the interment of a queen'. The rumour-mongers lost no time in getting to work: Richard himself was said to have poisoned the Queen who could bear him no more children. Worse still, he now planned to gratify an incestuous passion for his niece, Elizabeth of York. Such a marriage would, of course, have scuppered Henry's prospects. But it made no sense for Richard to marry the lady himself. His own claims to the throne were founded on the theory that all Edward IV's children were bastards. But the rumours stuck. Had the King not equipped his niece with gowns as magnificent as the Queen's during the recent Christmas festivities, and avoided his wife's bedside as she lay dying? Henry's supporters were probably genuinely frightened that the match might take place, and did all in their power to promote the scandal as a means of preventing it. Even

175

the faithful Cat and Rat were persuaded to subscribe to the rumours, and bluntly informed their master that the country – particularly the North – would not stand for it. Twelve doctors of divinity were paraded to tell Richard that the Pope would not grant him the necessary dispensation. By these tactics the King was eventually manœuvred into making the public denial the Lancastrians were hoping for. At the Hospital of the Knights of St John, in Clerkenwell, the Mayor and Aldermen heard from the King's own lips that the marriage had never crossed his mind. At the same time he wrote to the Mayor of York advising him to pay no heed to the 'divers seditious and evilly disposed persons' who 'enforce themselves daily to sow seeds of noise and slander against our person'.

Those evilly-disposed persons were doubtless also complaining loudly of Richard's financial exactions. The treasure bequeathed by Edward IV had all been spent in the suppression of Buckingham's rebellion and in the preparations of the previous summer. A pliant Parliament could usually be cajoled into granting a subsidy, but such taxes took a long time to

Chalice and paten of silver pierced gilt, of English manufacture and dating from the late fifteenth century.

collect. There was no alternative but to revert to the benevolences which caused so much unfavourable comment in Edward's day. Since Richard had gone out of his way to condemn benevolences in Parliament only twelve months before, their renewal caused widespread resentment. Nevertheless, between February and April his commissioners managed to scrape together some £20,000.

The great guessing game was about to begin. Where would Henry land and when would he come? Richard was not inclined to take any chances, and in June he once again took up his watch at the castle of Nottingham. His most able lieutenants were disposed in a great area covering the coasts from Essex to North Wales. The south-east was entrusted to Norfolk and his son the Earl of Surrey. Sir Robert Brackenbury, Constable of the Tower, took charge of London's defences. In Southampton harbour a well-equipped naval squadron lay at Viscount Lovell's command. The Tudors' family connections with South Wales and the lordship of Pembroke called for special defences in that area. William Herbert, Earl of Huntingdon, held Carmarthen and Brecon; Richard Williams held the strongholds of Pembroke, Tenby and Haverfordwest; and James Tyrell's men garrisoned Builth and Llandovery. On the adjoining hills beacons were laid, ready to flash across the valleys the news of Henry's coming.

On 22 June Richard put his commissioners of array on special alert. 'In all haste possible' they were to 'review the soldiers late mustered, and see that they be able persons well horsed and harnessed to do the King service, and if they be not, to put other able men in their places.' They were to be ready to move at an hour's warning 'upon peril of losing their lives, lands and goods'. At the same time the propaganda war was stepped up with another proclamation: the Lancastrian rebels were in the pocket of the King's ancient enemies, the French to whom they had pledged the towns of Calais, Guisnes and Hammes. Their leader was one Henry Tudor, of bastard blood on his mother's side as on his father's. If his cause prospered, this same Henry planned to strip the King's subjects bare in order to reward the traitors, adulterers and extortioners who followed him.

Despite these energetic preparations, Richard knew well that the issue could turn on the loyalty of a few men in high places.

Richard's Great Seal.

One such man was Thomas, Lord Stanley, who sought the King's permission in July to visit his family in Lancashire. As Steward of Richard's Household, Stanley had spent the best part of the last two years at the King's side, and was associated with him in all the principal acts of his reign. But he was also married to Henry Tudor's mother, Margaret Beaufort, the Countess of Richmond. It was an awkward dilemma: assent – and risk that Stanley would lead his three thousand Lancashiremen to Henry's camp; deny – and risk a mortal insult to the man who had taken Richard's part against his own Countess in 1483. Never at his best when it came to diplomacy, Richard settled on a compromise which invited both the treason and the insult. Stanley was allowed to go, providing he sent his eldest son, Lord Strange, to Nottingham in his place.

The waiting was now almost done. On 24 July informants brought word from France that the Tudor was making ready to embark at Harfleur. The Master of Rolls was quickly sent to London to fetch the Great Seal of England. On the same day that the Seal was delivered to the King at Nottingham, the rebel ships slipped their moorings and hoisted sail for the Welsh coast.

7 Bosworth 1484-5

WITH THE HELP OF fair weather and 'a soft southern wind', Henry Tudor, Earl of Richmond landed at Milford Haven in the county of Pembroke at sunset on 7 August. Nearly half of his twenty-six years had been spent in exile. It was his first visit to the land of his fathers since his uncle Jasper Tudor, Earl of Pembroke, had taken him abroad following the Lancastrian débâcle at Tewkesbury in 1471. With a proper sense of occasion, and a shrewd eye for propaganda, Henry's first recorded act was to kneel down and kiss the sands of Mill Bay.

The army he brought from France was hardly impressive. Jasper Tudor and the Earl of Oxford were the only two men of any consequence. Edward Woodville represented the family of his prospective bride. The rest of the English contingent were mainly the attainted rebels of Buckingham's abortive rebellion – Richard Guildford, John Cheyney, William Brandon, William Berkeley and a few others. The two thousand soldiers at his back were French convicts, persuaded to enlist by the promise of a free pardon. But it was not on them that Henry pinned his hopes. Since the early spring, his messengers had been sounding out possible sympathisers, rekindling the embers of Lancastrian loyalism, promising lands and titles to those who would betray their oaths to King Richard. In Wales espec-ially the seeds of treason had fallen on fertile ground. The Tudors were known in Wales, while the Yorkist kings were foreigners. As his banner Henry chose the red dragon of the old Welsh kings, from whom he claimed his descent.

On 8 August Henry marched unopposed into the county town of Haverfordwest. A delegation from the town of Pem-broke arrived to pledge its allegiance. Rumours that Sir Walter Herbert from Carmarthen was approaching with a large troop loyal to the King proved groundless. As Henry marched north through Cardigan and Aberystwyth to Merioneth, the towns and fortresses whose loyalty Richard had been at such pains to insure opened their gates to welcome his rival. From Merioneth his line of march swung to the east, through Newton and the Vale of Powys to the borders of Shropshire. Here he was joined by 'a great baulk of soldiers' under the black raven banner of Rhys ap Thomas, the Welsh chieftain who had promised Richard that the Tudor would cross the mountains into England only over his dead body. Shrewsbury opened its gates to the

invader on 15 August. Pushing on to Newport the next day, Henry's growing band of French and Welsh was joined by five hundred Shropshiremen under Sir Gilbert Talbot.

Thus far the enterprise had prospered. But Henry was in England now, less than sixty miles from Richard's crag at Nottingham, and still his step-father, Lord Stanley, had not joined him. So much depended on the notorious trimmer and on his scarcely less powerful brother Sir William, who held North Wales and much of Shropshire. At Stafford, on 17 August, Henry had his first meeting with Sir William. King

The red dragon of Wales, one of the heraldic supporters of Henry VII's arms from King's College Chapel, Cambridge. Henry chose the dragon as his symbol because of its associations with the old Welsh kings.

Richard, he was told, held Stanley's son, Lord Strange, a hostage at Nottingham. If the brothers declared for Henry now, he would surely lose his head. Glibly Sir William unfolded his strategy: Lord Stanley's army, presently encamped at Lichfield only fifteen miles away, would retreat before Henry's line of march until Richard's forces blocked the way. Richard himself would suspect nothing until the battle commenced, and Stanley's men fell on his unguarded flank. As proof of the Stanleys' good faith, Sir William arranged a secret *rendez-vous* between Henry and his brother at the village of Atherstone, south-east of Lichfield astride the old Roman road of Watling Street. It was a neat plan, but Henry saw that when it came to the battle, his own flank would be as vulnerable as Richard's.

By this time Richard had received an equally ambiguous token of Lord Stanley's intentions. The couriers who rode from Pembroke with the news of Henry's landing reached Nottingham three days later, on 11 August. His army, they reported, was pitifully small and ill-equipped. In the words of Henry VIII's historian, Edward Hall, this intelligence 'so inflated Richard's mind, that in a manner disdaining to here speak of so poor a company, [he] determined at first to take little or no regard to this so small a sparkle, declaring the earl [of Richmond] to be innocent and unwise because that he temerariously attempted such a great enterprise with so small and thin a number of war-like persons'. His Welsh captains, Sir Walter Herbert and Rhys ap Thomas would doubtless put the invader to 'shameful confusion'. All the same if Henry did emerge from his Welsh mountains, the opportunity to come to grips with the man who had kept Richard on the hook for the past two years was not to be missed. The King therefore lost no time in summoning his captains to his side – Northumberland from his manor of Wressell, Norfolk and Surrey from Essex, Lovell from Southampton, Brackenbury from London and Thomas, Lord Stanley from his Lancashire estates. The royal army would muster further south at Leicester, poised to intercept the Lancastrians if they planned a march on London.

In the event, the shameful confusion was not Henry's but Richard's. For on Monday 15 August his mounted scouts or 'scurriers' brought word that the Earl of Richmond had crossed the Severn at Shrewsbury and was heading in a straight line for Nottingham, his forces swollen by the Welsh levies raised to stop him. 'At which message,' according to Hall, 'he was sore moved and broiled with melancholy and dolour, and cried out, asking vengeance on them that contrary to their oath and promise had fraudulently deceived him.' Resisting the impulse to set out, as originally planned, on the following day, the King had to kick his heels for four more days, waiting for his army to reach its full strength.

More ominous news followed shortly. A message from Lord Stanley regretfully announced that the Steward was too sick with the sweating sickness to obey the King's summons. Fearing Richard's vengeance, Lord Strange tried to slip away from the castle. When he was apprehended in the nick of time, Strange confessed under interrogation that he, his uncle Sir William and Sir John Savage were indeed conspiring to ally themselves with Henry Tudor. But he would not implicate his father.

Rhys ap Thomas, Walter Herbert, Talbot and now Stanley – a fog of treason was closing in around Richard's well-laid martial plans. On Tuesday the 17th, as he sought to relieve the tensions of his enforced idleness by hunting in Sherwood Forest, two messengers from York arrived to cast doubts on Northumberland's loyalty too. Having learned of Henry's landing, the city fathers were anxious to know why the commissioners of array had not called on the men of York to send armed help to their King. Perhaps the reason was the plague that had recently swept the city. Or was Northumberland trying to restrict the levy to his own retainers, men who would put their loyalty to the House of Percy above their allegiance to the reigning House of York?

Late on Thursday the 18th the Lancastrian army was reported to have changed its line of march. Turning south-east from Stafford towards Lichfield, Henry's van now seemed to be headed not towards Nottingham, but towards Atherstone where Lord Stanley lay, and the main highway to London. Even if his muster was not yet complete, Richard must act now. The following morning the royal army, marching four abreast, left Nottingham by the southern gate and took the road for Leicester. 'With a frowning countenance and truculent aspect' Richard rode at the centre of the column, mounted on a great white courser, the yeomen of the Crown before him and wings of cavalry at his flanks. By 9 o'clock that same evening the King was at Leicester at an inn which displayed his own sign of the White Boar. The two halves of Richard's host were now united: together with Northumberland's contingent which was expected within the next twenty-four hours, they appear to have numbered more than ten thousand men. 'Here', states the Croyland Chronicle, 'was found a number of warriors ready to fight on the King's side, greater than had ever been seen before in England collected together in behalf of one person.'

This was, of course, an exaggeration, but Henry Tudor was heavily outnumbered all the same. His recruiting drive in Wales and Shropshire had added about three thousand men to the two thousand who landed at Milford Haven. Without the certainty of Stanley's support his prospects seemed decidedly bleak. The mass desertions confidently predicted by his agents in the spring had simply not materialised.

Distracted by these unpalatable thoughts, Henry apparently paused by the roadside on the evening of the 19th while his army marched on to Tamworth. The only others with him were a bodyguard of about twenty armed men. When night closed in he was shocked to discover, in Vergil's words, that 'he could not discern the trace of them that were gone before, and so, after long wandering could not find his company, he came unto a certain town [village] more than three miles from his camp, full of fear; who lest he might be betrayed, durst not ask questions of any man, but tarried there all night', as fearful of the present as he was of the perils to come. Reunited with his army on the morning of the 20th, Henry blandly assured his anxious followers that he had slipped away on purpose 'to receive some good news of his secret friends'.

20 August was in fact the day appointed for Henry's secret *rendez-vous* with the Stanleys at Atherstone, some eight miles beyond Tamworth and barely twenty miles from Richard's host at Leicester. Vergil's details of this meeting are sparse, but they do indicate that it went some way to allaying Henry's doubts about his step-father: 'taking one another by the hand, and yielding mutual salutation, each man was glad for the good state of the others, and all their minds were moved to great joy. After that they entered in counsel in what sort to arraign battle

with King Richard if the matter should come to strokes.' When the conference was over, Lord Stanley withdrew his troops to Stoke Golding and Henry's army took over Atherstone.

That same evening at Leicester, King Richard conducted a final review of his troops. All the most important Yorkist leaders were with him now, including the two late arrivals, Northumberland and Brackenbury. Early on Sunday morning a vanguard of archers and men at arms, wearing the silver lion badges of the Duke of Norfolk, led the royal army west towards the Lancastrian camp at Atherstone. The two armies would not clash on a Sunday, but Richard was anxious to narrow the gap as much as possible, both to forestall a Lancastrian dash down Watling Street, and to establish visual contact with the two forces led by the Stanley brothers. Twelve miles from Leicester, just beyond the village of Sutton Cheney, he found a position ideal for his purpose. Overlooking Redmore Plain, Sutton Cheney stood on high ground at the eastern end of a ridge, about one and a half miles to the west of Sir William Stanley's camp at Shenton, and just over two miles north of Lord Stanley at Stoke Golding. Less than three miles beyond Stoke Golding lay Watling Street, the highway to London.

As the afternoon wore on, Richard's scouts informed him that the Earl of Richmond's van had left Watling Street and taken the old Roman road towards Redmore Plain, soon to be renamed Bosworth Field. The long wait was over. Henry Tudor had decided to commit his cause to the test of arms. That night the campfires of Richard's enemies lit up the sky less than three miles from the King's tent.

Predictably enough, our two contemporary voices – Croyland and Vergil – attribute to Richard a sleepless night, interrupted by 'dreadful visions' and premonitions of disaster. At daybreak, says the Croyland Chronicler, his drawn features were even more livid and ghastly than usual. Moreover 'there were no chaplains present to perform divine service on behalf of King Richard, nor any breakfast prepared to refresh the flagging spirits of the king'. If he did indeed dispense with early morning Mass and breakfast, it was because a vital strategic manœuvre had to be performed before the Lancastrians stirred from their bivouacs. This was the occupation of Ambien Hill, the western end of the ridge on which Sutton Cheney stood.

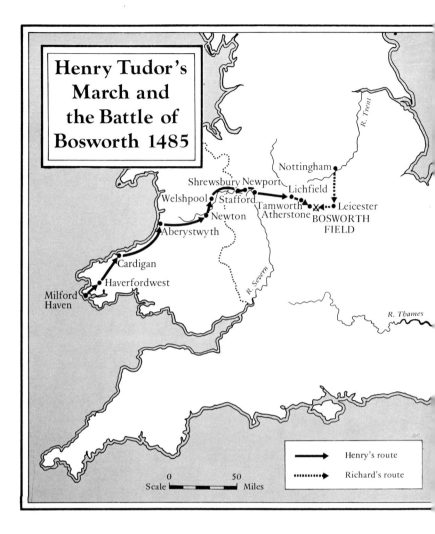

Henry Tudor's March and the Battle of Bosworth 1485

Ambien Hill jutted out some four hundred feet above the level of Redmore Plain: on its northern side the steep slopes would protect the right flank against Sir William Stanley's men, just as the swampy ground on the gentler southern slopes ·would deter his brother from an attempt on Richard's left.

As the Lancastrian van, under the Earl of Oxford, skirted the swamp and moved towards Ambien's western slopes, they were greeted by the sight of Norfolk's men already ensconced on the brow of the ridge above them. The archers crouched in the front ranks, equipped with their six-foot longbows of yew, oak or maplewood. The longbow, with a range of up to two hundred and fifty yards was still the favoured weapon of the common

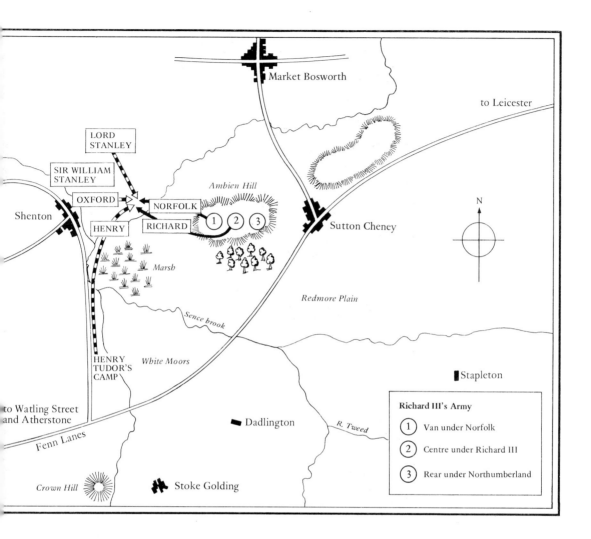

soldier, and an expert could discharge a dozen arrows within a single minute. However, since the end of the wars in France the general level of expertise had declined – so much so that in 1478 an act of Parliament specifically outlawed football and other frivolous pastimes which were held responsible for the decline. Like the archers, the ordinary infantrymen drawn behind carried swords at their sides, but their main weapon was a stout wooden pike, about the same length as the longbow and tipped with a heavy metal spearhead for jabbing their victims to death. The common soldier was lightly armoured, if at all. His tunic, or jack, was made up from layers of boiled hide, stuffed with hemp to give added protection. It was said that an English jack, which reached down to its owner's thighs, could stop an arrow or a swordthrust more effectively than a knight's hauberk of chain mail. On his head the common soldier wore a sallett, or plain metal helmet, without a vizor to protect his eyes and face.

The cream of Richard's army were his men-at-arms. They had come to the battlefield mounted, but they would fight on foot, clustered round the pennons of the simple knights, or the more gorgeous silken banners of the knights banneret to whom they were bound by their contracts of indenture. There was a gesture of bravado in this tradition – as in the story that the Earl of Warwick slew his horse on the eve of the battle of Towton, swearing that he would not live to run away. Less nimble than the common soldier, the man-at-arms was encased from the waist up in two metal plates, one to guard his chest, the other his back. He carried a variety of weapons – sword, dagger, pike, battleaxe or the formidable halberd which could stab like a pike or be swung like an axe. A few were equipped with fire-arms of wrought iron or brass, but loading the lead pellets was a cumbersome business and they were of little use when it came to hand-to-hand fighting.

Seven thousand men or more were stretched along the top of the ridge, from the summit of Ambien Hill to the outskirts of Sutton Cheney where the line was anchored by Northumberland's rearguard of three thousand. At the centre of the vanguard a knot of horsemen under the banner of the silver lion signalled the presence of the Duke of Norfolk, his son Thomas, Earl of Surrey and his chief lieutenants, Lords Zouche and Ferrers. At the centre of the ridge, a larger mounted concourse marked the King himself, surrounded by his close advisers Lovell, Ratcliffe and Catesby, by the knights and esquires of his bodyguard, and by the men who led the contingents of the North and Midlands, Lords Dacre, Graystoke and Scrope of Bolton.

Richard's mood was both determined and resigned. In Vergil's words: 'Knowing certainly that that day would either yield him a peaceable and quiet realm from thenceforth or else perpetually bereave him of the same, he came to the field with the crown upon his head, that thereby he might either make a beginning or end of his reign.' From his own bitter experience he knew that war was no chivalric adventure, as recounted in

the ballads of Crécy and Agincourt. If he won, he told his captains, he meant to crush every one of the rebels marching under Henry's banners. If he lost, Henry would do the same to them. In this spirit he sent his last message to Lord Stanley. Declare for Richard now, or Lord Strange would be instantly beheaded. Back came the answer that Lord Stanley had other sons, and would not join the King. Either because Richard relented when his bluff was called, or because his orders were disobeyed, Lord Strange survived his ordeal.

As the gap between the opposing vanguards narrowed, Henry Tudor too sent a last appeal to Lord Stanley, whose men were moving slowly forward towards the swamp. Would he now join forces with Oxford in the assault on Ambien Hill? Stanley still hesitated. He would make his own dispositions, and join his stepson when the time was ripe. The trimmer's steadfast

Miniature illustration from the *Imagination de Vraye noblesse,* showing in the foreground Imagination and the knight, and in the background, crossbowmen practising archery at the butts in a covered alley.

191

Arms and Armour at the time of Bosworth

The knights who fought for Richard and Henry Tudor at Bosworth wore plate-armour, riveted at the joints. Plate provided protection against sword and lance thrusts, and to a certain extent against primitive firearms, but was extremely bulky and uncomfortable to wear. Knights would carry swords, daggers and battle-axes. Men-at-arms wore armour to protect only the upper parts of their bodies, while common soldiers usually depended for protection upon tunics of leather stuffed with hemp, for they had to be agile in battle. On their heads they would wear salletts, and they would carry a variety of staff weapons, including pikes and halberds.

BELOW A sallet, a plain metal helmet, dating from 1460.
RIGHT A halberd, which could be used in a scything movement, or for jabbing the enemy.
BELOW RIGHT A staff weapon of the late fifteenth century.

RIGHT Monumental brass
of Sir William Mauntell
and his wife, 1487, from
Heyford, Northampton-
shire. Sir William is
shown in the type of
armour worn by
knights in the late
fifteenth century.

refusal to declare himself left Henry, in Vergil's words, 'no little vexed', but he was now too far committed to draw back. With Talbot's Shropshiremen on his right and Sir John Savage commanding the Welshmen on his left, Oxford planned to throw the entire Lancastrian army into the attack. Henry, who had no experience of war, would remain in the rear, protected by a slender screen of footmen and a single troop of horse.

The rebel troops reached the lower slopes and began to climb. As soon as they were within range Norfolk's troops unleashed a shower of arrows. Then Norfolk's trumpets sounded the order to charge, and the royal army streamed down the slopes. The Lancastrians were under strict orders not to stray more than a few feet from the standards of their company commanders. Under the shock of Norfolk's charge, Oxford's close-packed formations wavered but did not break. All around the lower slopes of Ambien Hill, the two front lines were locked in fierce hand-to-hand combat. Slowly at first, the Yorkists began to give ground. Norfolk himself thrust his way to the front in the effort to rally his men. Then disaster struck. Norfolk was down. Soon his men were in full retreat towards the top of the hill. Richard immediately gave orders for Northumberland to bring up his rearguard. But Henry Percy, taking his cue from Lord Stanley, had no intention of risking his neck in the dynastic blood feud which had already killed his father and his grandfather. When the battle was over, he would give his allegiance to the victor. Politely but firmly he let Richard know that he would stay put, to guard against a possible move by Lord Stanley's men.

The situation was dangerous but not desperate. The vanguard was badly mauled, but the Yorkist centre was still intact. Northumberland refused to move for Richard, but neither of the Stanleys had yet moved against him. Nonetheless Richard was too impatient to let the grim mêlée on Ambien Hill decide the day. While his best captain lay dead, the King's sword was still unblooded. The morale of his personal followers was sinking. Some faint hearts suggested flight: in the North there were still plenty of able-bodied men who would take his part against Henry Tudor.

Abruptly, Richard came to his decision. Less than a mile off on Redmore Plain his scouts had spotted the red dragon banner of his rival, screened by the small rearguard which Oxford had detached from his main force. If he could despatch Henry Tudor, the battle would be over. More than that, Henry's death would settle for ever the bloody feud between Lancaster and York. The orders were quickly given. At the head of his household knights and squires of the body – Sir Richard Ratcliffe, Hugh and Thomas Stafford, Sir Robert Brackenbury, Sir Robert Percy, Sir Ralph Assheton and about eighty others – Richard rode forward, skirting the battle on his left, down the north-western slope of Ambien Hill, and thundered out across the plain. His route took him straight across the path of Sir William Stanley, whom he had proclaimed a traitor less than a week before. As Sir William's men struggled into their saddles, Richard's cavalry crashed into the enemy ranks. The impetus of the charge carried them straight through the protective screen of infantry. Making straight for his target the King slew the Earl of Richmond's standard bearer, Sir William Brandon, with his own hand, and unhorsed the bulky figure of Sir John Cheyney who came to Brandon's aid. For a moment it seemed as if the King's desperate enterprise was about to be crowned with success.

But already Sir William Stanley's horsemen were colliding with the rear of Richard's little force. As the ring of steel closed in around him, Richard was overwhelmed and battered to the ground. John Rous, who had no cause to bless Richard's memory, had this to say of his last moments: 'If I may speak the truth to his honour, although small of body and weak in strength, he most valiantly defended himself as a noble knight to his last breath, often exclaiming as he was betrayed, and saying – Treason! Treason! Treason!'

After the battle Richard's body was recovered from the corpses piled around Henry's fallen banner and stripped of all its clothing. With a halter around the neck the naked corpse was strung across the back of a pack horse and taken off to Leicester. Here it lay exposed for two days, as proof of Henry's triumph, before it was buried without ceremony in the chapel of the Grey Friars. The tomb to which Henry contributed the sum of £10 – 1s, was destroyed at the dissolution of the monasteries, and Richard's bones were thrown into the River Soar.

'Although small of body and weak in strength, he most valiantly defended himself as a noble knight to his last breath'

195

8
Scorpio
Ascendant
1485

ALTHOUGH HE REIGNED only two years and two months, Richard is assured of immortality. He was the last English king to die in battle, the last of the Plantagenet line of kings, and the date of his death is said to mark the close of that otherwise indefinable episode known as the Middle Ages. Above all, he is the chief suspect in the longest and most emotive murder trial in English history.

Oddly enough, it was the imaginative efforts of the Tudor historians to blacken his name which most effectively ensured lasting fame and the great debate which continues to this day. Henry VII and his son Henry VIII after him, were always naggingly conscious of the flaws in their hereditary claims to the Crown. The Tudors were therefore particularly susceptible to the flattery of the propagandists who portrayed Richard as an inhuman tyrant, hunch-backed, treacherous and cruel, and who contrasted the dark winter of the House of York with the spring sunshine of the first Tudors. The first man to contribute to this tradition – a Warwickshire priest with antiquarian interests named John Rous – is especially interesting because he wrote both before and after Bosworth. His best-known work is an illustrated history of the earls of Warwick, which survives in two copies, one in English and the other in Latin, both of which were completed before 1485. In the English version Richard is described as 'a mighty prince and especial good lord ... in his realm full commendably punishing offenders of the laws, especially oppressors of the Commons, and cherishing those that were virtuous, by the which discreet guiding he got great thanks and love of all his subjects great and poor'. In the Latin version, which was presumably still in the author's possession in August 1485, this passage is edited out and Richard appears simply as 'the unhappy husband' of Anne Neville. Sometime before his death in 1491, Rous also compiled a *History of the Kings of England*, which he dedicated to Henry VII. The venomous flavour of this tract can be judged from the statement that Richard was born, after two years in his mother's womb, with a complete set of teeth, and hair down to his shoulders. 'At whose birth', Rous continues, 'Scorpio was in the ascendant, which sign is in the House of Mars; and as a scorpion mild in countenance, stinging in the tail, so he showed himself to all.'

Neither Rous's monster nor the 'serpent swollen with rage'

The tragical doynges of
Kyng Richard the thirde.

LOthe I am to remembre, but more I abhore to write, the miserable tragedy of this infortunate prince, which by fraude entered, by tyrannye proceded, and by sodayn deathe ended his infortunate life: But yf I should not declare the flagicious factes of the euyll princes, aswell as I haue done the notable actes of vertuous kinges, I shoulde neither animate, nor incourage rulers of royalmes, Countreyes and Seigniories to folowe the steppes of their profitable progenitors, for to attayne to the type of honour and worldly fame: neither yet aduertise princes being proane to vice and wickednes, to aduoyde and expell all synne and mischiefe, for dread of obloquy and worldly shame: for contrary set to contrary is more apparaunt, as whyte ioyned with black, maketh the fayrer shewe: Wherfore, I will procede in his actes after my accustomed vsage.

RICHARD the third of that name, vsurped ye croune of Englãd & openly toke vpon hym to bee kyng, the nyntene date of June, in the yere of our lord, a thousand foure hundred lxxiii. and in the .xxv. yere of Lewes the leuenth then beeyng french kyng: and the morow after, he was proclaymed a kyng and with great solempnite rode to Westminster, and there sate in the seate royal, and called before him the iudges of ye realme straightely commaundynge them to execute the lawe with out fauoure or delaie, with many good exhortaciõs (of the which he folowed not one) and then he departed towarde the Abbaye, and at the churche doore he was mett with procession, and by the abbot to hym was deliuered the scepter of sainte Edwarde, and so went and offered to sainte Edwarde his shrine, while the Monkes sang Te deum with a faint courage, and from the churche he returned to the palaice, where he lodged till the coronacion. And to be sure of all enemies (as he thoughte) he sent for fiue thousand men of the North against his coronaciõ, whiche came vp euill appareled and worse harneissed, in rusty harneys, neither defensable nor skoured to the sale, whiche mustered in Finesbury felde, to the great disdain of all the lookers on.

The fourth date of July he came to the tower by water with his wife, and the fifth daie he created Edward his onely begotten sonne, a childe of x. yere olde, prince of wales, and Jhon haward, a man of great knowlege and vertue (aswell in countaill as in battaill) he created duke of

CC.i.   Norffolke

and 'thirster after human blood' depicted in *The Life of Henry VII* by Prince Arthur's blind tutor, Bernard André, were sufficiently subtle or convincing for Henry's taste. In the last years of his reign he decided to commission a history of England from an Italian scholar trained in the Classical traditions of Renaissance humanism. Polydore Vergil's *History*, first published in 1534, was designed for the consumption of courts and scholars, and avoids the crude invective of his predecessors. The overall argument is that the Wars of the Roses were a divine punishment visited on the kingdom as a result of the original sin of Henry IV's usurpation in 1399, culminating in the tyranny of Richard's reign and eventually purged through Henry VII's union of Lancaster with York. In order to lend substance to this theme Vergil deftly adds to the list of Richard's villainies several new accusations, always safeguarding his integrity with the qualifications that he is reporting popular beliefs. Thus Gloucester is portrayed, along with Clarence, actually stabbing Henry VI's son Edward to death after the battle of Tewkesbury. Of Henry VI's death in the Tower he declares 'the continual report is that Richard, Duke of Gloucester, killed him with a sword whereby his brother might be delivered of all hostility'.

But the most influential account of Richard to appear in the early sixteenth century was Sir Thomas More's incomplete *History of King Richard III*, written in about 1513. Ironically, More's book, which ends with Buckingham's rebellion, was never intended for publication, nor was its primary aim to glorify the Tudor dynasty. More saw Richard as the antithesis of the humanist vision of a Good Prince, a symbol of evil rather than a person of flesh and blood, his crippled body a mirror image of his twisted soul: 'Malicious, wrathful, envious', 'little of stature, ill featured of limbs, crook backed', 'close and secret, a deep dissimuler, lowly of countenance, arrogant of heart, outwardly companionable where he inwardly hated, not letting to kiss whom he thought to kill', 'he slew with his own handes king Henry the Sixth', and 'lacked not in helping forth his brother Clarence to his death'. After doing away with the Princes in the Tower Richard 'never had quiet in his mind', 'so was his restless heart continually tossed and tumbled with the tedious impression and stormy remembrance of his abominable deed'.

OPPOSITE A page from Sir Thomas More's *Historie of the pitiful life and unfortunate death of Edward the Fifth and the then Duke of York to the tragicall doynges of Kyng Richard the thirde.*

Vergil and More provided the inspiration for all the later Tudor versions, including the chronicles of Edward Hall (1548), Richard Grafton (1568) and Raphael Holinshed (1578), and culminating in the 'poisonous hunchbacked toad' of Shakespeare's great melodrama.

Inevitably, such absurd exaggerations have provoked a flood of counter-claims in Richard's favour. Not long after the last of the Tudors was in her grave, Sir George Buc, James I's Master of the Revels, set to work on a five-volume biography, whose theme is that Richard's 'wisdom and courage had not then their nickname and calumny as now, but drew the eyes and acknowledgment of the whole kingdom towards him'. A more important milestone in Richard's rehabilitation is Horace Walpole's *Historic Doubts*, which argues most persuasively on the grounds of common sense that 'many of the crimes imputed to Richard seemed impossible; and, what was stronger, contrary to his interest'. At the end of the nineteenth century, Sir Clements Markham ingeniously turned the tables on Richard's conqueror by accusing Henry VII of the murder of the Princes. Markham's theories, which have been generally discounted since the analysis of the skeletons from the Tower, underline an important point about almost everything that has been written on Richard's life and reign: that the King's guilt or innocence in the murder of the Princes is an acceptable yardstick whereby we can judge everything else that he did. Fuelled with moral outrage, the hostile critic sees in every act of justice a cynical attempt to cultivate popularity; in every grant a bribe; in every gesture of conciliation the stirrings of an uneasy conscience. As recently as 1966 the All Souls antiquarian A.L.Rowse declared that 'anyone deriving his view of the whole story from Shakespeare would not be far out'; compared the execution of Lord Hastings with Hitler's Night of the Long Knives; and with a logic worthy of his fifteenth-century namesake John Rous, cites Henry's barbarous treatment of his rival's corpse as proof of Richard's villainy.

Even if we do succeed in peeling off the layers of prejudice, it is still not easy to arrive at a true assessment of Richard's character. His life coincides with a particularly barren patch as far as contemporary historians go. Most of the major events in his reign have to be reconstructed from unreliable Lancastrian

or Tudor sources whose bias is manifest. Even his physical appearance is elusive. His portraits show him with a rather careworn expression, thin pursed lips, brown eyes, a thrusting jaw and delicate tapering fingers. According to Sir Thomas More, who comments favourably on the good looks of Edward and Clarence, Richard was 'little of stature, ill featured of limbs, crook backed, his left shoulder much higher than his right'. This disparity of the shoulders, which John Rous also mentions, appears to be the sole foundation for the later myth of the ugly, hunchbacked cripple. The Elizabethan antiquarian John Stow specifically discounts the myth on the evidence of 'ancient men' who testified that Richard was quite handsome, although a little

The plight of the Princes in the Tower captured the imagination of many artists, especially during the Romantic period. Here Delaroche gives his version of their last days in the Bloody Tower.

203

below average height. Horace Walpole repeats an anecdote that the Countess of Desmond, after dancing with Richard, declared him to be the handsomest man in the room excepting his brother Edward. There is disagreement even about his height. The Scottish orator of 1484 made reference to Richard's shortness in his speech of address: yet the German diplomat Nicolas von Poppelau, who spent more than a week with the King at Middleham in May 1484 recorded that Richard was 'three fingers *taller* than himself, but a little slimmer, less thick set, and much more lean as well; he had delicate arms and legs, also a great heart'.

Nevertheless, there are sufficient grounds to rebuff or modify the outlines of the traditional Tudor villain. The most serious accusation – that he was consumed with ambition, 'a deep dissimuler' patiently waiting to snatch the reins of power from the fingers of his dead brother – has already been touched on in the preceding account of Richard's usurpation. His loyalty to Edward IV during his brother's lifetime is beyond dispute: as a devoted servant of the Crown Richard gains in stature from the contrast of Clarence's continual mischief-making. Nor could anyone have foretold that Edward's robust constitution would cave in at the age of forty. After Edward's death the Woodvilles showed themselves the first aggressors in their attempt to exclude the Duke of Gloucester from the position that was his by right of birth, by dint of his proven abilities and by the specific instructions Edward left in his will.

Nevertheless, the fact that Queen Elizabeth felt it necessary to safeguard her interests by forestalling Richard's protectorate shows that she had valid reasons to be afraid of him. The executions of Earl Rivers and Lord Richard Grey in late June 1483, bore out her misgivings. We know that Richard held her and her family responsible for Clarence's death, just as she had held Clarence responsible for her father's execution. But deeper motives were also at work. Mancini's reference to 'the good reputation' of Richard's private life supplies one clue. Richard's moral code is very succinctly expressed in a document addressed to his bishops in March 1484:

> Our principal intent and fervent desire is to see virtue and cleanness of living to be advanced ... and vices ... provoking the high indignation and fearful displeasure of God to be repressed and

annulled; and this ... put in execution by persons of lower degree to take thereof example ... but also thereby the great and infinite goodness of God is made placable and graciously inclined to the exaudition of petitions and prayers.

This high moral tone – which Richard himself transgressed to the extent of fathering at least two bastards – reappears in a number of other State documents. The confirmation of his claim to the throne enacted by Parliament in 1484 speaks of 'every good maiden and woman standing in dread to be ravished and defouled' during Edward's reign. The inference is that Richard saw himself as the 'person of high estate' who would 'put in execution' the reign of virtue. The permissive atmosphere of Edward's Court seems, in Richard's eyes, to have been symptomatic of a deep-seated corruption stemming from his brother's adulterous liaison with Elizabeth Woodville and abetted by his brother's companions in vice, the Marquess of Dorset and Lord Hastings. Richard's vision of the Woodvilles and of Hastings as a gang of moral degenerates unfit to wield any form of temporal authority, goes some way to explaining the vehemence of his retaliation. It also has ominous implications for Elizabeth's two sons, the unfortunate Princes.

This unattractive quirk of Richard's nature is well-attested by his treatment of Edward's favourite mistress, Jane Shore. This lady, who receives a glowing testimonial from Sir Thomas More, seems to have been quite free of the rapacity normally imputed to royal mistresses. 'The King would say that he had three concubines which in three divers properties diversely excelled: one the merriest, another the wiliest, the third the holiest harlot of his realm, as one whom no man could get out of the church lightly to any place, but it were to his bed. ... But the merriest was this Shore's wife, in whom the King therefore took special pleasure, for many he had, but her he loved.'

When Edward died, Jane took up with Lord Hastings. The proclamation of Hastings' execution for treason made a special point of the fact that these two had spent the previous night in the same bed. Jane was sent to prison, had her possessions confiscated and was compelled to undergo public penance for harlotry. Shortly after the outbreak of Buckingham's rebellion in October 1483, 'the unshameful and mischievous woman

'The merriest was this Shore's wife, in whom the King therefore took special pleasure'

nunate in neomenia tuba:
nitatis vr̄ ma preptū in isr̄l
deo iacob testimoniū in ioseph
urt de terra egypti: lingua quam no
uertit ab oneribus dorsum eiꝰ
cofino seruerunt in tribulacōe
ram te: et exaudiui te in abscondito

called Shore's wife' crops up in another proclamation, this time as the mistress of the rebel Marquess of Dorset. Even when she was languishing in Ludgate prison, Richard continued to be obsessed by this unfortunate woman. On hearing a rumour that his own Solicitor-General, Thomas Lynom, intended to marry her, he wrote to the Lord Chancellor with instructions to 'exhort and stir him to the contrary'. Lynom took the hint and the marriage was called off.

Richard's puritanism had its positive side too. The minute attention he gave to the affairs of York, and the legislative programme of the 1484 Parliament both demonstrate his scrupulous regard for the welfare of his subjects. It is no coincidence that the two most enduring creations of his reign were concerned with the administration of justice. In December 1483, one John Harrington was appointed clerk of a sub-committee of the Council which met in the White Hall at Westminster to

FAR LEFT Page from a breviary and antiphonary in the parish church of Ranworth, Norfolk, with a miniature of musicians. LEFT David playing the harp, accompanied by a choir, from an English psalter of *c.* 1460.

consider the 'bills, requests and supplications of poor persons'.
From this developed the institution later known as the Court
of Requests. The creation of the Council in the North in the
following year was even more significant. It replaced the King's
age-old dependence on feudal chieftains with a modern, stream-
lined replica of the parent Council at Westminster. The Tudors
gratefully adopted the institution as their own, and it proved
its value by outlasting the entire Tudor dynasty. It comes as
no surprise that the Mayor and Aldermen of York recorded
the news of Bosworth with these words: 'King Richard, late
mercifully reigning upon us, was ... piteously slain and
murdered, to the great heaviness of this city.'

In a letter excusing himself from an invitation to go hunting,
Sir William Stanley – an older man than the King – writes that
business is too pressing to get leave from 'Old Dick'. The epithet
suggests that Richard, with his conscientious enthusiasm for the
nuts and bolts of his administration, was regarded as a rather
over-earnest plodder, well-intentioned, old-fashioned and a
little dull. His private life, or rather the lack of it, supports this
view. It gave rise to none of the colourful anecdotes that
illumine the saintliness of Henry VI or the appetites of Edward IV.
We know nothing about his relationship with Anne apart from
the bare fact that they were both mad with grief at the death of
her son. A single letter to his mother, Cicely, who was to out-
live all her sons, suggests that he remained on polite but rather
distant terms with her. The following letter, which concerns
the appointment of a new steward to replace the treacherous
William Colyngbourne, is the only one of Richard's family
correspondence to survive:

> Madam, – I recommend me to you as heartily as is to me possible.
> Beseeching you in my most humble and affectuous wise of your
> daily blessing to my singular comfort and defence in my need.
> And, Madam, I heartily beseech you that I may often hear from
> you to my comfort. And such news as be here my servant Thomas
> Bryan, this bearer, shall show you to whom, please it you, to give
> credence unto. And, Madam, I beseech you to be good and gra-
> cious, Lady, to my Lord my chamberlain, to be your officer in
> Wiltshire in such as Collingbourne had. I trust he shall therein do
> you good service. And that it please you that by this bearer I may
> understand your pleasure in this behalf. And I pray God to send

208

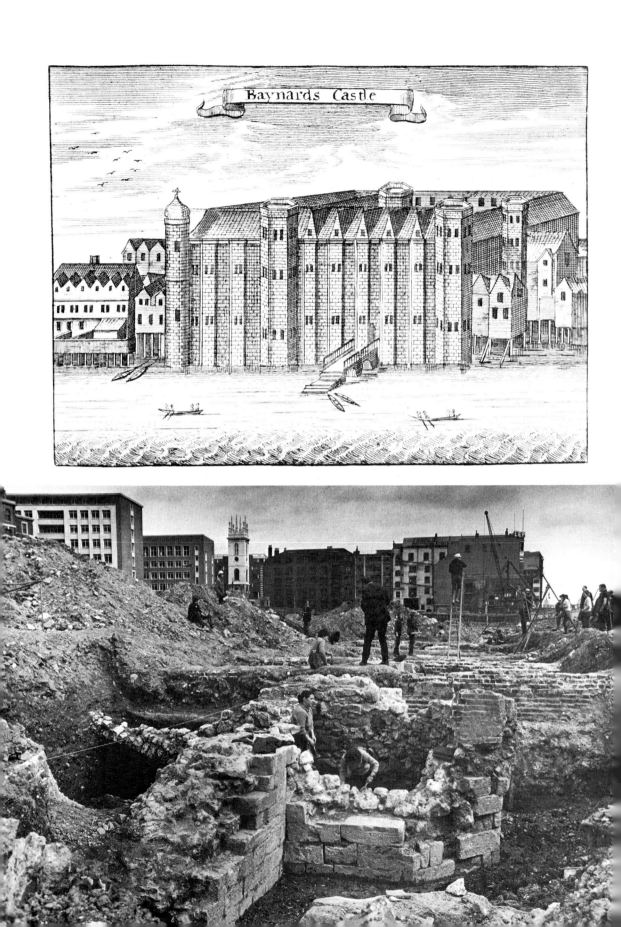

you the accomplishment of your noble desires. Written at Pomfret the 3rd day of June, 1484, with the hand of

Your most humble son,

Ricardus Rex.

Richard's favourite hobby was music. A foreign diplomat, Nicolas von Poppelau, who visited him at Pontefract or Middleham in May 1484, was greatly impressed by the singing at morning Mass. A gentleman of the royal chapel named John Melynek had earlier been commissioned to 'take and seize for the King all such singing men and children, being expert in the science of music, as he can find and think able to do the King's service within all places in the realm'. Able minstrels were also well rewarded, particularly those whom he was able to entice to his service from overseas. The King was also an enthusiastic builder, laying out considerable sums for altering and renovating the royal establishments of Windsor Castle, Westminster Palace, Baynard's Castle, the Tower of London, Nottingham Castle, the palace at York and the chapel at Pontefract. A gift of £300 went to the completion of King's College Chapel at Cambridge, and an annuity of 250 marks to St George's Chapel, Windsor. Even John Rous conceded that 'this King Richard is to be praised for his buildings'.

The two dominant strains in Richard's character – an assumption of moral superiority combined with a painstaking and conventional concept of duty – do resolve the puzzling contradictions touching on his personal code of honour. He could denounce the Treaty of Picquigny as a betrayal of chivalry and yet usurp the throne over the bodies of the rightful heirs. He could execute the Queen's brother, Earl Rivers, for treason, but he would not take the elementary precaution of marrying off the Queen's eldest daughter whose eligibility was so crucial to Henry Tudor's plans.

A 'thirster after blood' he was not. As Clarence's death shows, the steady escalation of violence and betrayal that characterises the Wars of the Roses coarsened Edward IV's amiable nature more than it did Richard's. Buckingham's rebellion was followed by less than a dozen executions, despite the fact that there was no pitched battle to take its toll of the King's enemies. The 95 attainders that followed compare favourably with the 113 enacted by Edward IV's Parliament after Towton in 1461.

OPPOSITE ABOVE
Baynard's Castle, which stood on the Thames near Paul's Wharf. This was the London residence of Richard's mother. Cicely Neville, but was often used by Richard in the months leading up to his accession to the throne.
BELOW Rescue excavations on Baynard's Castle in 1972, before redevelopment of the site.

Neither Richard nor any of his servants exhibited the cold cruelty of Edward's Constable, John Tiptoft, Earl of Worcester, who was nicknamed the Butcher of England and himself went to the block in 1470 asking that his head should be severed with three strokes 'in honour of the Trinity'. If Richard had taken a tougher line with the rebel gentry of 1483, Henry would have had to do without a number of the men who joined him on the road to Bosworth. These conclusions portray a Richard very different from the exotic ogre conjured up by More and Shakespeare. Yet the fact remains that he was defeated and killed by a rival with a shaky claim to the throne, a hazy acquaintance with the country he was invading and an inferior army at his back. Why?

The major calamity of his son's death in March 1484 undoubtedly played its part. After thirty years of intermittent civil war, invasions and depositions the majority of the gentry, merchants and yeomen classes were more interested in a settled succession than in the claims of the opposing branches of Edward III's quarrelsome family. When Prince Edward died

One of the greatest scholars of fifteenth-century England was John Tiptoft, Earl of Worcester and Constable of England. He studied at Padua University and returned to England loaded with precious Classical manuscripts which he eventually presented to Oxford University. But he was also a ruthless soldier, known as 'Butcher of England' during his period as Constable.

FAR LEFT He was executed on Warwick's orders in 1470 and buried with his two wives in Ely Cathedral.

LEFT Memorial brass to Joyce Charlton, John Tiptoft's wife, in Enfield Church.

213

there was little to choose between Richard and the unknown
Welshman who had promised to marry Elizabeth of York.

Bad luck is only a part of the story. Despite the disappearance
of so many famous names in the wars of Edward IV, it was still
the élite of great magnates who decided the issue of who should
be King, and it is his relationships with these men that reveal
Richard's greatest failing. 'Old Dick', for all his solid virtues
as an administrator and his undoubted courage on the battlefield, lacked Edward's knack of making friends. More's
observation that he had a 'close and secret' nature hits on an
uncomfortable truth. Perhaps it stemmed from a basic lack of
self-confidence in dealing with people. He never felt at home in
Edward's Court circle, distrusting both the easy familiarity of
men like Hastings and Dorset, and the waves of intrigue
emanating from the Queen's apartments. The extraordinary
circumstances of Richard's upbringing cannot have failed to
leave their mark on him, just as they did on his brother George.
But whereas George's shallow nature gave way to a mixture
of paranoia and bravado, Richard became wary, self-reliant and
inaccessible. Louis XI, who was a shrewd judge of character,
took an instant liking to Edward IV, but when he turned his
charm on Richard of Gloucester he met with a total lack of
response. Reserved and ill at ease with his peers, Richard chose
to put his trust in boyhood friends such as Francis Lovell and
Robert Percy, or able lieutenants, like Catesby and Ratcliffe,
who owed their positions to his continuing favour. While he
was Duke of Gloucester this self-sufficiency was a source of
strength. But the King was a public figure whose words and
gestures would be carefully marked. Richard's curt treatment
of Louis eight years previously was returned with interest in
the form of resolute hostility from the French.

Much more damaging were Richard's dealings with his own
aristocracy. Temporarily dazzled by Buckingham he succeeded
in driving Lord Hastings, his key supporter from the old régime,
into the arms of the Woodville opposition. Henry Percy, his
close associate in the North for more than ten years, was never
cultivated. Lord Stanley was arrested, released, loaded with
honours, kept close at heel for two years, then allowed to vanish
to his estates on the eve of the Earl of Richmond's landing with
polite threats of retribution on his son ringing in his ears. It is

no coincidence that the only magnate whose loyalty Richard retained was the Duke of Norfolk, an old warhorse whose outlook was as blunt as his King's.

Richard was not, to his cost, a political animal. His penchant for direct action in place of patient diplomacy brought him to die in a battle that should never have taken place. Nevertheless, it is as well to remember that for all his political mistakes there was nothing pre-ordained about the battle of Bosworth. With Northumberland and the Stanleys waiting on the sidelines, and Norfolk's troops matched against Oxford's, it was the superior generalship of the Lancastrian veteran and Richard's im-promptu cavalry charge that decided the day. Nor did Bosworth represent the verdict of the majority of Richard's subjects. The general consensus of support that Richard enjoyed from his northern subjects, from his Commons in Parliament and from the country at large during Buckingham's rebellion did not evaporate mysteriously on Henry's landing.

In later years, Henry VII's subjects might reflect that the change of kings wrought few far-reaching changes in their prospects or conditions. The personal style of government inaugurated by Edward IV and inherited by Richard, the tech-niques of estate management applied to Crown lands, the abandonment of chauvinistic and chivalric adventures overseas, the fostering of commercial interests abroad and at home, and the erosion of baronial power are as characteristic of Henry Tudor's government as they were of his Yorkist predecessors. For others the advent of the Tudors became a cause for regret. Four years after Bosworth Henry Percy was publicly murdered near Thirsk while levying a particularly burdensome tax for his new master. The Yorkshiremen thus delivered their own judgment on Percy's betrayal of Richard and on the rapacity of Henry VII. Morbid suspicion was Henry's other vice: in 1492 it claimed the life of Sir William Stanley, who was beheaded on a charge of conspiring with the pretender Perkin Warbeck. Three years later the Milanese ambassador reported that 'the King is rather feared than loved . . . if fortune allowed some lord of the blood royal to rise and he had to take the field, he would fare badly owing to his avarice; his people would abandon him'.

Dr Thomas Langton, Bishop of St David's and later of

Salisbury, recorded another verdict: 'He contents the people where he goes best that ever did prince; for many a poor man that hath suffered wrong many days have been relieved and helped by him .... God hath sent him to us for the weal of us all.' But he was writing about Richard.

Select bibliography

For the study of Richard and his contemporaries there is no more readable or scholarly guide than Paul Murray Kendall, whose four books are listed below with others of relevant interest.

H. S. Bennett, *The Pastons and their England* (1922)
Michael Bennett, *The Battle of Bosworth* (1985)
George Buck, *History of King Richard III*, 1619, ed. A. N. Kincaid (1979)
S. B. Chrimes, *Henry VII* (1972)
David R. Cook, *Lancastrians and Yorkists: The Wars of the Roses* (1984)
William Cornwallis, *Encomium of Richard III*, ed. A. N. Kincaid (1977)
James Gairdner, *History of the Life and Reign of Richard III* (rev. ed., 1898)
Anthony Goodman, *The Wars of the Roses: Military Activity and English Society 1452–1497* (1981)
P. W. Hammond, *Richard III: The Road to Bosworth Field* (1985)
Alison Hanham, *Richard III and His Early Historians 1483–1535* (1975)
E. F. Jacob, *The Fifteenth Century 1399–1485* (2nd ed., 1961)
R. H. Jarman, *We Speak No Treason* (1971)
Paul Murray Kendall, *Richard III* (1955)
   Warwick the Kingmaker (1957)
   The Yorkist Age (1962)
   Louis XI (1971)
C. L. Kingsford, *Prejudice and Promise in Fifteenth-Century England* (1925)
V. B. Lamb, *The Betrayal of Richard III* (1959)
J. R. Lander, *The Wars of the Roses* (1965)
Philip Lindsay, *King Richard III* (1933)
David MacGibbon, *Elizabeth Woodville* (1938)
Dominic Mancini, *The Usurpation of Richard III*, ed. C. A. J. Armstrong (2nd ed., 1969)

Sir Clements Markham, *Richard III: His Life and Character* (1906)

R. J. Mitchell, *John Tiptoft* (1938)

Thomas More, *The History of King Richard III*, ed. R. S. Sylvester (the Yale edition of the Complete Works of St Thomas More, vol. 2, 1963)

Richard Marius, *Thomas More* (1984)

Alec R. Myers, *England in the Late Middle Ages* (1952)

  'The Character of Richard III' in *History Today*, vol. 4 (1954)

Alec R. Myers, *The Household of Edward IV* (1959)

A. J. Pollard, *The Wars of the Roses* (1988)

Jeremy Potter, *Good King Richard? An Account of Richard III and His Reputation 1483–1983* (1983)

Sir James Ramsay, *Lancaster and York* (2 vols, 1892)

Charles Ross, *The Wars of the Roses: A Concise History* (1976)

  Richard III (1981)

A. L. Rowse, *Bosworth Field and the Wars of the Roses* (1966)

Giles St Aubyn, *The Year of Three Kings 1483* (1983)

Cora L. Scofield, *The Life and Reign of Edward IV* (2 vols, 1923)

Desmond Seward, *Richard III: England's Black Legend* (1983)

Horace Walpole, *Historic Doubts on the Life and Reign of King Richard III* (1768; reprinted 1974)

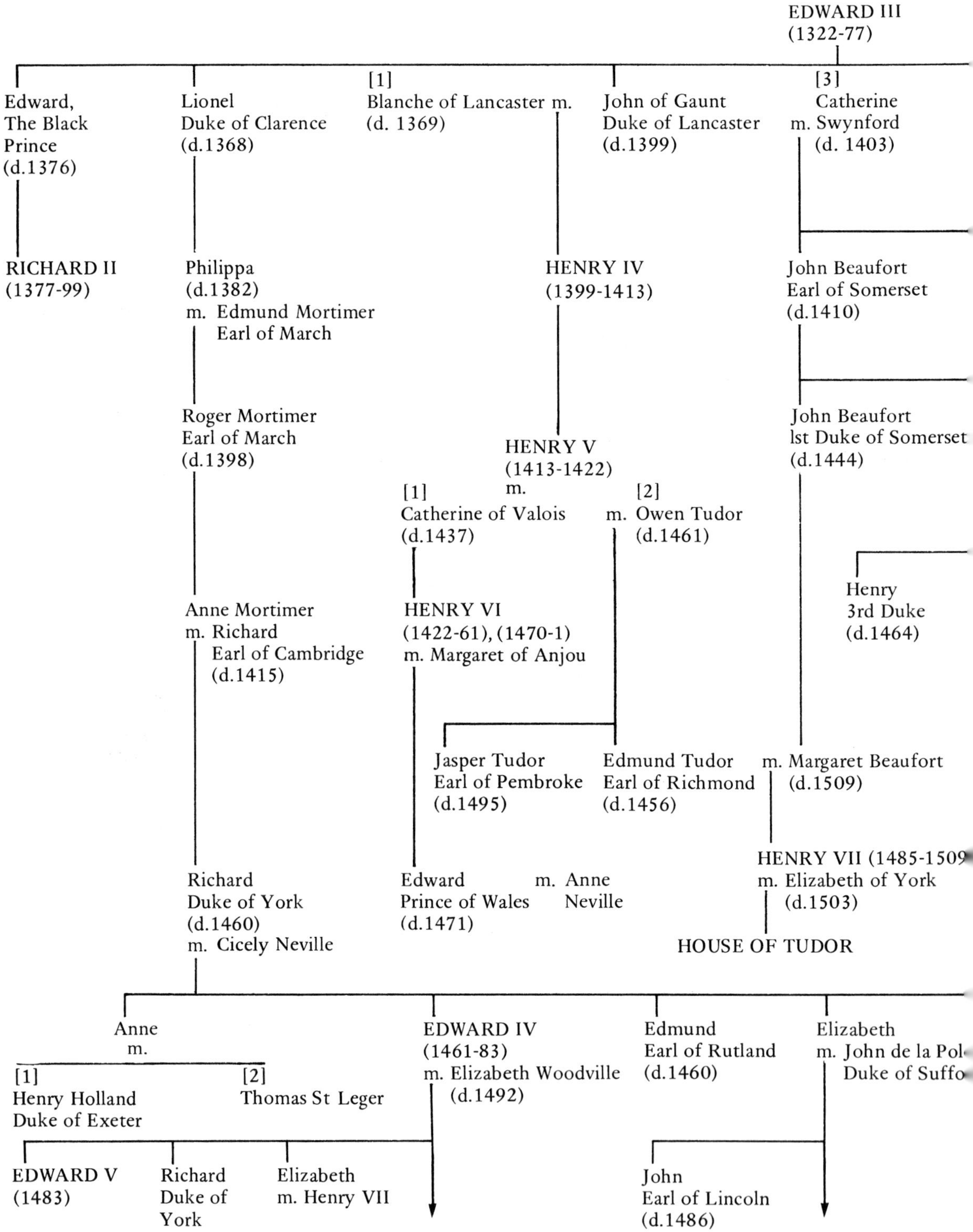

EDWARD III
(1322-77)

Edward,
The Black
Prince
(d.1376)

Lionel
Duke of Clarence
(d.1368)

[1]
Blanche of Lancaster m.
(d. 1369)

John of Gaunt
Duke of Lancaster
(d.1399)

[3]
Catherine
m. Swynford
(d. 1403)

RICHARD II
(1377-99)

Philippa
(d.1382)
m. Edmund Mortimer
Earl of March

HENRY IV
(1399-1413)

John Beaufort
Earl of Somerset
(d.1410)

Roger Mortimer
Earl of March
(d.1398)

HENRY V
(1413-1422)
m.

John Beaufort
lst Duke of Somerset
(d.1444)

[1]
Catherine of Valois
(d.1437)

[2]
m. Owen Tudor
(d.1461)

Anne Mortimer
m. Richard
Earl of Cambridge
(d.1415)

HENRY VI
(1422-61), (1470-1)
m. Margaret of Anjou

Henry
3rd Duke
(d.1464)

Jasper Tudor
Earl of Pembroke
(d.1495)

Edmund Tudor
Earl of Richmond
(d.1456)

m. Margaret Beaufort
(d.1509)

Richard
Duke of York
(d.1460)
m. Cicely Neville

Edward   m. Anne
Prince of Wales   Neville
(d.1471)

HENRY VII (1485-1509)
m. Elizabeth of York
(d.1503)

HOUSE OF TUDOR

Anne
m.

EDWARD IV
(1461-83)
m. Elizabeth Woodville
(d.1492)

Edmund
Earl of Rutland
(d.1460)

Elizabeth
m. John de la Pol
Duke of Suffo

[1]
Henry Holland
Duke of Exeter

[2]
Thomas St Leger

EDWARD V
(1483)

Richard
Duke of
York

Elizabeth
m. Henry VII

John
Earl of Lincoln
(d.1486)

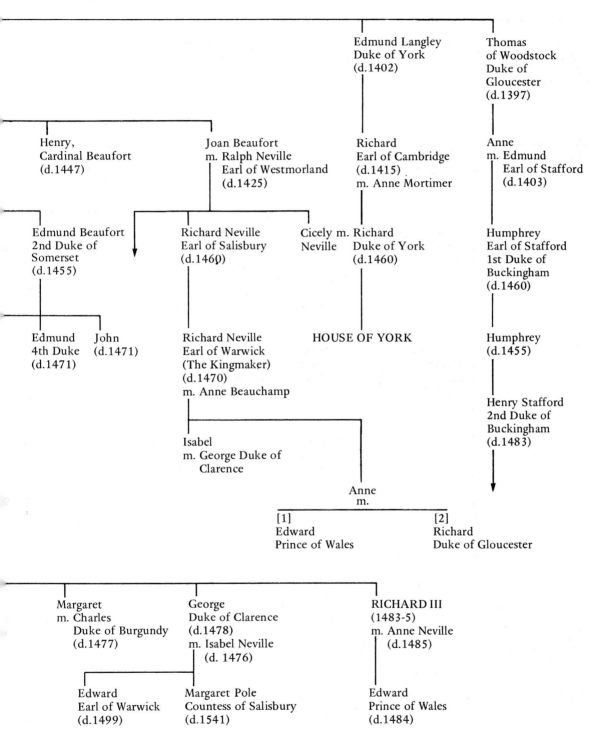

Edmund Langley
Duke of York
(d.1402)

Thomas
of Woodstock
Duke of
Gloucester
(d.1397)

Henry,
Cardinal Beaufort
(d.1447)

Joan Beaufort
m. Ralph Neville
   Earl of Westmorland
   (d.1425)

Richard
Earl of Cambridge
(d.1415)
m. Anne Mortimer

Anne
m. Edmund
   Earl of Stafford
   (d.1403)

Edmund Beaufort
2nd Duke of
Somerset
(d.1455)

Richard Neville
Earl of Salisbury
(d.1460)

Cicely m. Richard
Neville   Duke of York
           (d.1460)

Humphrey
Earl of Stafford
1st Duke of
Buckingham
(d.1460)

Edmund   John
4th Duke   (d.1471)
(d.1471)

Richard Neville
Earl of Warwick
(The Kingmaker)
(d.1470)
m. Anne Beauchamp

HOUSE OF YORK

Humphrey
(d.1455)

Henry Stafford
2nd Duke of
Buckingham
(d.1483)

Isabel
m. George Duke of
   Clarence

Anne
m.

[1]
Edward
Prince of Wales

[2]
Richard
Duke of Gloucester

Margaret
m. Charles
   Duke of Burgundy
   (d.1477)

George
Duke of Clarence
(d.1478)
m. Isabel Neville
   (d. 1476)

RICHARD III
(1483-5)
m. Anne Neville
   (d.1485)

Edward
Earl of Warwick
(d.1499)

Margaret Pole
Countess of Salisbury
(d.1541)

Edward
Prince of Wales
(d.1484)

Index

Official
Handbook

Bob Bayman
Piers Connor

Preface

The London Underground is one of the world's best known transport systems. It is used by Londoners and visitors alike. The Underground map, the bar and circle logo and the distinctive trains are instantly recognised even by strangers to the city. Even so, many of the system's lifelong users have little idea of what goes on to make the system work, how the equipment operates or the historical background to the world's first urban railway. This book attempts to provide a guide which answers many of the questions often asked about the Underground.

Photographic credits

London Underground Ltd   20, 23, 24 top right, 26 upper, 27 centre, 35 lower, 36, 42, 43, 44 lower, 47, 60, 61, 78, 79, 81, 82, 83, 84, 85, 86, 89, 91, 92

Capital Transport Publishing   Front and back covers, 1, 4, 5, 6, 17 bottom, 18, 22, 24 bottom, 25, 26 lower, 27 top, 27 bottom, 29, 30, 31, 32 left 34, 40, 41, 44 upper, 45, 46, 48, 49 upper, 50, 52, 53, 54, 55, 56, 57, 58, 59, 62, 63, 64, 65, 66, 68, 69, 70, 71, 72, 73, 74, 75, 76, 77, 93.

ABB Ltd   28

Bob Bayman   33

DCA   90

John Gillham   16 centre

John Glover   18 bottom left, 67

Brian Hardy   39 lower

Fred Ivey   38, 39 upper

London Transport Museum   6 inset, 7, 8, 10, 11, 12, 13, 14, 15, 16 bottom, 17 top, 17 centre, 19

John Laker   32 right

Brian Morrison   35 upper, 49 lower

ISBN 185414 169 4

Published by Capital Transport Publishing
38 Long Elmes, Harrow Weald, Middlesex

Printed by Bath Midway Press Ltd

© Capital Transport Publishing 1994

Contents

 # Introduction

Today the London Underground is one of the world's largest urban rapid transit systems. It serves 270 stations which provide services for up to twenty hours a day and is operated by London Underground Limited (LUL), a company wholly owned by the government-appointed authority known as London Regional Transport (LRT). LRT is also responsible for the provision of bus services in the greater London area.

Greater London has an area of 618 square miles and a population of over 7 million. Almost one million people travel into central London each day for work and over 60% of these use the London Underground system. Between 1983 and 1989, due largely to the availability of 'Travelcard' one-day and season tickets, there was an 84% increase in the demand for travel on the Underground so that more than ever before London relies upon the Underground system as part of the social and economic structure of the city, despite the minor downturn in traffic in the early 1990s resulting from economic recession.

The central area of London, bordered by the major main line railway termini and the Underground's Circle line which connects them, forms the commercial heart of the capital. The City, east of Holborn, is the financial district, while the West End contains the principal shopping and entertainment areas. Until the beginning of the twentieth century there was virtually no penetration of these areas by railways, but then various deep level Underground 'tube' lines were opened and now there is a network of lines covering both the City and West End zones and connecting them with many of the suburbs.

The greater London area is geographically divided into two halves by the River Thames. In the north-south division which this causes, by far the greater proportion of the Underground system is located in the northern area. Of the 270 stations on the system only 29 are located south of the Thames, due partly to the economic conditions of the development of railways south of the river and partly to the nature of the subsoil, which rendered tube construction difficult and expensive. In contrast with the railway companies north of the river, the southern companies depended very much on local passenger traffic for revenue and provided a close network of frequent services which was electrified almost entirely by 1930 and in some cases before 1914.

One of the features of the London Underground is that it operates rolling stock of two different sizes. This is because of the different tunnelling methods and sizes used during its construction. The original method, used for the Metropolitan and District lines, is known as 'cut and cover'. A cutting is excavated along the line of route and this is then roofed over and the surface restored, often with a roadway. Most of the resulting tunnels are wide enough to take two tracks, except at stations where they are further widened to take platforms and stairways.

The second type of tunnel is the deep level 'tube'. This method of construction was adopted to overcome the acute surface disruption caused by the cut and cover method and it took advantage of the blue clay upon which much of London is built. Single track circular tunnels of just under 3.4m diameter were bored at a level deep enough to avoid conflict with water mains, sewers and other underground services. Stations usually used a larger single track tunnel for each platform. The greater depth of these lines (an average of 20 metres) meant that lifts or escalators had to be provided for street access. The technology of deep level tube construction was available quite early but it had to await a practical means of propulsion without smoke and steam.

The head office of London Underground Ltd is at 55 Broadway, London SW1 in a large white stone building over St James's Park station. The building itself is an interesting architectural specimen finished in Portland stone and features sculptures by Eric Aumonier, Henry Moore, Eric Gill, Jacob Epstein and others. It was built in 1929 and has recently been refurbished.

History

The first underground railway in the world started operating when the Metropolitan Railway opened a line between Bishops Road, Paddington and Farringdon on 10th January 1863. At the Paddington end there was a connection to the Great Western Railway and, during the first few months of operation, the Great Western loaned locomotives and rolling stock to the Metropolitan. After one of the disputes which characterised the relationship between the two companies for many years, the Great Western withdrew its rolling stock and the Metropolitan prevailed upon the Great Northern Railway company to help it out until stock of its own could be built. By July 1864 the Metropolitan had enough of its own stock to operate the service without assistance.

Baker Street station in 1863 and today after its restoration as close as possible to original appearance.

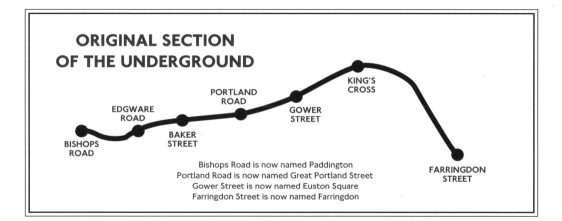

ORIGINAL SECTION OF THE UNDERGROUND

BISHOPS ROAD

EDGWARE ROAD

BAKER STREET

PORTLAND ROAD

GOWER STREET

KING'S CROSS

FARRINGDON STREET

Bishops Road is now named Paddington
Portland Road is now named Great Portland Street
Gower Street is now named Euston Square
Farringdon Street is now named Farringdon

Specially designed steam locomotives were purchased by the Metropolitan for working in their tunnels. They were built by Beyer Peacock of Manchester and were fitted with a system for condensing the exhaust steam to reduce the smoke appearing in the tunnels. The locomotives were of the 4-4-0 tank engine type and they became the standard for both the Metropolitan and District Railways. An example of one of them has survived to be preserved in the London Transport Museum, Covent Garden.

After the opening of the initial section in 1863, there were various extensions to the east and the line reached Aldgate in 1876. It was further extended round to a station called Tower of London (on the site of the present Tower Hill) in 1882. A westward projection was started from a junction at Praed Street between the stations at Paddington and Edgware Road. This line passed through a new Paddington station built exclusively for the Metropolitan (the present Circle/District line station), proceeded south to High Street Kensington and then curved east to South Kensington, which was reached in 1868.

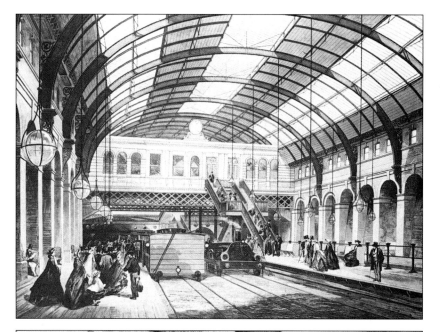

King's Cross station, Metropolitan Railway, 1863. Broad gauge trains supplied by the Great Western Railway were used at first.

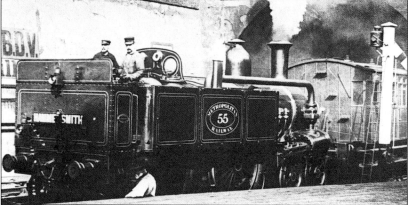

Metropolitan steam train at Aldgate.

Excavating the District Railway in front of Somerset House in 1869.

Below Cover of an early map sold by the District Railway.

At this point a second underground railway company entered the story. This was the Metropolitan District Railway, usually referred to as the District. The District built the southern section of the present-day Circle line between South Kensington and Mansion House, opening it in stages between 1868 and 1871. The present Embankment along the north shore of the Thames was built during this period as part of the construction of the District's tunnels between Westminster and Blackfriars.

The final part of the Circle was opened in 1884 when the joint construction by the Metropolitan and District of the link between Mansion House and the Tower was completed. The project included an extension to Whitechapel and a triangular junction with the present-day Circle line between Liverpool Street, Aldgate East and the Tower.

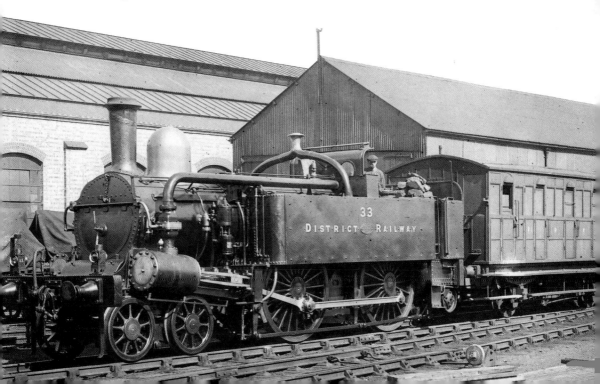

Both the District and Metropolitan became involved in the construction or operation of extensions radiating from the Circle line. Jointly with the Great Western, the Metropolitan operated a branch to Hammersmith which was opened in 1864. This line, like the first section of the Circle to Farringdon, was constructed to take the Great Western's broad gauge rolling stock. The track was laid as mixed gauge to allow both 4ft 8½in and 7ft 0¼in gauge rolling stock to operate. Traces of this can still be seen today in the wide gaps between tracks on the Hammersmith branch and the generous tunnel clearances between Paddington and Farringdon.

The District reached Hammersmith in 1874 and then built a further short extension to a junction with the London & South Western Railway at Studland Road near what is now Ravenscourt Park station. This gave the District access to Richmond to which point it began running trains in 1877. In 1879 it opened an extension from Turnham Green to Ealing Broadway.

In the following year the branch to West Brompton (opened 1869) was extended to Putney Bridge and, following the construction of a bridge across the river to connect with the London & South Western Railway at East Putney, District trains were allowed running powers to Wimbledon in 1889.

During this period the Metropolitan was also expanding. Apart from the line to Hammersmith already mentioned, a branch from Baker Street to Swiss Cottage was opened in 1868. This was extended to Willesden Green in 1879 and Harrow-on-the-Hill in 1880. Pinner was reached in 1885, Rickmansworth in 1887 and Chesham in 1889.

All the services on the Metropolitan and District Railways were originally steam operated, the District using the same 4-4-0 condensing tank locomotives as the Metropolitan. The District had 4-wheeled wooden carriages, usually formed into 9-coach sets for its trains. The Metropolitan also had some 4-wheeled stock but the bulk of its trains had 8-wheeled coaches, the four axles being on a rigid wheelbase. Bogie stock did not appear until 1898. However, by this time, a new form of motive power had come to the Underground for in 1890 electric traction was introduced with the opening of the City & South London Railway.

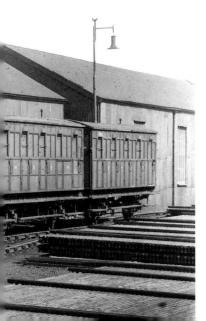

Far left **An early District train with four-wheeled compartment stock coaches.**

Left **District Railway tickets from the turn of the century**

9

The City & South London Railway was officially opened in 4th November 1890 by the then Prince of Wales, later King Edward VII, between Stockwell and King William Street in the City of London. It was the first tube railway in the world and the first underground railway to be operated by electricity. Although it was the pioneer of electric traction in London, the C&SLR almost missed this distinction. When work on the tunnelling of the line was started, it was envisaged that the system of traction would be cable haulage. It was to have been based on the system introduced in San Francisco for the now world-famous cable cars. By the time the C&SLR was opened however, electric traction had been substituted as its traction system, and the company led the way for London's future rapid transit systems. In 1898 the short tube line between Waterloo and the City was opened by the London & South Western Railway and the Metropolitan and District Railways began conversion to electric traction in the early 1900s. In 1900 the C&SLR opened extensions to Clapham Common in the south and to Moorgate in the north. The Moorgate extension allowed the original terminus at King William Street to be abandoned, being replaced by a station at Bank. A further extension of the line to Angel was opened in 1901 and another to Euston was opened in 1907.

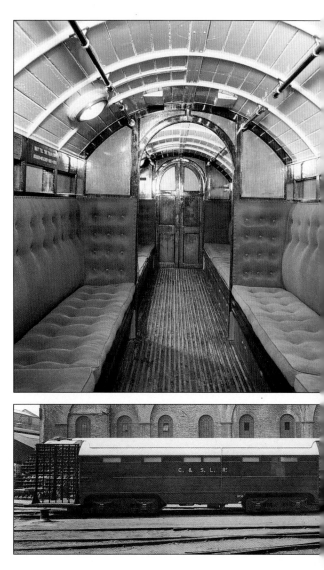

The C&SLR was opened with dc electric locomotives hauling trains consisting of three small carriages. The locomotives were only fourteen feet long. The carriages were specially designed to fit in the 10ft 2in diameter of the original tunnels. They were 26 feet long and weighed only 7 tons. Since they were to run only in tunnels, it was thought that they did not need full-size windows, so only small glazed panels were fitted to the bodysides just below gutter level. There were no other windows. Inside, there were longitudinal benches fitted with buttoned upholstery up to the base of the glazed panels. Entrances for the cars were provided at the ends, where double sliding doors gave access to open platforms. The platforms had gates which were closed between stations and opened by 'gatemen' to allow passengers to board and alight. The lack of proper windows meant that the gatemen had to announce the stations to the passengers and the noise level was such that the names had to be shouted if people were to hear them.

The original tube cars of the City & South London Railway. As the line was all in tunnel, windows were thought to be unimportant at first. The station name was shouted out at each stop by the 'gateman'.

The interiors of the cars with their tiny windows and buttoned upholstery were so claustrophobic that they were nicknamed 'padded cells' by the public. Later cars were improved by the provision of proper windows and the original cars were modified to match. One of the early vehicles was restored to its original condition in 1924 and is now preserved in the London Transport Museum. It makes an interesting comparison with the fluorescently lit interiors of modern Underground rolling stock.

BANK

KING WILLIAM STREET

BOROUGH

WATERLOO

ELEPHANT & CASTLE

KENNINGTON

OVAL

STOCKWELL

Above **Map of the first two deep-level tubes, the C&SLR and the Waterloo & City.**

City & South London Railway train after the line's extension to Moorgate.

Waterloo & City Railway car.

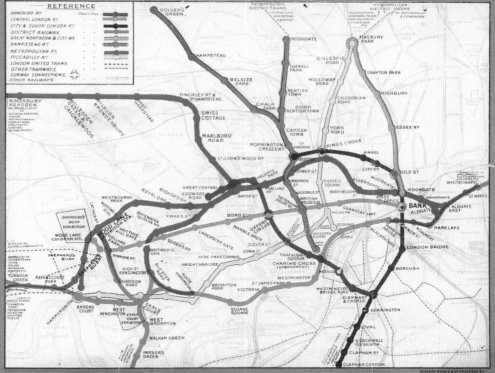

In spite of its primitive technology, the C&SLR, which is now part of the Northern (via Bank) line, was regarded as a success and it encouraged the building of other tube lines. In 1900 the Central London Railway was opened between Shepherd's Bush and Bank, cutting right across the central area within the Circle line and connecting the shopping district of Oxford Street with the financial district in the City. It also provided access to the then fashionable suburb of Shepherd's Bush. Like the C&SLR, this line opened with electric locomotives hauling passenger cars but the trains were up to seven cars long. However, after only three years of operation the locomotives were replaced by motor cars because of their excessive vibration. Multiple-unit traction then became the standard system of operation. This provided driver's cabs at each end of each train and eliminated locomotive changing at termini. With a service frequency of up to 30 trains per hour, the Central London Railway became London's first tube rapid transit railway.

In the years from 1900, tubes started to penetrate the heart of central London and by 1908, when this map was published, the core of today's Underground had taken shape.

The opening of the Central London Railway considerably threatened the Metropolitan Railway's traffic along the northern half of the Circle and the District's along the southern half and encouraged both railways to get together to electrify their lines. They began with an experimental dc electric service between Earl's Court and High Street Kensington in 1900. Following the experiment, they agreed to use a system of ac overhead electrification to be provided by the Hungarian company Ganz. Shortly after this decision however, the District was taken over by the American financier Charles Yerkes who wanted to introduce track level dc current supplies instead. Eventually, the Metropolitan and District agreed on the 630 volt dc supply system with 3rd and 4th current rails as still in use today.

12

More tube lines appeared following the opening of the Central London. The Bakerloo, Piccadilly and Hampstead lines were all opened during 1906-7. They formed the cores of the much longer lines now seen today. The Bakerloo was the first of the three to open, on 10th March 1906. It was originally known as the Baker Street and Waterloo Railway, although it originally ran from Baker Street to the station now known as Lambeth North and was extended to Elephant & Castle in August 1906. Extensions of the line to the north west were opened in stages, reaching Edgware Road in June 1907, Paddington in 1913, Queen's Park and Willesden Junction in 1915 and Watford in 1917. Between Queen's Park and Watford the Bakerloo trains ran over the new tracks specially constructed by the London & North Western Railway next to its main line for its own suburban electric service. At that time the Bakerloo was the longest of the tube lines and remained so until the opening of the Piccadilly extensions in 1932-33.

The Piccadilly line was opened as the Great Northern, Piccadilly and Brompton Railway in December 1906. It ran between Finsbury Park and Hammersmith and had a small branch from the main route at Holborn to Aldwych opened in November 1907.

The Hampstead line was the last of the lines to be opened as a result of the tube railway boom of the 1900s. It opened between Charing Cross and Golders Green (with a branch to Highgate) in 1907 and eventually became part of the Northern line after being combined with the rebuilt C&SLR.

Below **The Regent's Park entrance of the Baker Street & Waterloo Railway.**

Before the days of sliding doors, a gate-ended train is seen on the Hampstead Tube.

By the time they were opened, the Bakerloo, Piccadilly and Hampstead lines were all owned by Yerkes' holding company which was known as the Underground Electric Railways of London Ltd (UERL) which, by that time, also owned the District. The three tubes were formed into a common company called the London Electric Railway (LER). The UERL also absorbed the Central London and the C&SLR in 1913.

The three Yerkes tubes began their operations with multiple unit trains. As on the older tubes, the cars had open end entrances with iron lattice or grille gates. The first Metropolitan and District electric stock also had open ends but they quickly introduced enclosed entrances and middle doors to both improve weather protection and speed up station stops. The tube lines began introducing these improvements from 1915 and, from the early 1920s, they introduced air operated sliding doors on all new tube cars.

Both the Central London and the C&SLR had slightly smaller tunnels than the three LER tubes. A start was made towards standardisation during the 1920s when the C&SLR was enlarged to match the LER tunnel size and was extended south to Morden. The improvements to the C&SLR were designed to combine the line with the Hampstead. The two lines were connected at Kennington and Camden Town and the Hampstead line was extended from Golders Green to Edgware.

Circle line train with hand operated sliding doors opened and closed by passengers.

The Central London Railway was extended from Bank to Liverpool Street in 1912 and to Ealing Broadway in 1920 over a line built in a partnership with the Great Western Railway, but it had to wait until 1938 for its tunnels to be enlarged to normal tube size. This was done as part of the plans for long eastern and western extensions to Epping, Hainault, Ongar and West Ruislip. The second world war delayed these but they were opened soon after.

The idea of extending the tube lines to create suburbs and thus generate custom had begun in 1907 with the opening of the Hampstead tube to the open countryside at Golders Green. It was thought, rightly, that residential development would occur if good transport was provided. The idea had been imported from the United States with Yerkes and his engineers, who had seen the same phenomenon in cities like New York and Chicago.

The Piccadilly line was perhaps the classic example of the Underground Company's ideal of a tube line extended to serve the new suburbs, thus tapping new demand to fill the under-utilised tunnels through the central area. This line was substantially extended in the early 1930s to the west over two District line branches, whilst breaking new ground to the north with an extension part in tunnel and part on (or above) the surface.

The extension to Oakwood was the last under independent ownership; four months later the modest further extension to Cockfosters was the first to open under the auspices of the new London Passenger Transport Board, on 31st July 1933.

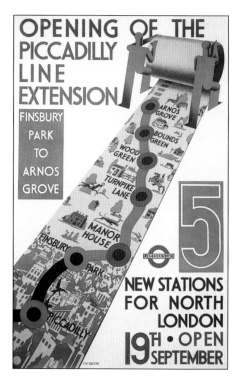

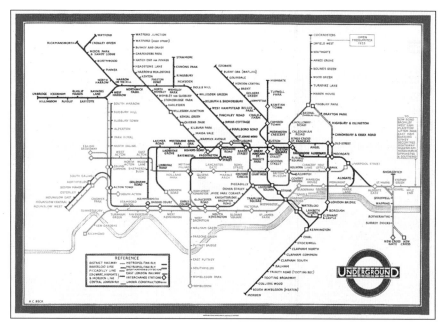

The first edition of the world-famous Underground map, designed in the early 1930s by H.C. Beck, a draughtsman in the Underground publicity office.

15

In 1933 the London Passenger Transport Board was appointed by the national government to take over the operation of the Underground railways and bus and tram services in what is now the greater London area. The name London Transport appeared for the first time on buses and trains to mark the passing of the Underground and bus companies from private to public ownership. The LPTB immediately began a programme of new works which included a new tube line between Baker Street and Finchley Road to relieve the Metropolitan's worst bottleneck, the extension of the Northern north of Highgate and the Central line extensions already mentioned. Much new rolling stock was acquired, including the 1938 tube stock which was withdrawn from the Underground in 1988 and some of which is now in use on the Isle of Wight.

The Underground Group built a large fleet of 'Standard' tube stock between 1923 and 1934. Thirties architecture is exemplified by Uxbridge station.

Below **Late-thirties train design for the 'surface' lines.**

Following the second world war there was a change of government and virtually all the railways in Britain were nationalised in 1948. London Transport remained much the same as before as far as the public was concerned. A bigger change occurred in 1970 when political control passed to the Greater London Council. Control reverted to the government from June 1984 when London Regional Transport was set up. London Underground Ltd was formed as a subsidiary of LRT on 1st April 1985.

The Victoria line, the first Underground line to be fully equipped for automatic train operation (ATO) was opened in stages between 1968 and 1971. Another new line — the Jubilee line — was formed from the Stanmore branch of the Bakerloo and a new tube built between Baker Street and Charing Cross. It opened in 1979. After many false starts, work commenced late in 1993 on an important extension to serve London's former Docklands.

Rolling stock developments in the early post-war period included new unpainted aluminium trains.

The Victoria line was completed in 1971 and was followed in 1977 by the extension of the Piccadilly line to Heathrow.

In 1977 the Piccadilly line extension to Heathrow Airport was opened. The building of a new terminal (Terminal 4) later became necessary and it was decided to include a link for the Underground. A single-track loop extension to the Piccadilly line was constructed and it opened in 1986.

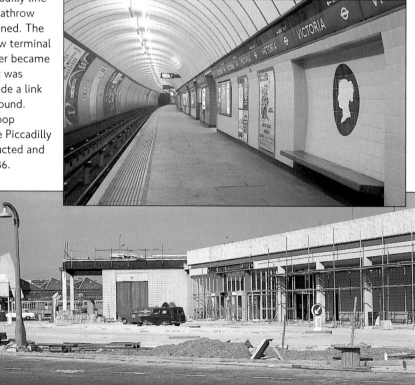

The London Underground has also had a distinguished history in the development of its public image and the approach to art. The best known symbol of the Underground is the bar and circle. About 1908, a version of the now familiar symbol, which had a solid red disc, appeared on station platforms as a way of displaying the station name. Shortly after the bar and disc device started to appear, a new corporate typeface was introduced on the Underground. It was designed by Edward Johnston and was used on new signs and publicity from 1916. It has remained in use with only minor modification to this day — as clear and crisp as ever — a tribute to the simplicity and clarity of the original design. Johnston also redesigned the bar and disc symbol so that it became the bar and circle device similar to that used today. During the expansion of the system in the 1920s and 1930s it was incorporated into exterior designs and is now universally used to say 'Here is the Underground'.

The London Underground has become renowned throughout the world as a leader in the use of high quality art in its publicity. Posters displayed on stations have been prominent in the use of works by artists specially commissioned by the Underground. This tradition started in 1908 with the appearance of posters such as Hassell's 'No need to ask a P'liceman', which depicted a policeman showing a lady the Underground map which had been recently introduced at stations. The famous Underground line diagram, now known as the Journey Planner, has become an internationally acknowledged masterpiece in its own right and its principles have been adopted by transport organisations throughout the world. It was originally designed by Harry Beck in 1931 and published two years later. The poster tradition continued throughout the 1920s and 1930s with work by such artists as Graham Sutherland, E. McKnight Kauffer and many others. The posters became so popular that they have been reproduced for sale to the public as well as revived for publicity purposes. Today the tradition continues as posters specially commissioned by the Underground continue to appear on stations advertising events and locations which can be reached by Underground.

Northfields,
one of the
1930s classics
designed by
Charles Holden.

 # Stations

Stations are regarded as one of the most important parts of the London Underground infrastructure. As a shopkeeper will provide an attractive window display to entice customers inside to buy his goods, so the Underground must provide attractive stations to persuade customers to sample its services. The diverse origins of many of the lines forming the Underground have left a legacy of variety in station design in addition to the variety of site needs ranging from deep-level tube lines in the centre of the city to stations serving small country towns in the outer suburbs.

The street access to every station is marked by the world-famous Underground logo. Before this came into use stations had used the traditional British form of displaying the name of the company and station on the exterior of the street level building and the name of the station at each end of the platforms. The tube lines incorporated the station name in the tiling of platform walls together with 'Way Out' signs. The bar and disc signs appeared on platforms from about 1908 and in 1937 a frieze was added repeating the station name along the length of the platform.

None of the earliest station buildings opened with the first Underground line on the north side of the Circle line between Paddington and Farringdon are still to be seen today in their original condition. However, a good idea of what they were like can be seen at Bayswater, where the original building of 1868 is still in use and still in many respects as built. All of the stations on the sub-surface lines are close enough to the surface to allow access by stairs to be sufficient for passengers to reach the platforms.

Many of the Circle stations were built in an open cutting and originally provided with an arched overall roof. One of the best remaining examples can be seen at Paddington, where the station has recently been refurbished to restore it to near its original condition. Of course the air space over stations like this can become a lucrative asset if developed as a property site. The most famous examples were the flats over Baker Street station known as Chiltern Court, which were completed in 1929, and London Underground's own headquarters at St James's Park which were opened the same year. In recent times more commercial development has taken place at a number of sites including large projects at Barbican, Mansion House and Gloucester Road. Most recently the site of the District and Piccadilly lines station at Hammersmith has been developed into a major shopping and office centre, opened in March 1994.

Gloucester Road station, built as a joint Metropolitan and District station in 1868 has been refurbished recently as part of a commercial development

When an extra pair of tracks was built in 1866 between King's Cross and Moorgate to cope with main line rail traffic wishing to use the Metropolitan's route, the stations had to be enlarged. Farringdon and Barbican (then Aldersgate) are still much as they were then and Farringdon still sports its magnificent twin overall roof. Another station with a fine overall roof is Earl's Court. The roof dates from 1878, whilst the Earl's Court Road entrance was rebuilt in 1906 by the District's architect Harry Ford in the style similar to that of Leslie Green for the three LER tubes which were contemporary with that period.

As lines were extended into the suburbs and the open air, so stations became similar to those of other railways. The buildings at Rickmansworth are typical of the 1880s expansion period on the Metropolitan, whilst the later suburban style of the 1920s can be seen at Croxley. The suburban flavour is much more apparent here, especially when compared with the Portland stone faced frontages of Charles Holden for the tube lines of that era (eg Clapham South to Morden).

The District also extended into the suburbs, particularly in west London, but few of the original station buildings have survived, having been rebuilt during the 1930s. One which has is at North Ealing, which dates from 1903, where the original station house incorporated a first floor flat built for the District Inspector.

Edgware Road (1907) provides an example of the dark red terracotta tile frontages of Leslie Green for the Bakerloo, Piccadilly and Hampstead lines. The Central London Railway chose a lighter shade of brick, as seen at Holland Park (1900). Metropolitan's suburban style is seen at Croxley (1925).

22

The expansion of the tube lines in the 1920s and 1930s created a new era for station design in London. Such was the quality of the designs introduced during this period that many of the buildings are now 'listed' and cannot be altered without good cause. The Portland stone buildings of the southern end of the Northern line have already been mentioned and further examples of Holden's first Underground style are to be seen at Hounslow West and Ealing Common. Another 1920s station entrance style, with elements of the Georgian and Roman, by the Underground's own architect, Stanley A. Heaps, can be seen north of Golders Green.

The 1930s produced the fine brickwork surface structures seen along the western and northern ends of the Piccadilly line. Southgate, Arnos Grove, Northfields, Sudbury Hill and Sudbury Town all show the large round or rectangular surface buildings typical of this time. It is interesting to compare them with the new brickwork stations provided by the London Midland & Scottish Railway at Dagenham East and Upminster Bridge for the Barking to Upminster electrification of 1932.

The Central line extensions mark the next big stage in the architectural development of the Underground. Opened in the 1940s, various modern designs appeared, notably at Hanger Lane, Loughton, Wanstead, Redbridge and Gants Hill. Many of the stations at the eastern end of the Central were taken over from the LNER at that time and date from the late 19th century.

Among a number of 'listed' stations from the inter-war period is Holden's Chiswick Park.

In recent years there have been few new station buildings but the late 1960s saw the opening of Blackhorse Road on the Victoria line in a style typical of the period, and Hatton Cross on the Piccadilly line Heathrow extension offers a mid-1970s example. Some stations have been provided with new or rebuilt structures like Bond Street, with the 'West One' shopping centre surrounding two of its entrances, and Surrey Quays and Shadwell, both of which have had new surface buildings in recent years. The latest new surface building has been at Hillingdon on the Metropolitan line, where diversion of the A40 trunk road required demolition of the old building.

The changes which can be seen today at many stations are the result of three separate projects; the new Underground fare collection system, a station modernisation programme and, since the Fennell Report on the King's Cross fire, additional work to improve safety at stations. The safety work has principally involved the removal of wood from escalator panels and the installation of fire detection and sprinkler systems. Many other less obvious improvements are being incorporated like new communications systems, removal of suspect materials, new cleaning methods, clear exit signage and training sessions for staff involving evacuation simulations.

The new ticketing system has caused many alterations to booking office design and entrance layouts while the much needed rehabilitation programme is changing the appearance of most stations. Improvements range from simple repainting to complete redecoration with new tiles, new lighting and new flooring.

Above **New designs for cigarette stubber and litter bin at Underground stations.**

Left **The Davies Street entrance to the recently rebuilt Bond Street station.**

Above right **The covered way from the newly rebuilt station at Hillingdon.**

Right **The redeveloped Hammersmith, completed in 1993.**

24

The station modernisation programme has aroused a lot of controversy amongst those who have complained that the Underground should retain its original decor and architecture. This ideal runs counter to the need to replace old materials with new, to renew broken tiling, improve lighting and signing systems, increase fire resistance, comply with new safety requirements and improve security and safety for passengers and staff. Costs, maintainability and durability under extremely arduous usage conditions all have to be considered as well as artistic and historical values. Nevertheless, a number of 'Heritage' stations have been designated, where original appearance is maintained as closely as possible.

This page **Recently restored brickwork at Gloucester Road (District and Circle) provides an idea of the appearance of many early stations when built, though in today's cleaner atmosphere it should remain like this a good deal longer. A combination of original and replica fittings graces the booking hall of Edgware Road (Bakerloo).**

Facing page upper **Restoration work at two other 'Heritage' stations, Tooting Bec and Hounslow West.**

Facing page lower **Comprehensive surveys of station signing have coupled modernisation with a programme of retaining the best of the old.**

Trains

London Underground operates two different types of rolling stock — tube stock and surface stock. The surface stock is similar in loading gauge to full-size British Rail main line stock but the tube stock is considerably smaller in order to fit in the single track circular tube tunnels. Although this size restriction imposes some special design requirements, particularly in the area of bodies and bogies, much of the equipment is standardised for both tube and surface stock.

The question is sometimes asked why a standard tube train design is not used on all tube lines and a standard surface stock design for all surface lines. There are a number of answers. To begin with, almost every line has individual characteristics. The Central and Victoria lines, for example, have 400ft platforms and can accommodate longer trains than the 350ft platforms standard on many other tube lines. The Victoria line has Automatic Train Operation (ATO) and therefore needs special stock. The Piccadilly line serves Heathrow Airport and its stock is provided with luggage spaces.

The surface lines also have differing characteristics which call for different stocks. The dense traffic on the Circle line, for example, is better catered for by stock with fewer seats and more doorways than the Metropolitan stock serving the outer suburbs to Amersham, Watford and Uxbridge.

Another reason for the different types of stock is that replacement has to be spread over many years. Suppliers could not re-equip the whole of the Underground in a few years with almost 4000 new cars and then remain idle for 30 years until new stock was needed again. Cars are therefore replaced in batches, usually on a line-by-line basis, taking into account changed traffic requirements, technical improvements and modern design expectations.

Below **New trains under construction at the Derby Works of ABB Ltd.**

Various types of car are used in various formations to give the type of train required for each line. Trains are formed with one, two, three or four units, each unit comprising two or more cars semi-permanently coupled together. Units have automatic couplers at their outer ends.

There are three basic types of car; a driving motor car, a non-driving motor car and a trailer car. A driving motor car has a cab and is equipped with traction motors. A non-driving motor car has the motors but no cab while the trailer has neither motors nor cab. Some non-driving motor cars are positioned at the coupling ends of units and are equipped with a small control cabinet at the outer end to allow the unit to be driven from that end in depots. It saves the space lost and the expense of a full driving cab at a little-used middle-of-the-train position. These cars, except in the most recently built trains, are known as uncoupling non-driving motor cars.

In order to allow tube cars to fit inside the small diameter tube tunnels they are 750mm lower in height than the surface stock cars. The floor height is only 600mm above rail level instead of 975mm. This restricts the size and layout of underfloor equipment and, because of this, originally all tube trains had motor cars with special equipment compartments behind the driver's cabs. By the mid-1930s designs had progressed to allow the main items of equipment to go under the floor. This removed the need for equipment compartments and gave up to 15% more passenger space per train.

Below The oldest trains in use on the Underground began work in 1960. Replacement of the stock on the Northern line is expected to be completed by 1998.

In spite of the improvements allowing the equipment to be positioned under the car floor, one problem has remained to this day. Wheels cannot be made small enough to fit completely below the floor. Tube cars are therefore designed with openings in the underframes to allow clearances for the wheels. Inside the cars, these openings are covered by longitudinal seating. This precludes the provision of doors in these areas.

Tube stock currently in use on the Underground can be divided into four broad types as far as design is concerned. The first type comprises the 1956/59/62 stocks which work the bulk of the services on the Northern line and until 1993 most of those on the Central. The bodies were the first tube trains to be finished in an unpainted aluminium alloy in place of the painted steel of the 1938 stock and this unpainted finish lasted very well until recent years when the scourge of graffiti vandalism arrived in London. Attempts to remove graffiti tend to leave shadows on the surface finish and this problem is now being addressed by painting the exterior of the cars.

The second group of tube stock is the 1967/72 type. The 1967 stock was introduced for the opening of the new Victoria line with automatic train operation (ATO). Although the car body was to the same general dimensions as the earlier tube stocks, there were a number of differences in style and layout such as wrap-round cab windows, double-glazed passenger windows and the provision of all-longitudinal seats in the trailer cars. The 1972 stocks, consisting of two versions known as Mk1 and Mk2, were 7-car versions of the 8-car 1967 stock. They were designed to operate on manually driven lines with a possible future conversion to automatic operation in mind. They never had this but the Mk2 stock is now working on the Bakerloo line under one-person operation with manual driving. The Mk1 stock remains two-person operated on the Northern line.

A Bakerloo line 1972 stock train, identical in appearance to 1967 stock on the Victoria line.

The 1973 tube stock for the Piccadilly line was, like the 1972 Mk2 trains, designed for eventual one-person operation, but because of the prevailing length of platforms on the line the overall train length had to be shortened to ensure the train operator's presence in the station with the train fully berthed. This was achieved by adopting a six-car formation with each vehicle some 1500mm longer than hitherto, a solution offering the added benefit of substantially lower purchase, operational and maintenance costs when compared with the earlier seven-car sets.

The 1983 tube stock, built for the Jubilee line.

A similar formation was adopted for the Jubilee line's 1983 stock trains even though platforms on the line are capable of accommodating eight cars of conventional stock. This latter fleet was designed with the wide single-leaf doors used on D78 stock, but this feature may preclude the trains being cascaded onto busy lines once the delivery of new trains renders them surplus from the Jubilee line.

The renewal of the rolling stock, signalling and power supplies for the Central line were all due within a few years of each other, so it was decided to combine them into a single project. The rolling stock element of the project is the 1992 tube stock built by BREL/ABB. The order was preceded by three prototype tube trains known as the 1986 tube stock which were used to try out various technical and design ideas prior to the ordering of the main batch. They were tested in passenger service on the Jubilee line from May 1988 until August 1989.

Outside mounted doors instead of internally fitted ones are a new feature and are emphasised by the application of the red finish. Passenger operated open and close buttons are provided. Another new feature is the extension of the side windows up into the car roof line. Restyled cab ends with dot matrix destination displays and deeper driving windows are also included. Each car has the traditional layout of double and single doors but these are wider than on existing cars. Seating is all longitudinal but it will be possible to alter the seat layout in the centre bays if necessary in the future. Large windows are provided in the car ends to improve passenger security.

The 85 eight-car trains have the solid state electric traction control system known as chopper control and every axle is motored giving smooth but rapid acceleration. Regenerative braking is provided to recycle energy. Air suspension, used for the first time on tube stock, gives an excellent ride even on indifferent track.

Driving cabs are normally provided at the outer ends of trains only but there are shunting control positions at the ends of every 2-car set. The driver has in-cab television viewing of the station platforms during approach and departure as well as during the station stop and, in addition to conventional public address, there are 'talk-back' facilities for passengers to communicate with the driver in an emergency. There are also automatic, digitised speech announcements at stations.

Passenger facilities have been designed to take account of the needs of disabled passengers and include the use of contrasting colours for grab poles and door close warning beeps.

The new trains recently introduced on the Central line.

Surface stock has neither the size nor space problems of the tube stock. The three types are, however, quite different in design. The oldest of the current types is the A60 stock. This was built for the Metropolitan line services to Uxbridge, Watford and Amersham (together with a second identical batch known as the A62 stock) and is designed to provide for the longer distance passenger. All seating is transverse and high-backed and double doors are provided at two positions on motor cars and three positions on trailer cars. This contrasts sharply with the four sets of double doors provided on the high-capacity C69 and C77 stocks built for the very heavily-trafficked Circle and Hammersmith & City lines. This stock is also used on the District line between Edgware Road and Wimbledon and on the Olympia branch.

The bulk of the District line service is provided by the latest surface stock, the D78 stock. This took the long car design first introduced on the 1973 stock and applied it to a surface stock. Each car has four large single-leaf doors on each side and a combination of longitudinal and transverse seating.

A unique feature of the D78 stock is that it has tube stock sized wheels. Traditionally, surface stock has always had 1067mm wheels, whereas tube stock has 790mm wheels. In an attempt to reduce the number of different types of wheelsets in use on the system, the D78 stock has the same type of wheels as the 1973 tube stock. The D78 stock also saw the introduction of a new type of bogie. It is of welded steel, box frame construction and is in the form of an 'H' with a rigid bolster. There are no headstocks. A similar type, but modified for use under tube cars, was produced for the 1983 tube stock. All stocks in current service have riveted steel bogie frames and rubber suspensions of various types.

Left **Metropolitan line A stock at Northwood.**

Right **District line D stock train at Richmond.**

During 1989 a series of trial modernisation schemes was carried out on various types of Underground rolling stock to determine the best way of refurbishing trains to comply with the new safety standards which have been adopted on the system. A number of different types of car were selected to test methods of replacing interior finishes with new fire-resistant materials, to determine ways of improving security, to improve the passenger alarm systems and to provide graffiti-resistant external finishes.

The trial units were displayed to the public for comments in September 1989 and the final scheme for each stock refurbishment was adopted following in-service testing of the prototypes.

One of the most striking features of the refurbished trains is the return to a painted finish. A combination of red front ends and doors with blue and white sides has now been adopted as the corporate colour scheme. The paint has been introduced to make the removal of graffiti easier and to eliminate the 'ghosting' on the cars which appears when graffiti is removed from the unpainted aluminium.

Various interior colour schemes were tried out on the prototype units but production trains share a common basic colour scheme of off white and pale grey, with trim to suit the colour and character of each line.

C stock is provided with new gears to reduce noise and new bogies to replace the original equipment which has been showing signs of the stress of many years of running over poor track. Other technical improvements include improved heating and ventilation, the provision of an automatic parking brake requiring no action by the crew and improved public address.

A refurbished train of C stock.

Train refurbishment before, during, and after. These views of C stock show the transformation in internal appearance, such that the refitted trains are often perceived as brand new. The refurbishment of structurally sound rolling stock offers substantial benefits at relatively low cost. This offers the possibility of retaining trains far longer than the nominal 35-40 year life expected hitherto, with one or more internal refits and new traction equipment during that extended lifespan.

Refurbished 1972 stock for the Bakerloo line. Similar stock, with different colour interior trimmings, operates on the Victoria line.

1973 stock is in course of modernisation for continued use on the Piccadilly line.

Train maintenance

Train maintenance on the Underground has always been conducted in a regular pattern of examination, detailed inspection and overhaul at pre-determined intervals. A daily safety check and interior sweep is applied to all stocks, followed by a weekly examination varying in type according to the stock involved. At between nine and fifteen weeks (again according to the stock) the train spends a day 'in the shed' having a close inspection and test. At much wider intervals ranging from nine months to four years, cars are lifted off their bogies for motor or wheel changing and bogie overhaul. Finally, a full-scale overhaul is conducted every six to nine years to restore the car to near new condition.

Each line has its own main depot where inspection sheds, a lifting shop and stabling sidings are provided. An exterior car washing machine is usually sited where trains can be washed as they return to the depot from service. Most roads in sheds are provided with pits under and at the side of trains to give access to the underfloor equipment. Not all the trains on a line are stabled at one point and many lines have two depots and various stabling sidings. At some places, trains are stabled in platforms overnight and cleaning and testing is done there.

Above **A Victoria line train over an inspection pit at Northumberland Park depot.**

Traction equipment

Series-parallel traction control is standard. Resistance switching is achieved by the use of cam-operated contactors, the camshaft being driven by an air-operated, oil-damped engine. All stocks use a single camshaft on each motor car, except for the 1967/72 tube stocks and C surface stocks, which use a separate camshaft for series notching and parallel notching. The two-camshaft system was introduced because of the more complex equipment required for rheostatic braking, introduced to Underground rolling stock at the same time. A larger single camshaft is used on the motoring and braking circuits of stock built since 1973. The 1983 tube stock has electric camshaft equipment. The dc motors of the 1992 tube stock are controlled by solid state Gate Turn Off (GTO) thyristors, reducing energy consumption and maintenance requirements. New trains for the Jubilee line extension will have ac motors for the first time on the Underground.

In the event of a fault on the control cable, it can be divided at the point where the units making up the train couple. It is then possible for the driver to operate the equipment on the good unit to move itself and its defective partner to a depot.

Air and auxiliary supply

The compressed air supply is provided by electrically driven compressors which automatically maintain the pressure at between 75 and 90 lb/in² on most stocks. Somewhat higher pressures have been adopted on some stocks in recent years. The compressors, between two and four per train depending on the length, are driven by the 630-volt traction supply, and are usually mounted under the trailer cars. Compressor control is synchronised to ensure all compressors operate together.

Brakes

All Underground trains have two braking systems, the service brake for normal use and the emergency brake. The emergency brake is provided to allow the train to be stopped if anything goes wrong with any part of the safety equipment or if an unsafe situation arises. A track level 'trainstop' device applies the emergency brake if a train overruns a danger signal.

Older stocks used the system whereby the emergency brake is applied if a passenger alarm handle is operated in the car. The difficulty of obtaining assistance if a train is stopped between stations has led to a new policy whereby most stocks are being equipped with an electronic passenger emergency alarm which alerts the driver but does not stop the train until the next station. This allows more rapid assistance because platform access is available, prevents the danger of trains being stopped in tunnels where there is smoke and allows outside help to reach the train more quickly.

The emergency brake was traditionally pneumatically controlled through the brake pipe and provided air-operated friction brakes acting on the wheel treads. Service braking was also controlled in this way until the introduction of electro-pneumatic control in the late 1920s. All Underground stock now has e.p. controlled service braking and, since 1967, new stocks have been provided with rheostatic braking on motor cars. From 1973, new stock had electrical control of emergency braking provided in place of the rather vulnerable brake pipe.

Door systems

All Underground passenger trains are fitted with air operated sliding doors worked from control panels at the operating position. This was usually at the leading end of the rear car but, with the introduction of stocks capable of conversion to one-person operation, door controls have now been provided in cabs. Some additional facilities to improve door service have been provided on modern stocks. The loss of car heating at terminal stations while trains are awaiting departure time has always been a concern and the C69 stock was the first to be equipped with a 'selective close' facility which allowed all the doors except one pair to be closed to retain interior heat. The D78, 1983 and 1992 stocks have passenger door control. This allows passengers to open only those doors which they need to use, a further way of reducing heat losses at stations. 'Open' buttons at each doorway are illuminated and enabled by the train operator as the train stops at the platform. The doors are closed by the operator and the system deactivated to allow the train to be started safely.

Engineers' trains

The Underground keeps a fleet of engineers' trains, particularly for track maintenance but also for other purposes. In recent years there have been a number of changes in the approach to engineers' trains and there has been something of a renaissance. From a rather motley collection of old and converted vehicles a new fleet of purpose-built wagons, special machines and improved locomotives has emerged.

Two of the fleet's cranes during the installation of a new crossover at Northolt.

The bulk of the engineers' trains on the Underground are hauled by battery/line electric locomotives. The oldest of these were built in 1951, the newest in 1985. They are usually used in pairs, one at each end of a train. This allows rapid turnround and easier shunting at worksites. It also prevents the failure of one locomotive from disabling the whole train.

A special brake block test locomotive is kept. This is the sole working survivor of the famous fleet of twenty Metropolitan electric locomotives which were built between 1921 and 1923 and which worked passenger trains on the Metropolitan line until 1961.

The engineers' vehicles used on the Underground range from conventional flat wagons and hopper wagons used for moving rails and ballast to worksites to specialist vehicles like tamping machines, gauging cars and a track recording train. Many of these have been specially rehabilitated, converted from passenger cars, or purchased new in a programme to bring the engineers' vehicle fleet up to date.

Although engineers' trains can be found all over the system, they are based on two main depots. One is at Lillie Bridge near Earl's Court, which is used only by engineers' trains; the other is at Ruislip where extra sidings for permanent way trains have been built to one side of the main passenger train depot.

An engineers' train made up of a battery loco front and rear, three brake vans and a gauging wagon.

A tube size gauging vehicle converted from 'Standard' stock.

 **Lines**

Circle line

The Circle line is basically a combination of the central sections of the Metropolitan and District lines, and it is managed with the Hammersmith & City. Thirteen miles in length and serving 27 stations, it connects most of London's main line railway termini.

Almost all of the Circle line service is operated over the Metropolitan and District lines. Only the short sections between High Street Kensington and Gloucester Road and between Aldgate and Minories Junction (east of Tower Hill) are used solely by Circle trains. The line's service is slotted between the District and Metropolitan services, making it difficult to timetable and vulnerable to delays by other trains. Its normal service pattern requires seven trains per direction operating at 7½ minute intervals on a 52½ minute round trip. At weekends and in the evenings the service widens to five trains per direction operating a 10 minute service on a 50 minute trip.

One of the Circle line's peculiarities is the fact that the constant running of trains on a circular route used to cause problems with uneven wheel wear. To overcome this, one train per day is diverted from Tower Hill to Whitechapel, where it reverses and then proceeds to Liverpool Street. This has the effect of turning the train round.

The rolling stock on the Circle is C69 and C77 stock and it is also used on the Hammersmith & City line and the District line's Edgware Road to Wimbledon service.

Facing Page
Farringdon station accommodates the Circle, H&C and Metropolitan lines as well as the Thameslink service of BR.

Above **A Circle line train at Paddington. The gaps in the tunnelling are a remnant of steam days.**

41

Tickets

Buying
your ticket

Fares

District line

Runs from Upminster in the east to Ealing, Richmond or Wimbledon
and has two small branches serving Edgware Road and Olympia.
The District covers 40 route miles and serves 60 stations.

The District is one of the most complex of all the Underground lines and consequently difficult to operate. Its main section forms the southern half of the Circle line plus a single route eastwards to Barking and Upminster. In the west there is a trio of main branches to Wimbledon, Ealing and Richmond. In addition, there is a shuttle service to Olympia and a Wimbledon/Putney Bridge service to Edgware Road. All these services pass through Earl's Court, which has become the hub of the line and the location of its control centre.

One of the main operating problems at Earl's Court is the passage of the Edgware Road service across the main line to the Wimbledon branch. A flyunder is provided for the westbound Ealing line to pass under the eastbound line from Wimbledon but trains still have to cross the eastbound line from Ealing to gain access to High Street Kensington and Edgware Road. A flyunder at the east end of the station allows trains from Edgware Road to pass under all the main line tracks.

Above **The original green tiling in the booking hall at Barons Court, on to which the needs of today's Underground have been grafted sympathetically.**

42

The Wimbledon branch is served by trains from the main District line as well as those from Edgware Road. The stations between High Street Kensington and Edgware Road are only able to accommodate six-car trains of C stock, not the longer six-car D stock trains used on the rest of the District. Some trains on the Edgware Road service terminate at Putney Bridge where a bay platform is provided for reversing. At Parsons Green some stabling sidings and a train crew depot are provided. There is also stabling accommodation in the triangle at Cromwell Road where the District and Circle lines meet. The West London Air Terminal was built above 'Triangle Sidings' in the early 1960s but the site is now occupied by a Sainsbury's supermarket.

At East Putney the District joins the Railtrack branch to Wimbledon. Special arrangements exist on Putney Bridge and between Turnham Green and Gunnersbury to separate the four-rail LUL and three-rail current rail systems. These automatically ensure a supply to each train as it crosses from one system to the other but without allowing the train to 'bridge' the gap between the two. British Rail does not run a regular passenger service over the line but uses it for access to the depot at Wimbledon Park. At Wimbledon, Underground trains use their own platforms to the west of those provided for BR services. East Putney, Southfields and Wimbledon Park stations were owned and operated by BR until transferred to the Underground in April 1994.

West Brompton, the picturesque first station on the Wimbledon branch, with the Earl's Court exhibition hall in the background betraying its urban setting.

The line to Richmond (once part of the London & South Western Railway's Richmond to Kensington branch) is shared with BR trains working between Richmond and North Woolwich via the North London line. On its journey from Richmond the line crosses the River Thames at Kew. A similar crossing occurs at Putney Bridge on the Wimbledon branch but the bridge at Kew is more visually attractive. At Gunnersbury the BR service continues towards South Acton while the District route forms an impressive flying junction with the four-track District/Piccadilly lines at Turnham Green. The line from Gunnersbury to Richmond is owned by Railtrack.

Between Acton Town and Barons Court the Piccadilly line occupies the two centre tracks and the District the two outer tracks. The District stops at all stations while the Piccadilly normally runs non-stop between Hammersmith and Acton Town.

Stamford Brook has an unusual station layout which has four tracks but only three platforms. The two westbound tracks are served from an island platform dating from 1912 which used to be the District station for both directions. Originally, there was no platform for the remaining two tracks, which were part of a separate line connecting the Richmond branch with the Hammersmith & City line. When the Piccadilly line was extended westwards from Hammersmith in 1932 a new platform was provided at Stamford Brook to serve what is now the eastbound District. The combination of the two platforms provides an interesting contrast in styles which has not been lessened by over sixty years of common ownership.

At the east end of Ravenscourt Park, the next station towards London, the remains of the viaduct connecting the line to the H&C at Hammersmith can be seen. The District/Piccadilly tracks drop sharply at this point to pass under the centre of Hammersmith. The District/Piccadilly station at Hammersmith was completely rebuilt in the early 1990s but remains separate from the Metropolitan station. A pedestrian subway connects the two.

The contrast in styles at Stamford Brook. A train of D stock draws into the 1932 built platform opposite the one of more traditional style dating from twenty years earlier.

Hammersmith station is at the centre of a large gyratory traffic system and has been completely rebuilt as part of a major commercial development.

44

Just east of Barons Court, the Piccadilly line enters its tunnel and runs below the District as far as South Kensington. The tunnel entrance is between the eastbound and westbound District tracks. Further east between West Kensington and Earl's Court there are two connections from the District, one to the Permanent Way depot at Lillie Bridge, the other to Olympia just before the underground junction with the Wimbledon branch.

Earl's Court, once described as the 'Crewe' of the Underground, handles five different District line services which split into three branches at the west end of the station and two at the east end. A few minutes' observation during the peak period from one of the passenger footbridges over the platforms shows just how complex the train service operation can be. The roof dates from 1878, whilst the Earl's Court Road entrance was rebuilt in 1906 in Leslie Green's standard style for the original stations on the Piccadilly, Bakerloo and Hampstead lines.

The District line's main junction, Earl's Court.

Once beyond Earl's Court, the line passes through Gloucester Road and South Kensington. Originally the District and Metropolitan had their own tracks side by side until they were combined at a junction east of South Kensington. At this station there were originally four through platforms and two bays. The southernmost bay has now almost disappeared under the structure housing the Piccadilly line escalators which can be seen from the present westbound platform. Between this and the eastbound platform traces of the former Metropolitan Railway bay can be seen.

East of South Kensington the line is in tunnel (except for Whitechapel) as far as Bow Road. The gaps in the tunnel roof along this section are a reminder that operation was originally with steam locomotives. Also of interest is the cross-platform interchange with the Central line at Mile End, the only example of tube and surface interchange at the same level in tunnel.

The shopping arcade at South Kensington, one of a number in similar style provided by the Metropolitan and District early in this century.

Art Nouveau on the District.

East of Bow Road the line rises steeply to the surface. This is the steepest gradient on the Underground used by passenger trains (1 in 32), though a steeper one exists at the Acton Town end of Ealing Common depot where the exit road is 1 in 28.

Beyond this point the line runs parallel with the former London, Tilbury & Southend line from Fenchurch Street. The BR 25kV electric trains run non-stop along this line except for a stop at Barking. District trains stop at all stations to Upminster. All four tracks along this route were originally owned by BR but now the District tracks are self-contained and all links with the fast tracks have been removed.

Some remnants of former links can be seen at Plaistow, where a bay platform is used by some District and Metropolitan trains. On the north side of the line is a large car dealers' workshop which was the site of the Plaistow engine shed. At East Ham a disused bay can still be seen on the north side of the platform and beyond the station the BR electric stock depot is built on the site of the former Underground depot. In contrast, a new interchange has been provided at West Ham to allow passengers access between the District and the BR service to North Woolwich: further rebuilding is now necessary to link the line with the Jubilee line extension.

Two important stations on the eastern part of the District line, both shared with BR, are at Barking and Upminster. Barking is a major interchange between various BR routes and the Underground. Upminster is the easternmost station on the District and has a large depot beyond it, not visible from the platforms, built in 1958 to replace the old site at East Ham. At the other end of the line the main depot is at Ealing Common, built in 1905 for the electrification of the District Railway and formerly the workshop for the line as well.

Recent refurbishment at Stepney Green, where sturdy pillars support attractive brick arches.

East London line

*Whitechapel to New Cross or New Cross Gate. The line serves
7 stations and covers 4 miles. Its management is shared with
the Jubilee line.*

The East London line provides a shuttle service between the low-level platforms at Whitechapel and New Cross alternately with New Cross Gate. There is a small depot at New Cross. The service is extended to Shoreditch at peak times and on Sunday mornings. A feature of this line is that it utilises the tunnels built under the River Thames by Brunel. These consist of twin tunnels which were opened in 1843 for pedestrians. They were provided with rail tracks in 1869 and these were connected at the southern end to the London Brighton & South Coast Railway at New Cross. In 1876 a link was established at the northern end to the Great Eastern Railway just outside Liverpool Street station. The East London was electrified in 1913 and its passenger services were then operated by the Metropolitan Railway.

The stations on the East London line have been improved and modernised in recent years. At Rotherhithe a pair of escalators has been installed under a curved plastic transparent roof and the surface building restored. At Wapping, which is the deepest station (60ft) on the so-called sub-surface lines, the old lifts, installed in 1915, were replaced. At both Surrey Docks (renamed Surrey Quays in 1989) and Shadwell stations the surface buildings were replaced by new ones in 1983. A new station will be built at Canada Water, near the old Canada Dock, to provide interchange with the extension of the Jubilee line. This is due to open in 1998.

The East London line has seen many different types of rolling stock over the years, including 1938 tube stock between 1974 and 1977. Both the District and Metropolitan lines have provided the normal surface stock. At present, A60/62 stock from the Metropolitan is used.

Above and top right **The contrast at Shadwell between the surface building, built 1983, and the original tunnel below, dating from 1876.**

Right **Canal Junction, where the East London line splits into two branches. The train carries a livery style unadopted for general use.**

48

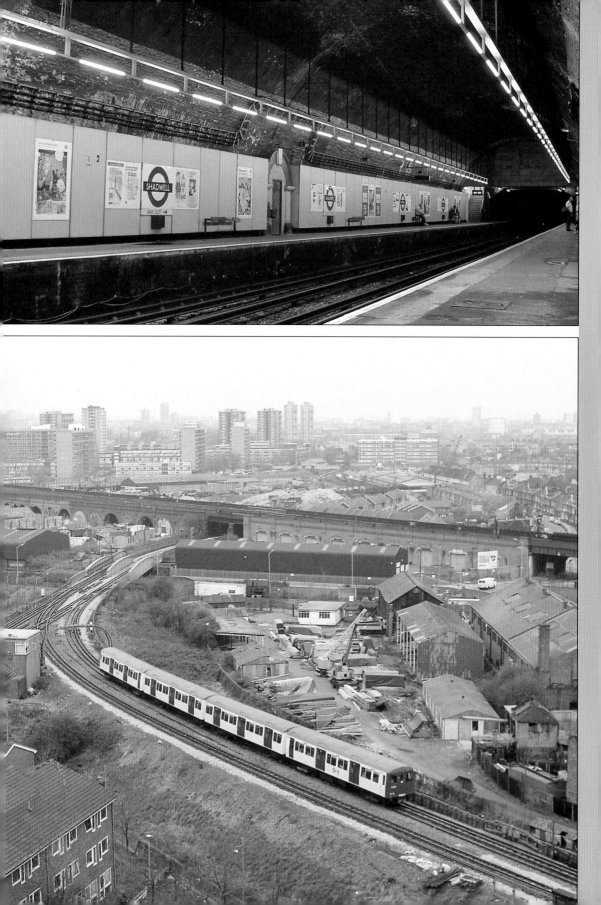

Hammersmith & City line

*Hammersmith to Whitechapel, with a peak hour extension to Barking.
This line serves 19 stations (28 in rush hours); and covers 9 miles
(16½ in peaks). The line is managed with the Circle line
with which half its length is shared.*

In addition to sharing the Circle line's rolling stock, the Hammersmith & City line shares the route along the north side of the Circle, which is the oldest part of the Underground. The section from Hammersmith to Farringdon was built to accommodate the broad gauge trains operated by the Great Western Railway in the 19th century. This can still be detected today at places along the route which show generous spaces between tracks and in tunnels. West of Westbourne Park the tracks are further apart than needed today and many of the tunnel sections east of Edgware Road are much wider than sections built later.

The main depot for the Circle and Hammersmith stock is at Hammersmith. It was built for the electrification of the line in 1906 and has changed little since. It is located outside the station on the east side of the main line.

Above **A train of C stock pulls into the Paddington Hammersmith & City line platform with the trainshed of the main line station in the background.**

On the west side of the main line at Hammersmith an office block was built on the site of the former goods yard and, to accommodate additional stabling tracks should they ever be required, the block was constructed on a raised platform with pillars spaced to allow tracks to be laid between them. Further up on the same side there was a connection to the former London & South Western Railway's Kensington and Richmond line, over which the Metropolitan Railway operated services to Richmond via Turnham Green until 1910. This connection was removed in 1914.

At Westbourne Park, the H&C joins the BR main line route into Paddington. There are no longer any track connections between the two railways but the H&C passes under the BR lines and then runs parallel to them between Royal Oak and Paddington. The H&C platforms at Paddington are structurally part of the BR station and are separate from the Circle line platforms. The H&C and Circle lines join at the junction at Praed Street before entering Edgware Road station. This is a four-platform station where the District line service to Wimbledon terminates. On the south side of the station (which is in a cutting) is Griffith House, one of a number of offices used by LRT around London. The amount of railway property at this point is explained by the former presence of Metropolitan Railway steam locomotive and carriage depots and sidings.

Further along the line beyond King's Cross is a section where two extra tracks, known as the 'City Widened Lines', run parallel with the Underground line as far as Moorgate. These extra tracks were originally built by the Metropolitan Railway to allow local passenger and freight trains to run off the Midland and Great Northern Railways at King's Cross to Moorgate without conflicting with Metropolitan Railway services and to have a cross-London connection via Farringdon to the southern railway companies. Between King's Cross and Farringdon the Widened Lines cross under the H&C and Circle tracks.

In 1982, the Widened Lines were electrified at 25kV and disconnected from the Underground. In May 1988, the connection with the south London routes at Farringdon was reinstated after being disused for many years and new dual-voltage electric trains now provide a service between the Bedford line and several destinations south of the Thames with Underground interchange at Farringdon.

At Moorgate and Aldgate facilities for reversing Metropolitan trains are provided in addition to the through tracks. Aldgate is located on the west leg of a triangle of lines connecting the Metropolitan, Circle and District lines.

At Aldgate East an interested observer at the west end of the station can watch the routes being changed for District and Metropolitan trains. Air-operated point machines are standard on the London Underground and these can clearly be heard operating here. The relationship between route setting, signal clearance and train movement is easily visible.

Towards the next station, Whitechapel, is a junction giving access to the East London line. There was originally a station here known as St Mary's, which was closed in 1938. Whitechapel is the normal terminus for H&C trains but these are extended over the District to Barking in rush hours.

Metropolitan line

Runs from Aldgate or Baker Street to Amersham,
with branches to Chesham, Watford, and Uxbridge
with a total mileage of 41½ serving 34 stations.

The Metropolitan line is more suburban in character than the rest of the Underground and it has some fast trains at peak hours. Only the section south of Finchley Road is in tunnel; the remainder is in the open.

Originally the tunnel section had three stations between Finchley Road and Baker Street but these were closed in 1939-40 when the Bakerloo (now Jubilee) line was opened along the same route but in deep level tube tunnels. The sites of these disused stations can still clearly be seen as the trains make the steep climb up the gradient from Baker Street.

Baker Street station has seen much rebuilding in recent years with the opening of the Jubilee line and the restoration work on Circle line platforms 5 and 6. The work on the remainder of the station is now complete and gives the whole complex a combination of 1860s restoration on the Circle, 1930s on the main station, 1970s on the Jubilee line platforms and 1980s on the Bakerloo platforms.

Above **The terminus of the single track branch to Chesham, with the water tower from steam days on the left and the old signal box just visible in the background.**

The tunnels between Finchley Road and Baker Street are, for the most part, in single track bores. This is because the first railway along the route was single-track only and doubled later. At Finchley Road the two Metropolitan tracks part to allow the Jubilee line tracks to emerge from the 1939 tube tunnel originally built for the Bakerloo extension from Baker Street. The Jubilee line serves the stations between Finchley Road and Wembley Park which were operated by the Metropolitan before the 1939 changes. Now the Metropolitan trains normally run non-stop between these two stations. On the west side of the line runs the BR service to Marylebone.

At Neasden, on the east side of the Metropolitan line, is Neasden Depot. This is the main depot for the Metropolitan and Jubilee lines and is the largest on the Underground. It was formerly the site of the Metropolitan Railway works, main depot and power station. After the depot was rebuilt to its present configuration in the late 1930s only a small steam shed was retained. This is still visible at the north end of the yard although the last steam locomotives were withdrawn in 1971. There has been much re-equipment of Neasden in recent years, including new automatic train washing machines and a new signalling system using solid state interlocking.

At Wembley Park, north of which the 1932 Metropolitan Railway Stanmore branch diverges, the signal box then installed and equipped with centralised train control still stands at the country end. The control equipment has long since been removed and Jubilee line tube trains now serve the branch, which still shows evidence of its origins. The station has had successive rebuildings to cope with traffic demands of the Wembley Exhibition of 1924-25, subsequent suburban growth and the crowds going to Wembley Stadium. From here as far as Moor Park trains may run fast or stop at all stations as required, since four tracks are provided. At Harrow the configuration changes so that, instead of the slow tracks being between the two fast tracks as they are south of the station, north of the station they are east of the fast tracks. North of Harrow the fast tracks are shared with BR Aylesbury trains.

At Baker Street the Metropolitan ticket hall was refurbished in 1987. Units once occupied by a bookstall and a tea room are now used as a booking office, but their fascias have been restored.

The north western suburbs of London served by the Metropolitan line were largely developed between the wars and owe much to the former Metropolitan Railway's astute combination of 'Metro-land' publicity, its policy of operating a separate land development company and its electrification and improvement of train services in this period. The Uxbridge line, which diverges north of Harrow-on-the-Hill, was built in 1904 and electrified with the main line to Baker Street in 1905. Further electrification from Harrow to Rickmansworth was completed in 1925 and, under the London Transport regime, electric trains reached Amersham and Chesham in 1960.

The Uxbridge branch passes through an area intensively developed with suburban type estates in the 1930s, most of the houses being somewhat cheaper and smaller than those of the earlier Metro-land developments along the main line. Today only a few fields remain, at the western end, to remind the traveller what the whole area outwards from Willesden looked like before 1920. Most of the stations along this branch of the line follow the style produced for the Underground in the 1930s by Charles Holden, although other architects also had a hand in their detailed design; but Ruislip, which retains much of its 1904 appearance, offers a pleasant contrast.

At Rayners Lane the Metropolitan line is joined by the Piccadilly line branch from Acton Town. Normally Piccadilly trains reverse at Rayners Lane using a centre siding provided west of the station. This is a typical example of the centre siding used all over the Underground and the observer on the platform can clearly see how it is used and how the signals operate to control it. Few other places offer such opportunities as many of the frequently used examples are in tunnels.

At Harrow-on-the-Hill the Metropolitan diverges to Uxbridge by one branch and Amersham, Watford and Chesham by the other. Interchange with the Chiltern line services of BR is also provided. The early 1940s station contrasts with recent office development in central Harrow.

Between Ruislip and Ickenham there is a siding on the south side of the line. This is used both for reversing Piccadilly line trains which terminate at Ruislip and as a transfer route for stock being moved to the Central line depot at West Ruislip. At Hillingdon, a striking new station has recently been built.

At Uxbridge a set of sidings is provided on the north side of the station. Both Metropolitan and Piccadilly trains are stabled here. The present station was built in 1938, the original station site being adjacent to the present sidings. There is a steep gradient into the station and the cutting walls gave considerable problems for a number of years. They had to be specially strengthened in 1954. The station itself is of particular interest. It has a three-track design with the centre track being provided with platforms on both sides. The roof has an interesting clerestory design very similar to that provided at Cockfosters at the other end of the Piccadilly line. There is also a fine stained glass window overlooking the booking hall incorporating the coats of arms of Uxbridge Urban District Council and of Middlesex and Buckinghamshire Counties.

The light and airy new station at Hillingdon, provided as part of a road improvement that required the demolition of the old one.

Sculpture surmounts the station at Uxbridge, the terminus of one of the Metropolitan's suburban branches.

55

The line between Harrow and Moor Park was quadrupled in 1960-61 as part of the modernisation plan for the Metropolitan which included the electrification to Amersham and the introduction of new rolling stock (the A stock) which is still in use on the line today. All the stations as far as Moor Park have platforms serving only the slow lines. Speeds over the fast lines of this section are higher than elsewhere on the Underground, 70mph being the permitted maximum. The grades are quite steep in some places however and this speed is rarely reached except between Northwood and Harrow.

Just north of Moor Park the short branch to Watford diverges to the right and the tracks are reduced to two from this point. The connections to the Watford branch form a triangle. Trains normally use the southern connection, proceeding from Moor Park to Watford.

The Watford branch was built in 1925 at the time of the electrification from Harrow to Rickmansworth. The station at Watford is about a mile away from the town centre but it serves a housing area known as Cassiobury Park. The line, which was expensive to build and produced disappointing traffic results, passes through a spectacular cutting at the approach to Croxley station and then high over a canal just outside Watford. It was originally intended to run the four tracks through to Rickmansworth and traces of the spaces levelled and bridge widths installed can be seen on the northbound or 'down' side of the line.

Annual steam specials have become a feature in 'Metroland' in recent years. An Ivatt Class 2 locomotive is seen at Watford in May 1993 on such a trip.

56

From Rickmansworth, the line climbs steeply through the Chiltern Hills to Amersham, now the most westerly point on the system. The whole area is quite rural but with scattered areas of development. At Chalfont & Latimer there is a single track branch to Chesham which is normally operated by a single unit of A stock shuttling between the two places. At peak times two through trains operate while the shuttle train is held in the short terminal platform at Chalfont.

The Metropolitan line now terminates at Amersham but a service continues to Aylesbury provided by BR. The station has three platforms, expanded from the simple two-track station of the conventional type originally provided. North of the station a pair of reversing sidings is provided for Metropolitan trains. The normal Metropolitan service to this point is half-hourly and is supplemented by an hourly service to Aylesbury from Marylebone.

Just after leaving Watford, the Metropolitan line crosses the Grand Union Canal. The viaduct, built in 1925, will be abandoned if the line is diverted to Watford Junction.

The 1889 station at Chorleywood.

Bakerloo line

From Elephant & Castle to Harrow & Wealdstone.
The Bakerloo covers 14 miles and serves 25 stations.

Since the opening of the first part of the Bakerloo line in 1906, it has expanded, contracted and then expanded again to its present length. From its original northern terminus at Baker Street under the Metropolitan line station, it had expanded north to Queen's Park by 1915 and in stages to Watford by 1917. The Watford service used tracks built by the main line railway. In 1939 a new branch was built north of Baker Street which ran directly under the Metropolitan line to Finchley Road. At Finchley Road it rose to the surface and connected with the Metropolitan. This allowed Bakerloo trains to take over the Metropolitan's Stanmore service.

Until the opening of the Jubilee line in 1979 the Bakerloo operated both Stanmore and Watford services. However, the building of the new Jubilee tube from Charing Cross to Baker Street and its connection to the Stanmore branch of the Bakerloo line meant that the Bakerloo was confined to its Watford branch. In 1982 the Watford service was withdrawn and Queen's Park became the usual northern terminus once more. However, there were occasional journeys to and from Stonebridge Park to allow access to the new depot there and in 1984 some rush hour trips were extended to Harrow & Wealdstone. The present all-day service to Harrow & Wealdstone began in May 1988, Queen's Park remaining the Sunday terminus until October 1989.

The southern terminus of the Bakerloo is at Elephant & Castle, known to the staff simply as 'The Elephant'. Between the next station, Lambeth North, and Waterloo is a connection to London Road depot. This was once the main depot of the Bakerloo but is now only a stabling point for nine trains.

Above **The Bakerloo line platforms at Baker Street acknowledge the street's most famous 'resident'.**

58

From Elephant to just south of Queen's Park the line is in tunnel. Of interest along this part of the route is the sharply curved platform at Waterloo, the crossover at Piccadilly Circus and the connections with the Jubilee line at Baker Street. At Piccadilly, the two separate station tunnels become one at the northern end of the station where the crossover is located. Trains passing in both directions can be seen from either platform, an unusual sight in a tube station.

At Baker Street, connections between both northbound and southbound Bakerloo and Jubilee lines are provided to allow stock transfers. At Queen's Park, the line rises to the surface and uses two platforms between the two tracks on the Euston to Watford line. A small depot is provided which is unusual in being divided into two parts. At the south end there is a two-track shed capable of accommodating four trains. At the north end another four-berth shed is provided. This has four tracks, two sidings and two connecting tracks which allow Bakerloo trains access to the tracks to Watford. Bakerloo trains on trips north of Queen's Park have to pass through the shed, a unique experience for passengers on the Underground. At night, one of these tracks is used for stabling a seventh train.

Top **Drawings of early tunnelling equipment decorate the platforms and passages at Paddington.**

Above **Original tiled names intact at Regent's Park and Marylebone.**

59

Central line

Ealing Broadway or West Ruislip to Hainault or Epping.
The line covers 46 miles and serves 49 stations.

As first built in 1900 the Central line provided a cross-London route along the main east-west axis from the Bank to the western suburb of Shepherd's Bush. It was originally worked with locomotive-hauled trains but changed to multiple-unit traction in 1903. It was the first line to use multiple unit control of trains. An extension to Ealing was opened in 1920.

The original traction system used a three-rail configuration having a centrally positioned positive current rail and the tunnels were slightly smaller in diameter than those subsequently adopted for later tube lines. The Central line therefore remained non-standard until its conversion to normal tube dimensions and the four-rail traction system in 1938-40. At the same time the original platforms were lengthened to take eight-car trains. Many of the station tunnels in the central area show evidence of the lengthening work undertaken at that time.

The eastern and western extensions of the line were begun in 1936 but were delayed by the war and not opened until 1946-49. At the eastern end of the line a large loop was formed partly by new tunnel construction and partly by taking over existing railways. Between Newbury Park and Wanstead the tunnels were used during the war to accommodate the manufacture of aircraft parts.

Above
Snaresbrook was reached by the Eastern Counties Railway in 1856, long before the Central line was thought of. The ECR rebuilt the station in the late-Victorian period. It was taken over by the Underground in 1947.

60

Many of the open-air stations at this end of the Central line were taken over from the LNER and date from the 19th century. Snaresbrook and Barkingside still have their original buildings and they contrast sharply with those built in the 1940s like Wanstead, Loughton and Redbridge. The platforms at Redbridge are the shallowest on the tube lines, only 26ft below the road. From 1957 until closure in September 1994 a single-track section of railway between Epping and Ongar was operated by Central line trains. Ongar remains at present the start point for the measurement of the whole system. Distance markers are provided every 200m all over the Underground to provide reference points for operators and engineers.

The main line from Epping is joined at Woodford and Leytonstone by the two connections to the Hainault Loop. South of Leytonstone at Stratford there is interchange between the Central and the BR services and Docklands Light Railway.

Largely as built by the ECR, Leyton's original station building is visible above the canopy on the right.

At Bank, the next station west from Liverpool Street, interchange is provided with the Northern line, the Waterloo & City line, the Docklands Light Railway and with the District/Circle station at Monument. Bank has some very sharp curves which require quite severe speed reductions.

The straight route of the Central line over the central London section enables the 'hump profile' on which this and other tube lines were built to be seen clearly. Each station is approached on a rising gradient and left on a falling gradient to assist braking and acceleration respectively.

The sharply curved station at Bank, the original eastern terminus.

Modern mosaics at Tottenham Court Road.

The line rises to the surface at White City. This station was rebuilt in 1947 to replace the original station which served the area which was known as Wood Lane. The approach to the open section was via a sharp curve under Caxton Street known as the Caxton Curve. It has a radius of 400ft. It originally formed part of a loop which allowed trains to leave Shepherd's Bush, rise to the surface station at Wood Lane and then return to Shepherd's Bush. The loop also allowed access to the depot. When the line was extended to Ealing in 1920, the westbound line was on the right hand side of the eastbound line because of the configuration of the loop. This situation still exists at White City. Access to the depot is now from the station instead of from the loop. Further west, the lines are crossed on a flyover to return to the standard British left hand running layout. Just west of North Acton station, another flyover provides a grade separated junction for the divergence of the Ealing Broadway and West Ruislip branches.

The branch to West Ruislip runs parallel to another BR line, but only Greenford, South Ruislip and West Ruislip are served by both BR and Underground trains. All the other stations are used by the Central line only. At Greenford, a small bay platform is provided between the Central line platforms to allow interchange between the BR shuttle service and the Underground. A feature unique to the Underground is that an escalator is provided to go *up* to the trains.

Between Ruislip Gardens and West Ruislip is a large depot. In accordance with the Underground's policy of always providing two exit tracks to each depot where possible, it has a connection to both stations. Recently, a new permanent way depot has been provided adjacent to the main rolling stock depot and there is also a connection to the Metropolitan line at the rear of the depot.

West Ruislip station marks the western limit of the Central line and is the terminus of the Underground's longest possible continuous journey. It is 34.1 miles long and takes 1 hour 28$^{1}/_{2}$ minutes from Epping (off-peak).

Above left
Unusual tubular steel lamp and name sign unit at White City.

Above **A modern waiting room under GWR canopies at North Acton.**

Jubilee line

Charing Cross to Stanmore; serves 17 stations in its 14 miles. It runs parallel with the Metropolitan between Baker Street and Wembley Park.

The Jubilee line was opened throughout for public use on 1st May 1979. It was made up of two parts: a new tunnel section built between Baker Street and Charing Cross, plus that section of the Bakerloo line between Baker Street and Stanmore which had been worked by Bakerloo trains since 1939. Physical connections for trains as well as simple passenger interchange between the two lines are provided at Baker Street.

The Jubilee line is controlled from the new signal control centre at Baker Street. The new installation is part of a scheme to modernise the signalling of the whole of the Metropolitan/Jubilee lines complex using computers. Although the traditional fixed line diagram is provided in the control room showing the whole of the Jubilee line (and parts of the Metropolitan), all the control functions are carried out using colour VDUs, tracker balls and 'mice'. Using these the operator can control trains by editing the timetable if something goes wrong. A train trip can be selected and modified in advance. Then the system is left to signal the train in accordance with the instruction as it arrives at the site where the change is required.

The Jubilee line runs in tunnel from Charing Cross to Finchley Road, where it rises to the surface between the Metropolitan tracks, providing cross platform interchange at that station. All the rest of the line to Stanmore is in the open and between Finchley Road and Wembley Park it runs parallel with the Metropolitan. It shares with that line the depot at Neasden.

Above **Nelson at Charing Cross, the closest station to Trafalgar Square. The Jubilee line will be diverted away from here when the extension to Docklands and Stratford opens.**

Stations on the line have a variety of styles ranging from late-1970s at Baker Street and south to Charing Cross, through late-1930s at Kilburn and Dollis Hill, early 1930s Metropolitan suburban at Kingsbury, Canons Park and Stanmore, to 1920s Metropolitan urban at Willesden Green and 1880 Metropolitan rural at Neasden.

At the Charing Cross terminus the Jubilee faces east. The original hope was that there would be extensions to Fenchurch Street, Surrey Docks and Lewisham with further extensions over the BR route to Hayes in Kent. These did not find favour with the government of the time but construction of an extension to Docklands and Stratford was started in December 1993, to be partly financed by private capital.

The platforms at West Hampstead, rebuilt when the Bakerloo line was extended to Stanmore in 1939. The street entrance is late-Victorian.

At Kilburn, southbound Jubilee line trains make use of an iron bridge built by the Metropolitan Railway in 1915.

Northern line

*Morden to Edgware, Mill Hill East or High Barnet via Bank or
Charing Cross; serves 49 stations and 36 route miles.*

The Northern line possesses the longest section of continuous tunnel on the
system, 17 miles 528 yards between Morden and East Finchley (via Bank). For
many years this was the longest railway tunnel in the world.

The line has two main routes across London. One is via the West End
(Charing Cross). The other is via the City (Bank). The City route uses the
tunnels built for the City & South London Railway, the oldest of the tubes,
and these had to be enlarged in the 1920s to match the tunnel diameter of
the other tube lines. Some stations show variations in tunnel diameter where
platforms were extended to accommodate longer trains.

In some areas traces of the old arrangements still exist. At Clapham North
and Clapham Common there is a narrow island platform in a single large
station tunnel accommodating both tracks. A similar layout existed at Angel
until mid 1992, when a new station opened at a cost of over £70 million. A
dramatic traffic increase had rendered the old layout potentially unsafe.

At Euston (southbound City platform) the former C&SLR terminus tunnel
originally accommodated two tracks and an island platform. Now it serves
only one track and like Angel has a wide platform unusual for a tube station.
Further south over a section of the line between Bank and Borough the
original tunnels were crossed over for ease of operation and led to the
station tracks having 'right hand running' instead of the standard British left
handed arrangement. This arrangement may also be seen at White City,
Central line and on the Victoria line at Warren Street and King's Cross.

Above **The
recently rebuilt
southbound
platform at Angel.
In the five years
prior to rebuilding,
use of this station
had more than
doubled.**

At each end of the City section there is a junction with the West End branch. At Camden Town the connection is a series of underground tunnels which allow trains to run from either the City or the West End to either of the north London branches of the line. One serves Edgware via Golders Green, the other High Barnet and Mill Hill East via Finchley Central.

A Northern line train enters the depot at Morden, the southern end of the line. The terminal station can be seen in the background.

There is a simpler junction at Kennington. Here a reversing loop (for Charing Cross branch trains) and siding are provided and the line continues south to Morden, the southernmost point on the system.

A variety of services can operate on the Northern line. Trains going north from Morden may run via Bank or Charing Cross to Edgware or to High Barnet or Mill Hill East. Whilst this may seem advantageous to the passenger, allowing a choice of routes, it is very difficult to operate. The running time between Kennington and Camden Town is four minutes greater via Bank than via Charing Cross, making the provision of a regular service difficult.

The diversity of routes means that trains must always arrive at a converging junction at the right moment to avoid missing their turn through the junction. At both Camden Town and Kennington there are two platforms for each branch. Cross-platform interchange is provided for City and West End trains at the latter.

The line south of Clapham Common was extended to Morden in 1926 and the surface stations along this section are in a standard pattern of Portland stone evolved by Charles Holden, easily adaptable to varying site conformations and designed to show up well when floodlit at night. The whole of this section is in tunnel except for the terminus at Morden. Beyond the station is Morden depot. Although it is quite a large depot it is not the main one for the line. This is located at Golders Green, the site of the original terminus of the Charing Cross, Euston and Hampstead Railway opened in 1907.

67

The CC,E&H Railway originally ran from Charing Cross (the station now called Embankment) to Golders Green with a branch to Highgate (the present Archway station). It had a terminal loop at Charing Cross, opened in 1914, which became disused when the line was extended south to Kennington to meet the enlarged City & South London Railway in 1926. The present sharply curved northbound platform at Embankment is located on the former loop. This platform was the origin of the system of automatic warning lights and a recorded 'Mind the gap' message now found at many curved platforms.

Floodgates are provided at Embankment where they can be used to close off the under river tunnels should they be breached. Floodgates are also provided at other vulnerable points on deep level and sub-surface lines.

The Northern line has the deepest station below street level on the system. This is Hampstead, which is 192ft below the surface. Special high speed lifts are provided here, since it is too deep to provide escalators at a reasonable cost. Just north of the station the Underground is at its deepest — 221ft below the surface of Hampstead Heath. The deepest point below sea level on the whole system (67ft) is also on this line, south of Waterloo, although this will be surpassed by the extension of the Jubilee line.

At Golders Green the line reaches the surface and its access to the main depot which lies adjacent to the station. The depot buildings are typical of the 1905-7 style adopted for the original electrification depots and are similar to those at Ealing Common, Lillie Bridge and London Road. Unfortunately, the depot at Golders Green was originally designed for five-car trains. The line now uses seven-car trains and some tracks in the depot cannot take a full length train, making it difficult to operate. The building boom which took place in the area after the line was opened has effectively cut off any expansion of the site.

Embankment, showing the tight curve and the floodgate equipment installed here and at other stations next to the Thames.

North of Golders Green the line is in the open except for a short tunnel at the Burroughs near Hendon. It is interesting to follow the line on foot between Golders Green and Brent Cross stations to examine how in 1923, a victim of its own success, it had to be projected through an area already covered with new houses. At Brent Cross there were originally passing loops on each side of the station but these have been removed. At Edgware there are stabling sidings next to the terminus and there are still traces of the work done in preparation for an extension to Elstree abandoned at the beginning of the second world war.

The other branch of the Northern line goes north from Camden Town to Finchley Central, where the line splits. A single track serves the short branch to Mill Hill East while the main line continues along the very attractive route to High Barnet. The branch to High Barnet was taken over from the main line railway in 1940 and the stations still retain the characteristics of their original owner, the Great Northern Railway. The line to Mill Hill East has an attractive brick arch viaduct over Dollis Road where the Underground reaches its highest level above ground at 60ft.

For the extension to Mill Hill East and High Barnet a small depot was built at Highgate including some sidings at the side of Highgate Wood. With the decline in services during the early 1980s the depot was closed in 1984. However, because of the recent increases in traffic levels the depot has been reopened to accommodate the extra trains provided for the restored services.

Mornington Crescent station was closed in mid 1992 to carry out lift replacement and a renovation scheme, but work had to be suspended by the end of the year because of funding difficulties, and the station remains closed indefinitely.

The station at West Finchley, little changed from LNER days. Opened in 1933, it looks older because it was furnished with secondhand structures from other parts of the railway.

Piccadilly line

Cockfosters to Heathrow Airport or Uxbridge.
The line covers 43 miles and serves 51 stations.

The Great Northern, Piccadilly & Brompton Railway, later known as the Piccadilly line, opened in 1906 between Hammersmith and Finsbury Park. The extensions at each end were largely undertaken during the 1930s. The Piccadilly serves Heathrow Airport using the extensions completed to Heathrow Central (Terminals 1/2/3) in 1977 and to Terminal 4 in 1986. The platforms on the sections of line used by both Piccadilly tube trains and District surface stock trains have to be a special compromise height to allow a reasonable step between either type of train and the platform. Stations between Acton Town and Hounslow Central also have platforms of this height. Until 1964 these too were shared with the District line.

Hounslow West, until 1975 the terminus of the branch, now has its 1920s ticket hall connected to below-ground platforms built fifty years later by a covered passage and staircase. A wheelchair lift was added to the staircase in September 1993, a unique feature, immediately before wheelchair-bound passengers were accepted onto the system.

The Piccadilly line from Heathrow passes the line's main rolling stock depot at Northfields and is then provided with four tracks east from there. Two tracks between there and Acton Town are used during off-peak periods for train testing. The westbound fast track is fitted with water sprays which can be used for braking and adhesion trials.

The extensive additions to the Piccadilly line during the 1930s provided it with a good number of classic station designs by Charles Holden. Sudbury Town was one of his earliest.

Heathrow Terminal 4, the most recent addition to the Piccadilly line.

The section of line between Hounslow West and Hatton Cross was largely built by 'cut-and-cover' methods similar to those employed for the very first underground railways.

At Acton Town, the Uxbridge/Rayners Lane route, combined with the District's Ealing Broadway branch, meets the line from Heathrow. Here Piccadilly line trains are diverted to the two centre fast tracks for the non-stop trip to Hammersmith. Late at night, early in the morning and on Sundays they call additionally at Turnham Green.

The line is in tunnel between Barons Court and Arnos Grove. Of interest along this section is the Leicester Square to Covent Garden portion of the line, which represents the shortest distance between stations on any line (0.16 miles). At King's Cross there is a single line connection between the eastbound Piccadilly line and the northbound Northern line. Built in 1927, this is the only connection available between the Northern line and the rest of the Underground for stock transfer purposes.

At Finsbury Park there are connections between both tracks of the Piccadilly line and the Victoria line as well as cross-platform interchange. It is occasionally possible to compare the stopping sequence of the automatic Victoria line train with the manual stop of the Piccadilly train when two trains arrive together.

71

At Arnos Grove there is a three-track station with the centre track having a platform on each side. When a train arrives, the doors are opened on both sides to expedite unloading. Other examples exist around the system, both at termini and at through stations like Golders Green and White City.

Southgate is an unusual station in that it has the only tube tunnel platform on the Underground from which the end of the tube tunnels can be seen. The next station north is Oakwood, which has a connection at its north end to Cockfosters depot. Oakwood station, like all the Piccadilly stations built for the northward extension of the line from its original terminus at Finsbury Park, is in the 1930s style of Charles Holden. Many of these designs are now so highly regarded as specimens of the best public architecture of the period that they have become protected structures.

Hot-air balloons at Finsbury Park.

Southgate shares with Hounslow West the facility for seeing light at the end of the tunnel, in this case a tube tunnel.

Arsenal station, the only Underground station named after a football club, has recently had its large mosaic logo - the largest on the system - restored. Gunners fans arrive for a match.

Original tiled sign at Holloway Road indicating the direction of travel to the original western terminus of the line.

Illustrations of items housed at the nearby British Museum decorate the platforms at Holborn, one of the more successful 1980s modernisations.

Victoria line

Walthamstow Central to Brixton; serves 16 stations and is 14 miles in length. It is all in tunnel except for Northumberland Park depot.

The Victoria line was the first completely new tube line to be built across central London since the tube building boom of 1905-7. It was opened from Walthamstow to Highbury & Islington in September 1968, to Warren Street in December that year, to Victoria in March 1969 and to Brixton in July 1971. It was designed to relieve congestion in the north-east to West End corridor. From its opening, Automatic Train Operation (see next chapter) has been employed on the line. The trains have a one-person crew in the leading cab, responsible for door operation and re-starting from a station. Acceleration, signal checks and station stops are all performed automatically. The traditional 'hump' profile (described earlier) was used in the building of the line where permitted by prevailing conditions. At Finsbury Park (southbound) the gradient, unusually, starts within the platform tunnels.

As mentioned in the introductory chapter to this book, the nature of the subsoil south of the Thames makes tunnelling particularly difficult and expensive. The Victoria line extension to Brixton was the first extension of the tube into south London since the Northern line's extension to Morden in the mid-1920s. An important design objective was the avoidance of curves below 20 chains radius. Many of the earlier tubes had followed street routes to avoid the payment of 'easements' to the owners of property under which a line passed. This meant many sharp curves, like the approach to Piccadilly Circus from Oxford Circus (Bakerloo) which follows the curve of Regent Street. Speed restrictions were therefore necessary which still plague the system today. The Victoria line has no sharp curves, allowing higher speeds than average on the system.

Above **The southbound Victoria line platform at Finsbury Park was originally built for the old Great Northern & City Railway. This was designed to take main line size rolling stock, hence the larger than normal tube tunnel. The 'hump profile' of the track bed, which assists braking and acceleration, is particularly evident here.**

The design of the route also incorporated many cross platform interchanges. Some involved special diversions. At Finsbury Park, the former westbound Piccadilly platform became the northbound Victoria line tunnel and the opposite directions for both lines used the former Northern City line platforms. The Northern City line formerly ran between Finsbury Park and Moorgate but was curtailed at Drayton Park when construction work at Finsbury Park started. In 1975 the line was taken over by BR for incorporation into its Great Northern electrification scheme. Cross platform interchange between it and the Victoria line is provided at Highbury & Islington, where reconstruction like that at Finsbury Park was undertaken.

South of Highbury the Victoria line tunnels cross to give right-hand running. This allows cross-platform interchange at Euston with the Northern line (via Bank). This was another site which involved diversion of existing routes. South of Warren Street the tunnels again cross to regain left hand running.

Cross platform interchange with the Bakerloo is provided at Oxford Circus and with the Northern at Stockwell but at Green Park and Victoria the line is at a different level from that of other lines. Victoria has a pair of reversing sidings beyond the station and at Brixton and Walthamstow two stabling sidings are provided beyond the termini.

The Victoria line is one of the most heavily used lines on the London Underground. Although plans for its extension south east from Brixton were drawn up at one time, it is not capable of carrying any extra traffic and this rules out any extension, at least under the current signalling regime.

The northbound Victoria line platform at Oxford Circus is in a different style from the rest of the line's stations. Vitreous enamel panels replaced the original tiling following fire damage in 1984. A snakes-and-ladders/escalator theme is used for decoration.

Waterloo & City line

Waterloo to Bank, with no intermediate stations. Length 1¹/₂ miles.
Managed as part of the Central line

This short railway was London's second tube line, having opened in 1898. It was the brainchild of the London & South Western Railway which by the end of the nineteenth century was already becoming an important commuter route but which, like most of its rivals, was unable to reach the City — then a proportionately more important employment centre than now.

The original wooden-bodied trains survived until 1940 when they were replaced by specially designed tube-sized cars embodying the relatively crude technology of the Southern Railway's surface stocks, which had been superseded on the Underground several years earlier. These trains were themselves to survive until 1993, some cars to the end bearing 'Southern Railway' motifs inside, recalling pre-nationalisation days of the early 1940s.

Waterloo station, Waterloo & City line. The small depot and workshop can be seen beyond the platform.

The Bank end of the line. Trains on the Waterloo & City are similar to those on the Central line apart from the number of cars and the livery.

An inclined travolator links the Waterloo & City line with the other part of Bank station.

In 1993 the line closed for several weeks for some remaining civil engineering works and resignalling to take place. When it reopened on 19th July 1993, it was equipped with new trains — in effect units of Central line 1992 tube stock added to the Underground order and sold on to Network SouthEast, the only significant difference being in external livery.

The line is wholly in tunnel and physically isolated from all other railways. Until 1990 cars were moved to and from the line by hydraulic lift at Waterloo. This facility had to be removed as part of the preparations for the international platforms for Eurostar services so that the 1940 cars and their replacements had to be lifted by mobile crane. It is anticipated that the new trains will be left in place for life.

Uniquely amongst London's tube lines, the Waterloo & City (or 'Drain') remained outside London Transport ownership. In April 1994 however, with the impending privatisation of BR, it was transferred to London Underground and is now managed as part of the Central line, although there is no physical connection.

 # Operation

Signalling

The basis of the Underground's signalling system is the automatic operation of signals using track circuits to detect the presence of trains. Interruption of a track circuit by a train (or for any other reason) will cause the signal protecting the entrance of that section of track to show a red aspect. When the section is cleared the signal will display a 'proceed' aspect. A co-acting trainstop operates in conjunction with each signal. When the signal shows a 'stop' aspect, the trainstop is raised and will act on a tripcock of any train attempting to pass. Operation of the tripcock on a train causes an emergency brake application.

The Underground signalling system is of the two-aspect type. A driver is told 'proceed' or 'stop' (green or red). Yellow lights are usually only used as repeaters for red signals where the view is restricted. Platforms are also provided with repeaters to assist guards or station staff in preventing a train being given a start signal against a red signal. Disc signals are used for shunting manoeuvres with most recent installations using fibre optic displays.

Signals are positioned in such a way that an allowance is made for possible overruns. In case a train should be 'tripped' as a result of passing a red signal, a safe braking distance is provided between the signal and the section it protects. At certain places where a junction or dead end reduces this overlap, as it is called, a speed limit is enforced by a combination of signals and speed controlled trainstops. At certain locations where there are speed limits, these are also enforced by speed controlled signals. Terminal platforms have speed controlled trainstops and at Earl's Court and Baker Street there are examples of 'draw-up' signals which restrict train speeds under conditions of reduced overlaps.

Signals at junctions also operate automatically but with the addition of levers or other control methods to provide route setting. These signals are known as semi-automatic signals. Those provided at diverging junctions use three white indicator lights above the green aspect to display that a diverging route is set.

For automatic control of route setting, the description of the approaching train is used to set the route required. The reversing siding at Wood Green was the first example of the use of this equipment when it was opened in 1932. A more sophisticated version was needed to regulate routes at main junctions, and a trial installation was put in at Camden Town in 1955. A further refinement was the introduction of the programme machine. The programme machine was used to check the train description with the timetable and the time and, if all matched up, to set the route and pass on the train to the next area. The machine itself contains a plastic roll with holes arranged in codes for each train. Electrical contacts are made through the holes as the roll steps up for each train. The circuits set up in this way operate the routes.

The first programme machines were installed at Kennington and Euston in 1958. These were considered sufficiently successful to continue the idea using a central control room, located first at Leicester Square for part of the Northern line. When the Victoria line was opened in 1968, a new control room was opened at Cobourg Street, Euston, for that line and the Northern line control moved there later.

The programme machine allows a number of different operating modes. 'First come-first served' at a converging junction can be used instead of 'programme only' which only allows trains through in the correct timetabled order. At a diverging junction a train can be signalled on either 'describer only' or 'work according to programme'. Manual can also be selected. Facilities are also provided for a train to be cancelled from the programme or for an extra train to be inserted.

The latest computerised control centre was opened in 1994 for the Central line in conjunction with the entry into service of new trains.

The first computerised scheme was put in at Watford, controlled from the signal cabin at Rickmansworth. Heathrow and the north end of the Piccadilly line were next to get this equipment, followed by the whole of the Jubilee and Metropolitan lines. Refinements continued for the Bakerloo line (1989) and the Central line (1994) with work now under way for the Jubilee line.

Automatic Train Operation

The Underground first began trials with ATO (Automatic Train Operation) in 1961. The objective was to achieve more uniform train performance and better service regulation. Following a trial on the District line in 1963, and then the full-scale conversion of the Woodford to Hainault shuttle service in 1964, it was decided to instal ATO on the Victoria line, opened in 1968.

For station stops a series of patches with command frequencies indicating speed required at each spot tell the train how to brake in order to ensure that it stops in the correct place in the platform. Once stopped, the train operator will work the doors and then restart the train using push buttons on his control desk. Lineside signals are not normally provided except at junctions and at stations. Block sections are marked by headway posts. In addition to the signal brake command spots, special 'coast' commands are provided to reduce energy consumption.

ATO for many years remained unique to the Victoria line. This is because it was found possible to convert lines to one-person operation (OPO) without the need for resignalling which would be necessary if ATO were to be installed. For the Central line, however, ATO is being provided because of the need to increase capacity, and the opportunity given by the coincident expiry of trains and much of the line's signalling.

The Central line's ATO equipment could be regarded as perhaps the ultimate development of the Victoria line system, as updated progressively for Hong Kong (1979) and Singapore (1987). The Jubilee line will benefit from a new technology, however, and a contract was placed with Westinghouse in 1993 for their new transmission-based Westrace system.

One-Person Operation

Since the late 1960s most new rolling stock has been supplied with the eventual conversion to single-manning in mind. This has principally involved the provision of door controls in the driver's cab instead of in the passenger saloon where the guard was traditionally situated. Now, modifications to the trains to allow the driver to operate the doors instead of the guard, and the installation of train radio and visual aids on platforms, have allowed all the surface lines and the Piccadilly, Bakerloo and Jubilee tube lines to have one-person operation (OPO).

The first lines to go over to OPO were the Circle and the Hammersmith & City lines in 1985. The C stock used on these lines had the guard's door controls located in the driver's cab and the conversion to OPO was achieved by adding train radio and placing cameras, closed-circuit TV screens and mirrors on platforms to allow full observation from the leading cab. The circuit detecting 'all doors closed' is now linked to the traction control, preventing the train from starting until the circuit is complete.

Some additional provisions have been made for the OPO conversion of tube lines. To allow for rapid removal of a train stalled due to incapacity of the driver a special radio alarm signal has been fitted to the driver's controller handle — the famous 'deadman's handle'. If this is released and not reset within a predetermined time not only does the train stop but also an automatic alarm is sent to the line control room.

Communications

For many years the telephone was the principal means of communication used on the Underground. Apart from connecting signal cabins, stations and depots with each other and the line controller, it was used for emergency situations when signals had failed or current had been discharged. The twin copper wires installed in tunnels to allow drivers to discharge current may also be used for emergency telephone communication between driver and controller.

The use of the telephone is restricted to a fixed location or a stationary train. Radio offers a more flexible communications link, particularly with trains and with staff who have to be on the move. Now that the technical difficulties with providing radio communications in tunnels have been overcome by use of a 'leaky feeder' system, trains have been provided with radios. Before the introduction of radio, the only line which had mobile communication with trains was the Victoria line. This used a system known as carrier wave which used the current rails as the transmission medium. Whilst adequate, it did not provide the flexibility of modern radio equipment which was finally installed in June 1992. A current programme for the introduction of radio communications at 42 tunnel stations will mean that firemen and police will have communications links to the surface which allow more rapid response to emergencies. It will also mean better communications for station staff. Each controller has radio and telecommunications links with all fixed locations and trains on his line. He can call individual trains on the move as well as stations, depots and engineering staff. He can also call on outside services, Police, Ambulance and Fire, as necessary. Links between lines and other undertakings like the bus services and British Rail are maintained through a Network Command Centre.

Combined mirror and closed-circuit television unit on the Victoria line. These units are installed at the ends of platforms to provide the train operator with a view of the doors on his train.

Response to a passenger's enquiry via a Help Point at Hammersmith.

Lifts and Escalators

The cut and cover lines were built near or on the surface and were therefore provided with stairs down to platforms from street level. However, when the deep level tube lines were opened, it became necessary to provide lifts. On the first tube, the City & South London Railway, hydraulically-powered lifts were provided but on later lines most were electric. To fulfil its purpose in providing mass transport, the Underground pursued a policy of replacing lifts by escalators from the 1920s onwards. Sixty years later however the social conscience was turning towards the concept of catering for as much of the population as possible, including those with impaired mobility. Apart from satisfying social needs, this policy has some commercial benefits in widening the potential customer base to the many who have pushchairs and other bulky items. Thus by 1990 it was realised that both lifts and escalators were desirable, and new station designs began to include both facilities. There are currently only 68 lifts in operation at 27 stations (in 1907 there were 249 lifts in service), but this number will rise again in the coming years.

The recently modernised lifts at Belsize Park.

Originally, lifts were manually operated by staff. The first semi-automatic system was installed at Warren Street in 1928 as a trial and the first fully automatic lifts were introduced at Earl's Court in 1932. The first lifts ran at a vertical speed of 100-120ft/min but by the early 1920s this had increased to 180-200ft/min and in 1924-5 some high speed lifts were introduced at Angel and Leicester Square which ran at 290ft/min. In 1937 Goodge Street had 600ft/min lifts installed and in 1954 Hampstead (the deepest station on the system) had 800ft/min lifts fitted.

Over the years all of the original lifts have been replaced or abandoned. The last in use was at Aldwych on a short branch of the Piccadilly line from Holborn, closed in September 1994. Very low passenger demand made replacement of the lifts here too expensive. Mornington Crescent station was closed temporarily in summer 1992 for lift replacement and renovation, but funding problems caused work to be suspended indefinitely later in the year, and the station remained closed.

Escalators were first introduced on the Underground at Earl's Court in 1911. At that time they were of the 'shunt' type which required passengers to step on or off from the side of the machine. The first example of the modern escalator or 'comb' type, allowing a straight step on or off the landing, was installed at Clapham Common in 1924. A survey carried out in 1966 showed that the capacity of an escalator is not related solely to speed. At speeds above 160 ft/min it was found that capacity began to fall because of the hesitancy of some passengers to board a fast moving machine. Since then the top speed has been set at 145ft/min. The first escalators were inclined at an angle of just over 26% to the horizontal (because the prototype was built at that angle and the rest had to conform) whereas all later types were designed at 30°. Escalators have a height range of between 15ft rise at Chancery Lane and 90ft rise at Angel, where the escalators are 196ft 10ins long — the longest in western Europe.

The Northern line has the longest escalators on the system, these being at Angel station.

All escalators are provided with special safety devices. Emergency stop switches for passengers' use are the only readily visible devices but there are others. One is a non-reversing device which prevents an escalator running in the 'up' direction from running backwards. A worn-link detector is also provided. The main chains which drive the steps have special detectors which stop the machine if either of the two chains should break. There are also two brake systems and an overspeed device. Since the King's Cross fire, additional safety systems and procedures have been installed. All the wooden panelling on escalators has been removed and replaced with aluminium and all escalators now have fire detection, alarm and sprinkler systems.

Power for lifts and escalators is supplied from traction substations at 600 volts dc or 415 volts — 3 phase — 50hz depending on the type of motor involved. Supplies are provided from the substations on both sides of a section so that the loss of one will not totally disable the system at the station.

Track and Electricity Supply

Until recently the Underground used 95lb/yd Bull Head rail but this is now being replaced by flat bottomed rail of the type long since standard on the main line railways. Conductor rail is of keystone section in tube tunnels and flat bottomed elsewhere. Concrete sleepers are in use at various places, and in the new tunnel on the Terminal 4 loop of the Piccadilly line concrete sleepers are fitted with a 'boot' made of bonded cork granules to reduce vibration.

In 1993 some sections of track and the underlying sub-structure were replaced entirely in the Pinner-Northwood and Ladbroke Grove areas, providing a vastly improved ride for passengers and offering substantial savings in future maintenance costs. As funding permits similar work will be carried out in other areas suffering from poor track.

Night-time track maintenance at Oxford Circus, Bakerloo line.

Normal maintenance in tunnels and track bed cleaning are done in the short period between the last train at night and the first in the morning, about 4½ hours. During this period the current is switched off and the line is given over to the engineers. In the morning a special 'Line Clear Procedure' is used to ensure all workers and equipment are accounted for before current is switched on.

The main maintenance depot is at Lillie Bridge near Earl's Court. It has access to the District line at West Kensington and at Olympia. It houses most of the facilities associated with permanent way, drainage and signal engineering. Although it is a rather cramped site, its central position gives the depot an advantage as all lines can be reached quite easily.

In addition to Lillie Bridge, there is a rail-welding plant at West Ruislip depot. This allows rail lengths up to 300ft to be carried by special 'long rail' trains to site. They can be unloaded from these trains and laid in a continuous operation.

In 1903-7, the District, Metropolitan and new tube railways introduced the four-rail system in use today with separate positive and negative rails. This was introduced to overcome fears of corrosion of underground pipes and cables which could result from a three-rail system. The negative rail is positioned in the centre of the running rails with the positive rail on the outside. The current is supplied at 630 volts dc. Traction current from power stations at Greenwich and Chelsea is fed to the track from remotely-controlled substations located every few miles along each line. Except for terminal sections, which are single-end fed, each section is fed from the substation at each end.

Ticketing

All self-service passenger operated ticket machines are wall mounted and are serviced by staff from within secure areas at the rear. The free-standing ticket offices originally located at the centre of many booking halls have been replaced by wall ticket offices.

All tickets valid on the Underground (including those issued by British Rail) are of credit card size and are magnetically encoded. This enables improved control to be achieved when tickets are inserted in the automatic gates, as well as assisting travelling ticket checkers, who are provided with portable ticket verifiers providing extensive information about the ticket and its recent use. Experiments with a 'touch and pass' system which would enable long-period season ticket holders to use the gates without letting go of their tickets have taken place as part of the development of new technologies.

The design and operation of the automatic ticket gates was carefully reassessed following the King's Cross fire report. Gates were modified to ensure that they would open under all conditions of power failure and that they could be opened with an emergency push button release for an evacuation. A special review has been undertaken by a firm of independent consultants who have confirmed the safety of the system.

Initially, automatic gates were installed throughout Farezone 1. In 1991 two stations outside Zone 1 — Stockwell and Brixton — were provided with gates in view of the high levels of fraud experienced there. The gates were originally earmarked for currently deferred congestion relief work at King's Cross and Victoria. The success of the exercise has led to plans for further installations in outer areas.

Above left **Ticket office and machines at Hounslow West.**

Above **A new type of ticket gate has recently been designed. It has a reduced pedestal width, enabling more gates to be fitted in a given space.**

 # Future

Just as in the past, the fortunes of the Underground will in future be inextricably linked with those of London as a whole. As London faces competition with other cities to retain and enhance its status, especially as a financial centre, it will need a first class transport system to support it. This should bode well for the Underground, especially given rising public interest in reducing pollution and making our transport 'greener'. Some 70% of the Underground's demand arises from employment: travel was thus depressed during the first years of the decade, but stabilised during 1993 and can be expected to rise again as the economy improves.

The Underground will be expected to appeal to a wider sector of the market if it is to fulfil social and financial targets. Thus, standards of security must encourage evening travel and allow people to travel alone without fear. Similarly, people with a wide range of disabilities are now expecting a freedom of movement not hitherto experienced on public transport.

Above **Work on the Jubilee line extension to Canary Wharf and Stratford. A 200-ton tunnel boring machine is lowered into place at North Greenwich.**

A new culture

By the 1990s much of the Underground's culture had stagnated for many decades: for example the conditions of service governing most front line staff had been unchanged since 1922. In response London Underground evolved its Company Plan, launched in November 1991, to improve safety, quality and efficiency. Major changes were successfully negotiated with the Unions during mid-1992, with the result that between December 1992 and summer 1993 virtually all staff employed in service delivery and day-to-day maintenance adopted new conditions of service appropriate to today's circumstances. The whole thrust of the changes was to focus all staff on meeting customer needs.

This step now enables managers to undertake the long process of changing the culture to improve the human touch for both passengers and staff and to deliver a high quality service. This is to be achieved through a process of carefully targeted training, and by continuing the process started in 1988 of empowering local managers to make key decisions. In doing this, the Underground intends to follow a policy of continuous improvement, avoiding the need for further major upheavals in future. It is intended that these changes, if coupled with much needed but well focused investment in run down assets, will result in the system becoming financially self-sufficient in the early years of the next decade.

Services to meet customer needs

Present frequencies and service patterns have changed little on most lines over the years, yet there have been significant changes in demand, especially in the off-peak periods and to the timing of the peaks themselves. For example, the traditional evening rush now starts earlier and finishes later than a few years ago, with a second peak in many areas at around 19.00 hours. Efforts are now being made to tailor service levels much more accurately to the demand: one consequence was the substantial improvement in mid-day off peak services to the outer ends of the Northern line implemented in April 1993, with a decision for similar changes taking place on the Piccadilly, District and Metropolitan lines during 1994.

Expanding stations

Many stations on the existing system are close to becoming congested at peak periods and, although the improved reliability of train services and the economic recession of the early 1990s have offered some respite, it is likely that major capacity enhancement will be needed at several stations within the next few years. The solution to congestion varies from one location to another, but normally will involve opening new access to platforms with an additional ticket hall, thus meeting emergency evacuation ideals as well as extending the useful catchment area served. Some 25 sites are currently under active consideration, ranging upwards in cost to over £60m to provide a new ticket hall and escalator access at Holborn. Where capacity is adequate, much can still be done to improve facilities and design to enhance safety, security and the general environment. The provision of closed circuit television, video recorded, and Help Points is proving invaluable in reducing crime, and will now be steadily extended.

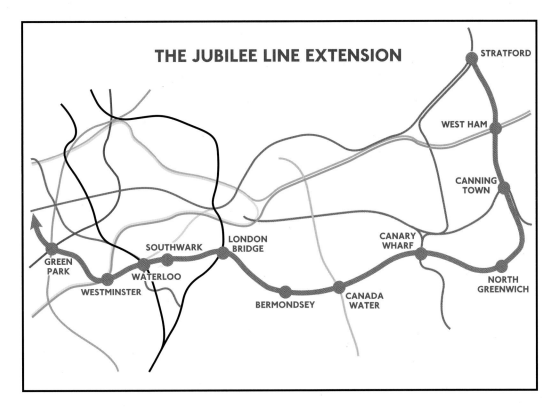

THE JUBILEE LINE EXTENSION

STRATFORD
WEST HAM
CANNING TOWN
CANARY WHARF
SOUTHWARK
LONDON BRIDGE
GREEN PARK
WATERLOO
WESTMINSTER
BERMONDSEY
CANADA WATER
NORTH GREENWICH

Downstream to Docklands

Much of the thrust of the Underground in the coming years is intended to better serve existing markets. If the system is to continue to support London effectively it is just as important that it is adapted to feed developing areas.

The initial drive will be the extension of the Jubilee line from Green Park to Waterloo, thence along the South Bank to Docklands and onward to Stratford. This line is jointly funded by the Government and the private interests at Canary Wharf; the first extension to the network to be so financed. Construction of the line started in earnest in the late autumn of 1993 and should open in spring 1998.

Many of the features of this extension will be new to London. The tunnels themselves are being bored to a larger diameter than hitherto to permit the provision of a side walkway throughout, assisting maintenance and giving greater flexibility when it is necessary to detrain passengers between stations. Signalling will be transmission based. This form of signalling permits higher frequencies than conventional track-circuit based systems.

The trains will have six cars and be similar dimensionally and in door layout to 1973 stock. The bodyshell construction will, however, be similar to the new Central line trains, while propulsion will be through ac motors for the first time on the Underground. The car interiors are designed by Warwick Design, responsible also for the production refurbishment design of Piccadilly line 1973 stock trains: the two will bear a strong family resemblance. The contract for supply has been awarded to GEC-Alsthom.

It is perhaps in the design of the stations that Londoners will see the greatest departure from normal Underground practice. There will be a strong emphasis on space, with large banks of escalators (104 on the eight below-ground stations of the extension alone and 12 above ground, against 295 for the entire Underground today). Full provision will be made for wheelchair bound passengers, with the installation of 26 lifts, and a better environment for all will result from the admission of daylight to lower levels, as in some Singapore stations. Shared also with that railway are platform edge doors, which will improve safety as well as reduce draught problems for users. Architecturally, the stations will make a bold statement about the Underground's presence not seen since Charles Holden's designs of the inter-war years.

The design for Canada Water station.

Interior mock-up of the new trains for the Jubilee line before their construction.

89

CrossRail and North East/South West Metro

Looking beyond the Jubilee extension there are two further major schemes which, once opened, would probably mark the completion of the central London Underground map for many decades to come.

As conceived, CrossRail would introduce 12-car trains of main line size from Shenfield (and possibly beyond) in the east to Reading and Aylesbury in the west, through tunnels owned by London Underground and with stations at Liverpool Street/Moorgate, Farringdon, Holborn, Tottenham Court Road, Bond Street and Paddington. By the time a Bill was deposited in Parliament in November 1991, plans for Holborn station had been shelved, but there was the prospect of adding Heathrow Airport as a western destination through the proposed BAA Heathrow Express link with Paddington, at least during off-peak periods. In May 1994 the Bill failed to survive Committee stage in the Commons — a controversial move, not least since the project had the declared support of both government and opposition. After much work attempting to revive the Bill it was acknowledged two months later that it was dead, and a decision was taken to proceed instead under the new Transport and Works Act. This is a radically different process, and replanning meant that an application could not be made until the early months of 1995.

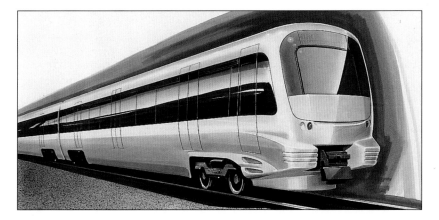

Train design for the planned CrossRail line. The livery details have yet to be finalised.

CrossRail stations would be massive by the standards we know now: that at Tottenham Court Road, for example, would stretch under some 25% of the area of Soho. Modern tunnelling techniques would permit large ticket halls, and passages designed for smooth flows of people, with none of the right angled junctions and turns we experience today. All stations would have at least two ticket halls and, as with Jubilee extension stations, daylight would be admitted to low levels.

Looking still further into the future, London Underground intends to seek powers to construct a new line from south London and Victoria to King's Cross on an alignment to the east of the Victoria line, thereby affording much-needed relief. It would benefit from new tunnelling technology, proven in London on the early Jubilee line extension works. Beyond the central area, the line is planned to continue to Angel, Dalston and Hackney and over existing tracks, possibly via the North London line to Stratford, London City Airport and North Woolwich.

East London, Croxley and more at Heathrow Airport

Some more modest, but thoroughly worthwhile, schemes are also under consideration. Closest to fruition is the extension of the East London line to the north, from Whitechapel (abandoning Shoreditch) to Bishopsgate, where in future interchange would be possible with a new Central line station and thence over the disused BR Broad Street line viaduct through Hoxton and Haggerston to Dalston Junction. A further extension would take the line by way of Canonbury to Highbury, to forge a very useful interchange with other lines and open up a new route from the northern suburbs to Docklands.

Subsequently it is intended to extend to the south as well, with a new alignment from a point south of Surrey Quays to join an existing Southern Region line to serve North Deptford, Queens Road Peckham, Peckham Rye and terminating at East Dulwich. A new depot is due to be built at Silwood, south of Surrey Quays — this will form part of phase one, with the extension to Dalston. An application for powers for phase one under the Transport and Works Act was made in 1993 — the first in London by this process. The stations will be simple and in keeping with the line's character, but will have distinctive architecture to form a focus in the communities served. Rolling stock for the line is likely to come from elsewhere on the system.

Smaller still is a project to connect the Metropolitan Watford branch to the BR Croxley line at Croxley Green. Only some 200 metres separate the lines at present: forming a connection would transform two backwater branches into a new trunk route feeding the much expanded centre of Watford.

Meanwhile at Heathrow, BAA is planning its new Terminal 5 at Perry Oaks, on the western fringes of the airport. This terminal would need public transport services as well as the expansion of motorway links, and design work is starting on a possible further extension of the Piccadilly line and Heathrow Express to serve a station within the terminal. Plans for the extension were prepared for submission under the Transport and Works Act in November 1994, to run concurrently with the planning process for the terminal itself.

Basic infrastructure

Along with planned improvements to rolling stock, the track and, more particularly, signalling are capable of major upgrading to provide a high quality service. Existing track forms are expensive to maintain and offer at best an indifferent ride for passengers. As track needs relaying it will now be possible to use more modern techniques giving reduced wear and tear along with big improvements in comfort. The increased mechanisation of maintenance will also ensure that the new standards are maintained, but at reduced cost.

Track renewal near Ladbroke Grove.

Many new possibilities are offered by the latest signalling techniques. Transmission based systems can bring trains much closer together than now, and in greater safety. With bi-directional use it would be possible, with enough crossovers, to run trains through the night in each tunnel in turn on a single line basis, while the other was undergoing inspection and maintenance. Improved supervision of the service would also provide a breakthrough in regular intervals without the penalty of delaying trains to space them out evenly, and would enable services to recover from incidents far more quickly than now. This type of system offers much for the Northern line modernisation in years to come, but would also dramatically improve capacity where the limits of the current signalling system have been reached, either through high frequency (as on the Victoria line) or complexity (the Circle line and adjoining services). It would also ease the operation of semi-fast or skip-stop services, for instance to Heathrow Airport.

Money

Since 1988 the quality and safety of services has improved materially, in part through investment, but substantially through the efforts of front line staff and managers. This process will go on, but the Underground will continue to be dependent on heavy investment for some years to come if the dramatic improvements needed to serve London are to be achieved. Given the shortage of funding from the public purse, opportunities are now being pursued for introducing private sector financing of some projects, many of which could offer a very good return on investment. With adequate investment there is now little doubt that within the foreseeable future the system could offer not only a service to rival the world's best, but that it would do so without subsidy.

Holloway Road, opened 1906

North Ealing, opened 1903

 **Chronologies**

Present station names have been used in this list

Metropolitan and Hammersmith & City lines (including north half of Circle line)
1863 Opened on 10 January as the Metropolitan Railway from Farringdon to Paddington
1864 Extension to Hammersmith with branch from Latimer Road to Kensington (Olympia)
1865 Extension from Farringdon to Moorgate
1868 Branch opened from Baker Street to Swiss Cottage
1868 Part of Circle line opened from Edgware Road to South Kensington
1875 Extension from Moorgate to Liverpool Street
1876 Extension from Liverpool Street to Aldgate
1877 Branch opened between Goldhawk Road and Richmond, over District Railway route between Ravenscourt Park and Richmond
1879 Extension from Swiss Cottage to Willesden Green
1880 Extension from Willesden Green to Harrow-on-the-Hill
1882 Extension from Aldgate to Tower Hill
1884 Branch opened from Aldgate East to East London Railway
1885 Extension from Harrow-on-the-Hill to Pinner
1887 Extension from Pinner to Rickmansworth
1889 Extension from Rickmansworth to Chalfont & Latimer and Chesham
1892 Extension from Chalfont & Latimer to Aylesbury
1894 Extension from Aylesbury to Verney Junction
1899 Branch to Brill taken over
1904 Branch opened from Harrow-on-the-Hill to Uxbridge
1906 Closure of branch from Goldhawk Road to Richmond
1906 Closure of branch from Aldgate East to East London Railway
1906 Extension from Aldgate East to Whitechapel
1925 Branch opened from Moor Park and Rickmansworth to Watford
1932 Branch opened from Wembley Park to Stanmore
1935 Closure of Brill Branch
1936 Closure of section between Aylesbury and Verney Junction (reopened between Aylesbury and Quainton Road from 1943 to 1948)
1936 Extension from Whitechapel to Barking
1939 Transfer of Stanmore branch to the Bakerloo line
1940 Closure of branch from Latimer Road to Olympia
1961 Closure of section between Amersham and Aylesbury upon electrification of the line between Rickmansworth and Amersham

District line (including south half of Circle line)

1868   Opened on 24 December as the Metropolitan District Railway between South Kensington and Westminster

1869   Branch opened from Gloucester Road to West Brompton

1870   Extension from Westminster to Blackfriars

1871   Extension from Blackfriars to Mansion House

1871   Branch opened from High Street Kensington to Earl's Court

1874   Extension from Earl's Court to Hammersmith

1877   Extension from Hammersmith to Richmond, over London & South Western Railway route between Ravenscourt Park and Richmond

1879   Branch opened from Turnham Green to Ealing Broadway

1880   Extension from West Brompton to Putney Bridge

1883   Branch opened from Acton Town to Hounslow Town

1883   Extension from Ealing Broadway to Windsor over Great Western Railway route

1884   Re-routed at Osterley to a new western terminus at Hounslow West

1884   Extension from Mansion House to Whitechapel and East London Railway; completion of the Inner Circle (Circle line)

1885   Service between Ealing Broadway and Windsor withdrawn

1889   Extension from Putney Bridge to Wimbledon

1902   Extension from Whitechapel to Upminster (over London, Tilbury & Southend Railway route from Bromley-by-Bow to Upminster)

1903   Branch opened from Ealing Common to South Harrow

1905   Branch opened from Acton Town to South Acton

1905   Operation over East London Railway withdrawn

1910   Extension from South Harrow to Uxbridge

1910   Some journeys extended to Southend-on-Sea and, shortly after, to Shoeburyness, over London, Tilbury & Southend Railway route

1933   Services on Uxbridge branch withdrawn (taken over by Piccadilly line)

1939   Journeys to Southend and Shoeburyness withdrawn

1946   Service introduced between High Street Kensington and Olympia

1959   Closure of South Acton branch

1964   Closure of section between Acton Town and Hounslow West (covered by Piccadilly line)

East London line

1869   Opened on 7 December as the East London Railway from Wapping to New Cross Gate

1876   Extension from Wapping to Liverpool Street (Great Eastern Railway)

1880   Branch opened from Surrey Docks to New Cross

1913   New Cross/New Cross Gate to Shoreditch section taken over by Metropolitan upon electrification of the line. Closure of section beyond Shoreditch

Northern line

1890   City & South London Railway opened on 18 December between Stockwell and King William Street (near Bank)

1900   Extension north to Moorgate with new station at Bank and south from Stockwell to Clapham Common

1901   Extension from Moorgate to Angel

1907   Charing Cross, Euston & Hampstead Railway opened between Charing Cross and Golders Green with branch from Camden Town to Archway

1907   City & South London Railway extended from Angel to Euston

1914   Extension from Charing Cross to Embankment

1923   Extension from Golders Green to Hendon Central

1924   Extension from Hendon Central to Edgware and from Euston to Camden Town

1926   Extension from Clapham Common to Morden and from Embankment to Kennington

1939   Extension from Archway to East Finchley

1940   Extension from East Finchley to High Barnet over Great Northern Railway route

1941   Branch opened to Mill Hill East over Great Northern Railway route

Waterloo & City line
1898   Opened on 8 August as the Waterloo & City Railway between Waterloo and Bank

Central line
1900   Opened on 30 July as the Central London Railway between Shepherd's Bush and Bank
1908   Extension from Shepherd's Bush to Wood Lane (near White City)
1912   Extension from Bank to Liverpool Street
1920   Extension from Wood Lane to Ealing Broadway
1946   Extension from Liverpool Street to Stratford
1947   Extension from Stratford to Newbury Park and Woodford, partly over Great Eastern Railway routes
1947   Branch opened from North Acton to Greenford over Great Western Railway route
1948   Extension from Greenford to West Ruislip over Great Western Railway route
1948   Extension from Newbury Park to Hainault and from Woodford to Hainault and Loughton over Great Eastern Railway routes
1949   Extension from Loughton to Epping over Great Eastern Railway routes
1957   Shuttle service between Epping and Ongar taken over from BR upon electrification
1994   Closure of shuttle service between Epping and Ongar

Bakerloo line
1906   Opened on 10 March as the Baker Street & Waterloo Railway between Baker Street and Lambeth North; extended to Elephant & Castle on 5 August
1907   Extension from Baker Street to Edgware Road
1913   Extension from Edgware Road to Paddington
1915   Extension from Paddington to Willesden Junction, over London & North Western Railway route between Queen's Park and Willesden Junction
1917   Extension from Willesden Junction to Watford Junction over LNWR route
1939   Branch opened from Baker Street to Stanmore, over Metropolitan line route between Finchley Road and Stanmore
1979   Baker Street to Stanmore branch transferred to Jubilee line
1982   Closure of section between Stonebridge Park and Watford Junction
1984   Service restored between Stonebridge Park and Harrow and Wealdstone

Piccadilly line
1906   Great Northern, Piccadilly & Brompton Railway opened on 15 December between Hammersmith and Finsbury Park
1907   Branch opened from Holborn to Aldwych
1932   Extension from Hammersmith to South Harrow over District Railway route
1932   Extension from Finsbury Park to Arnos Grove
1933   Extension from Acton Town to Hounslow West over District Railway route
1933   Extension from South Harrow to Uxbridge over District Railway route
1933   Extension from Arnos Grove to Cockfosters
1975   Extension from Hounslow West to Hatton Cross
1977   Extension from Hatton Cross to Heathrow (Terminals 1,2,3)
1986   Extension at Heathrow to Terminal 4
1994   Closure of shuttle service between Holborn and Aldwych

Victoria line
1968   Opened on 1 September between Walthamstow Central and Highbury & Islington; extended to Warren Street on 1 December
1969   Extension from Warren Street to Victoria
1971   Extension from Victoria to Brixton

Jubilee line
1979   Opened on 1 May between Charing Cross and Stanmore, over Bakerloo line route between Baker Street and Stanmore

Statistics

The Underground's Passengers
Passengers carried annually (1993/94)   735million
Passengers carried daily (Monday to Friday average)   2.4million

Stations
Busiest stations and estimated annual numbers of journeys starting or ending:

1. Victoria	61.0m	4. King's Cross	37.0m
2. Oxford Circus	46.0m	5. Waterloo	33.0m
3. Liverpool Street	38.0m	6. Piccadilly Circus	30.0m

Station with the most platforms used by Underground trains:
Baker Street — 10 (6 Metropolitan, H&C and Circle; 2 Bakerloo; 2 Jubilee)

Lengths and Distances
Length of route served by Underground trains; 249miles/401km, comprising 143 miles in the open (57½%), 86 miles in tube tunnelling (34½%) and 20 miles in cut-and-cover tunnelling (8%).

Longest continuous tunnel	17.3miles/27.8km
East Finchley to Morden, via Bank (Northern line)	
Longest journey without change	34.1miles/54.9km
West Ruislip to Epping (Central line)	
Longest distance between adjacent stations by rail	3.89miles/6.26km
Chesham to Chalfont & Latimer (Metropolitan line)	
Shortest distance between adjacent stations by rail	0.16miles/0.26km
Leicester Square to Covent Garden (Piccadilly line)	

Elevation
The highest point above mean sea level on the system is at Amersham (approx 500ft/150metres); the greatest elevation from ground level is on Dollis Brook viaduct, Dollis Road on the Mill Hill East branch of the Northern line (approx 60ft/18metres).

Depth
The maximum depth below mean sea level is on the Northern line just south of Waterloo station (70ft/21.3metres); the maximum depth below ground level is on the Northern line near Whitestone Pond, Hampstead (221ft/67.4metres); Hampstead is the deepest station (192ft/58.5metres)

Lifts and Escalators
The deepest lift is at Hampstead (181ft/55.2 metres), the shortest one is at Chalk Farm (30ft 6ins/9.3 metres). The longest escalator is at Angel (vertical rise 90ft/27.4metres) and the shortest is at Chancery Lane (15ft/4.6metres). The station with the most escalators is Oxford Circus, where there are 14.